"A superb treatment of a [...] in commending this excellen [...]

—**Daniel L. Akin**, president, Southeastern Baptist Theological Seminary

"Landon Dowden's *Ezekiel* is the best available pastoral commentary on this significant book of the Bible. Dowden provides a responsible exegesis of Ezekiel, grounds it in the hope of the gospel, applies it to the lives of ordinary people, and communicates it in a lucid and lively manner. Highly recommended."

—**Bruce Ashford**, provost and dean of faculty, Southeastern Baptist Theological Seminary

"Landon Dowden has provided an insightful commentary on the book of Ezekiel as seen through the eyes of a pastor wanting to inform the Christian community concerning the key theological principles found in this pivotal Old Testament book. He faithfully adheres to the purposes of the Christ-Centered Commentary series by focusing on the practical theological issues that the Israelite community of faith faced five to six centuries before Christ's ministry, and then relating them to those faced by the Christian community in the present. Such principles as the character and attributes of God, the nature and content of God's Word, the call to repentance, His discipline of His people, and His demand for holiness from His people are given careful and practical considerations.

"The structure of providing guides for interpretation through questions for furthering the reader's understanding of the meaning of the text is well developed. Each subsection begins by asking an essential question that demands a faith response of the Christian. Major sections conclude with a series of practical questions that can facilitate personal devotional reading and group interaction. Above all the commentary is designed to glorify Christ, who was God's goal of history for all ages."

—**Dennis Cole**, professor of Old Testament and Archaeology, occupying the Mcfarland Chair of Archaeology, at New Orleans Baptist Theological Seminary

"Landon is a master craftsman in creating expository messages. He has taken a book of the Bible many have shied away from preaching and has made it accessible and applicable to everyday disciples. Add this resource to your preaching repertoire and be well equipped to develop and deliver expository, Christ-exalting sermons."

—**Robby Gallaty**, Senior Pastor, Brainerd Baptist Church, Chattanooga, Tennessee

"Landon Dowden is a friend and former student, so I had to fight a 'hometown hero' instinct to objectively evaluate and/or endorse his work when the opportunity arose. I probably cast a more critical eye as I read than I would have done had I not been so familiar with Dr. Dowden and his ministry. Still, I was impressed. Some commentators either write for an academic audience or for preachers who are just trying to get a word for Sunday morning. The expositor's commentary is exactly what it promises. It is technical enough to appreciate the excellent scholarship, but also comprehensible for a layperson who is preparing a Bible study class. As I would have expected, Dr. Dowden gives radical attention to what the text actually says, not what we would like for it to say. I will look forward to collecting the whole set."

—**R. Allen Jackson**, Professor of Youth Education and Collegiate Ministry, New Orleans Baptist Theological Seminary

"Landon Dowden is known for his faithful exposition and dynamic sermon delivery. I rejoice to see his work now in print. If you desire to study Ezekiel in your own devotional life or to expound it to others (and you should consider both!), then pick up this fresh, readable, insightful, God-centered, Christ-exalting commentary. It's outstanding! I plan on using it for years to come."

—**Tony Merida**, lead pastor, Imago Dei Church, Raleigh, North Carolina

"For years I have taught a doctoral seminar in expository preaching with Dr. Dowden. I have marveled at how he helps pastors become better preachers, and I have often thought how wonderful it would be if every preacher had the opportunity to learn from him. Now that his commentary on Ezekiel is available, they do! This book is a gold mine of gospel preaching from Ezekiel and a superb model of Bible exposition. Dr. Dowden is an exemplary expository preacher, Bible teacher, and teacher of preachers. Buy everything he writes and study it."

—**Alan Moseley**, professor of Old Testament and Hebrew, Southeastern Baptist Theological Seminary

CHRIST-CENTERED

Exposition

OT / COMMENTARY

AUTHOR Landon Dowden

SERIES EDITORS David Platt, Daniel L. Akin, and Tony Merida

CHRIST-CENTERED

Exposition

EXALTING JESUS IN

EZEKIEL

HOLMAN
REFERENCE

NASHVILLE, TENNESSEE

Christ-Centered Exposition Commentary: Exalting Jesus in Ezekiel

© Copyright 2015 by Landon Dowden

B&H Publishing Group
Nashville, Tennessee

ISBN 978-0-8054-9697-0

Dewey Decimal Classification: 220.7
Subject Heading: BIBLE. O.T. EZEKIEL—COMMENTARIES\
JESUS CHRIST

Printed in the United States of America
1 2 3 4 5 6 7 8 9 10 • 20 19 18 17 16 15
VP

SERIES DEDICATION

Dedicated to Adrian Rogers and John Piper. They have taught us to love the gospel of Jesus Christ, to preach the Bible as the inerrant Word of God, to pastor the church for which our Savior died, and to have a passion to see all nations gladly worship the Lamb.

—David Platt, Tony Merida, and Danny Akin
March 2013

AUTHOR'S DEDICATION

To Tara, Arabella, Adalaide, Adoniram, and Alastair,
my five precious gifts from God.
May God strengthen you to know and proclaim
He is Yahweh!

TABLE OF CONTENTS

ACKNOWLEDGMENTS

Without any triteness I am grateful for a God whose steadfast love overcomes all of my rebellion. I pray that His atonement and adoption always steal my breath. I am grateful He aided me not just to get through the book of Ezekiel but also to see that it is lodged in me. Any fruit that comes from this commentary will be a work of His grace alone.

I will forever be grateful for both the sacrifices and the support of my family. My beautiful gift from God, Tara, has given up time together so that I could study, prepare sermons, study some more, and write this commentary. You will never have to hear again the phrase, "I need to work on the Ezekiel commentary!" Thank you for all the care you have given the children and me during this season. My additional blessings from God—Arabella, Adalaide, Adoniram, and Alastair—have given up lots of playtime with Daddy. I love each of you so much and pray God will use you for His glory and the good of others. Thank you also to my mother, Barbara, to my sister, Larilyn, to my in-laws, TK and Rita, and to Aunt Frances for your prayers, your encouragement, and all of your help with the children. I love you and thank God for you.

I am blessed to shepherd the Church at Trace Crossing. What is found on these pages you bore as a trial run. Thank you for desiring God's Word and being willing to journey through a sermon series in Ezekiel. I'm certain some of you thought Christ would return before we finished the series or I finished this work! Thank you for every prayer and note of encouragement. I especially want to thank my fellow elders and our staff, whose sacrifices made it possible for me to have time to study and write. Thank you to Barton Ramsey, in particular, for always being trustworthy in the pulpit.

With regard to exposition, I owe a deep gratitude to my mentor, Jim Shaddix. No one has taught me more about seeking to rightly divide God's Word. I am grateful for the Lord's good providences in bringing me to New Orleans Baptist Theological Seminary and for Dr. Shaddix's bringing me into his home. Every faithful sermon I (and many others) deliver is a fruit of his investment into my life and preaching.

Lastly, thank you to Danny Akin, Tony Merida, and David Platt for the opportunity to contribute to this great commentary series. Thank you for your trust and for enduring my whining. I count it among my highest privileges to call each of you friend.

Landon Dowden

SERIES INTRODUCTION

Augustine said, "Where Scripture speaks, God speaks." The editors of the Christ-Centered Exposition Commentary series believe that where God speaks, the pastor must speak. God speaks through His written Word. We must speak from that Word. We believe the Bible is God breathed, authoritative, inerrant, sufficient, understandable, necessary, and timeless. We also affirm that the Bible is a Christ-centered book; that is, it contains a unified story of redemptive history of which Jesus is the hero. Because of this Christ-centered trajectory that runs from Genesis 1 through Revelation 22, we believe the Bible has a corresponding global-missions thrust. From beginning to end, we see God's mission as one of making worshipers of Christ from every tribe and tongue worked out through this redemptive drama in Scripture. To that end we must preach the Word.

In addition to these distinct convictions, the Christ-Centered Exposition Commentary series has some distinguishing characteristics. First, this series seeks to display exegetical accuracy. What the Bible says is what we want to say. While not every volume in the series will be a verse-by-verse commentary, we nevertheless desire to handle the text carefully and explain it rightly. Those who teach and preach bear the heavy responsibility of saying what God has said in His Word and declaring what God has done in Christ. We desire to handle God's Word faithfully, knowing that we must give an account for how we have fulfilled this holy calling (Jas 3:1).

Second, the Christ-Centered Exposition Commentary series has pastors in view. While we hope others will read this series, such as parents, teachers, small-group leaders, and student ministers, we desire to provide a commentary busy pastors will use for weekly preparation of biblically faithful and gospel-saturated sermons. This series is not academic in nature. Our aim is to present a readable and pastoral style of commentaries. We believe this aim will serve the church of the Lord Jesus Christ.

Third, we want the Christ-Centered Exposition Commentary series to be known for the inclusion of helpful illustrations and theologically driven applications. Many commentaries offer no help in illustrations, and few offer any kind of help in application. Often those that do offer illustrative material and application unfortunately give little serious attention to the text. While giving ourselves primarily to explanation, we also hope to serve readers by providing inspiring and illuminating illustrations coupled with timely and timeless application.

Finally, as the name suggests, the editors seek to exalt Jesus from every book of the Bible. In saying this, we are not commending wild allegory or fanciful typology. We certainly believe we must be constrained to the meaning intended by the divine Author Himself, the Holy Spirit of God. However, we also believe the Bible has a messianic focus, and our hope is that the individual authors will exalt Christ from particular texts. Luke 24:25-27,44-47 and John 5:39,46 inform both our hermeneutics and our homiletics. Not every author will do this the same way or have the same degree of Christ-centered emphasis. That is fine with us. We believe faithful exposition that is Christ centered is not monolithic. We do believe, however, that we must read the whole Bible as Christian Scripture. Therefore, our aim is both to honor the historical particularity of each biblical passage and to highlight its intrinsic connection to the Redeemer.

The editors are indebted to the contributors of each volume. The reader will detect a unique style from each writer, and we celebrate these unique gifts and traits. While distinctive in their approaches, the authors share a common characteristic in that they are pastoral theologians. They love the church, and they regularly preach and teach God's Word to God's people. Further, many of these contributors are younger voices. We think these new, fresh voices can serve the church well, especially among a rising generation that has the task of proclaiming the Word of Christ and the Christ of the Word to the lost world.

We hope and pray this series will serve the body of Christ well in these ways until our Savior returns in glory. If it does, we will have succeeded in our assignment.

David Platt
Daniel L. Akin
Tony Merida
Series Editors
February 2013

Ezekiel

God's Glory and Discipline

EZEKIEL 1:1-28

Main Idea: Even in discipline God does not abandon His people but sustains them for the sake of His glory.

I. **God Always Has a Purpose for Disciplining His Children (1:1-2).**
   A. God's discipline of His children is never arbitrary but always deserved.
   B. God's discipline of His children is always a means of grace.
II. **God Always Provides When Disciplining His Children (1:3).**
   A. His prophet
   B. His word
   C. His hand
III. **God Is Always Present Through the Disciplining of His Children (1:4-28).**
   A. What does Ezekiel see and hear?
   B. Why does Ezekiel see this vision?
   C. What can we see?
      1. God is holy and rightly judges sin.
      2. God knows everything and is everywhere.
      3. God is sovereign and unique.
      4. God is glorious and merciful.
   D. Ezekiel's reaction and ours

Prior to my being asked to write a commentary on Ezekiel, I honestly had not spent a lot of time in this book. Also prior to Platt, Akin, and Merida's asking me to write a commentary on Ezekiel, I considered these men my friends. But I digress. As I prepared to lead the people I have the privilege of pastoring through a sermon series on Ezekiel, I found that three of my favorite pastors had neither recorded nor published any sermons on Ezekiel and a fourth pastor has only five sermons from Ezekiel on his church website. I won't reveal their names so as not to incriminate them for avoiding such a great text. I learned that rabbis had discouraged their students from teaching through Ezekiel before the age of 30, but my suspicion is they were scared God might

3

ask them to do some of the things He asked Ezekiel to do. Imagine if you were Ezekiel's neighbor! Despite the lack of preaching frequency in Ezekiel, this book has much to say to contemporary audiences about God's glory, God's discipline, God's sovereignty, God's judgment, God's mercy, God's faithfulness, and God's restoration. The value of preaching through Ezekiel can even be seen from its opening chapter.

Have you ever felt like your ability to sin is greater than God's ability to save? Have you ever felt like you have overextended your sin limit on God's daily mercies? Have you ever felt like "I've done it now" and your sin is going to cause God to finally say, "I'm done with you! I quit"? Or perhaps you have felt like God has abandoned you in your sin and left you alone to experience the full consequences of your rebellion. If you have ever had any or all of these feelings, then Ezekiel is the word from the Lord you need to hear.

God will not tolerate the sin of His people, but it is also true that He will not abandon them. The gospel reminds us why: God will not leave us because He left His Son; God will not abandon us because He abandoned His Son; God will not forsake us because He forsook His Son; and God will not condemn us because He condemned His Son. Even in the midst of the worst consequences due to our sin, God still offers a word of hope and restoration. The ultimate fulfillment may never occur in this life, but it will occur. The way God chose to remind His people in Ezekiel's day that He would not forsake them was to give them a magnificent vision of Himself.

God Always Has a Purpose for Disciplining His Children
EZEKIEL 1:1-2

The book opens with Ezekiel and other Israelites living as exiles in Babylon. Daniel and those with him were most likely deported to Babylon in 605 BC, while Ezekiel was most likely exiled in 597 BC (House and Mitchell, *Survey*, 220). We do not know the exact city Ezekiel lived in while in Babylon, but some see Tel-Abib as a possibility. We are informed in the opening verses that Ezekiel and the others have been in exile for five years. On this particular day, Ezekiel is by the **Chebar canal**.

He begins by letting us know that in the thirtieth year, in the fourth month, on the fifth day of the month, he was among the exiles by the Chebar canal and the heavens were opened and he saw visions of God. The date appears permanently etched in Ezekiel's memory. For many of us, it might be similar to asking, "Where were you when the *Challenger* shuttle exploded?" or "Where were you when the towers fell in New York?" For me August stands out because this is the day my parents separated and a few years later it was the same date on which one of my good friends was drowned. We all have dates and experiences that are seared into our memories. In Ezekiel's case there is no doubt why he remembered so many details surrounding the vision he was given. God was going to reveal Himself in a way Ezekiel could have never imagined in his wildest dreams.

What about you? Can you remember a day when God spoke to you when you were least expecting it? Perhaps you were not even speaking to Him, but He captured your attention. Ezekiel is a reminder that God can do extraordinary things on what seems to be ordinary days. The day of the first vision had such an impact on Ezekiel that he never forgot it but could pinpoint specifically when it occurred and where he was. Where he was is a good question. Why was he in Babylon?

God's Discipline of His Children Is Never Arbitrary but Always Deserved

God's people were in Babylon because God was disciplining them for their sin. None were innocent and nothing was arbitrary. From 2 Kings 24 we learn that God used Nebuchadnezzar to come against and conquer His people because of the rebellion and all the evil their leaders had done in His sight (2 Kgs 24:9). God is holy. He reigns for His glory and our good. All of our sin is a rejection of His reign and an assertion of our own. The length of the exile would be 70 years. Many of those exiled would die in Babylon, and others would be born there. Imagine a father having to explain to his son why he was born in Babylon instead of Judah. Always remember: it may be *my* sin, but it is always *our* consequences. Sin always has a cost. For God's people exile would be a heavy price to pay.

If you want to know how the Israelites were feeling during this exile, then all you have to do is read Psalm 137. In this psalm we learn that God's people wept when they remembered Zion and they hung up their musical instruments because they didn't feel like singing anymore. They were separated from the temple and its sacrificial system. But more importantly, they were cut off from God's presence—at least, that is what they thought. If God was in the temple and the temple was in Jerusalem, then how could they meet with Him? For Israel it was a period of deep mourning. Whether their mourning was from proper or improper motives remains to be seen. What about us? When God disciplines us, do we mourn because we've been caught or because we have grieved Him? All of God's discipline is grace to us.

God's Discipline of His Children Is Always a Means of Grace

Amazingly, God does not abandon the children He disciplines but instead sustains and sanctifies them through it. Jeremiah 24 is a record of God's purpose for the Babylonian exile. Listen to what He says about those He sent away to the land of the Chaldeans:

> *I will keep My eyes on them for their good and will return them to this land. I will build them up and not demolish them; I will plant them and not uproot them. I will give them a heart to know Me, that I am Yahweh. They will be My people, and I will be their God because they will return to Me with all their heart.* (vv. 6-7)

Did you see it? His aim in the discipline is the heart of His people. He will give them a heart that is wholly His and that knows He is the Lord. The point of Israel's knowing that God is Yahweh is emphasized more than 60 times in Ezekiel. This will occur through the discipline and not around it.

God disciplines because He loves us and wants to produce righteousness in us and through us (see Heb 12:3-11). God's discipline is always in the right amount and has as its aim our repentance and not just our remorse. If we were honest, short discipline and minimal repentance would often be our preference. Our focus in discipline is often restoration instead of removing what led to the discipline. We often think to ourselves, "How quickly can I get out of this?" instead of, "How quickly can I deal with what brought me to this place?" As will be revealed through the book of Ezekiel, Israel's hope of restoration would not be because of any self-merit but because of God's mercy. All Israel and the rest of us deserved was judgment.

God Always Provides When Disciplining His Children
EZEKIEL 1:3

His Prophet

We do not have a lot of details about the one God would choose to be His mouthpiece, but we do know a few facts. Ezekiel was a **priest**. Some believe he was most likely 30 years old. We also know Ezekiel did not go searching for God but God came to him. Mark Dever points out,

> God takes the initiative. He is the one who comes to us. . . . Ezekiel didn't open the heavens and go to God. . . . Like Moses and the burning bush. Like Isaiah in the temple. Like Paul on the road to Damascus. So with Ezekiel. None of these men were out looking for God or trying to initiate contact with Him. This God takes the initiative. He comes to us. (Dever, *Message*, 641)

The same initiative is seen in the incarnation. God seeks His lost sheep.

Though Ezekiel was a priest, God had a new occupation for him: prophet. Most likely Ezekiel had been looking forward to serving in the temple and having a long and fruitful ministry as a priest. God, however, had different plans for him. No temple. No priestly service. No problem. God wanted Ezekiel to serve as His mouthpiece to those in exile. What about us? Are our lives wide open to His call? Are we those who say, "Whatever You want, Lord!" If we are not, then our lack of trust and obedience is to our own detriment. Ezekiel the prophet in Babylon is shown a vision of God that Ezekiel the priest may have never seen in Jerusalem.

His Word

God didn't just have something to show Ezekiel, but He had something to say. **The word of the LORD** came to Ezekiel. As a matter of fact, the word of the Lord would come to Ezekiel a lot—the phrase is recorded over 49 times in the book. In the initial vision Ezekiel hears the voice of the Lord twice (vv. 25,28). Stuart contends,

> The purpose was not simply to dazzle Ezekiel, but to point to a message. God is on the move, He is allowing Himself to be seen, He is appearing even in what people thought was a godforsaken place. What an enduring message of hope! How important it is for us to remember that God is never confined, never limited, never distracted, never disinterested in His people. (Stuart, *Ezekiel*, 28–29)

Ezekiel would never lack God's message for God's people. Yahweh knew exactly what His people needed to hear.

His Hand

As Ezekiel receives the vision, the Lord's hand was on His prophet. This is not a sign of oppression but of empowerment. In the remainder of the book, Ezekiel will refer to the Lord's hand as many as four more times. As a matter of fact, his name bears testimony to this thought of empowerment, for *Ezekiel* means, "God strengthens" (Taylor, *Ezekiel*, 68). Ezekiel would have God's sayings and His strength. All of the resources Ezekiel needed for his new ministry, God provided.

God Is Always Present Through the Disciplining of His Children
EZEKIEL 1:4-28

What Does Ezekiel See and Hear?

Though it does not appear that God spoke to His people during the first five years of their exile, His silence did not mean His absence. The vision given to Ezekiel will confirm not only that God is not limited to the temple in Jerusalem but also that He will in fact be with and sustain His people in exile. So what exactly does Ezekiel see and hear? He sees "an impressive picture of God's giant, fiery, air chariot driven by the King of kings himself, which had touched down right there at the obscure town of Tel-Abib" (Stuart, *Ezekiel*, 31).

Why Does Ezekiel See This Vision?

Ezekiel receives the vision so God's people will know He is Yahweh. One would think they already knew this, but if they did, they have not been acting like it. In Ezekiel every bit of judgment and every ray of hope have the purpose of reintroducing God to His people (Dever, *Message*, 649). Seeing God clearly allows us to see everything else rightly, including ourselves. Thomas notes, "God's aim is not to constrain man's submission by force, but to ravish our affections with irresistible displays of the treasure of His glory. When God is our treasure, submission is our pleasure" (Thomas, *God Strengthens*, 30). Obedience driven by delight is far better than obedience driven by duty alone.

What about us? Is our view of God the same as His? Can the people in our worship services see Him rightly in His Word? Are our pulpits declaring His greatness? Tony Evans does not think so. He contends,

The God most of us worship is too small. The God of most
Christians seems anemic, weak, and limited. He does not
have the capacity to make a difference, to turn things around.
The God most of us serve resembles more the flickering of a
candle than the burning of the noonday sun. (Evans, *Awesome*,
93)

In Ezekiel Yahweh will make Himself known so that Israel and the
nations will know exactly who He is.

What Can We See?

First, from Ezekiel's vision we can see that *God is holy and rightly judges sin.*
God will not ignore sin forever. He will see that every sin is punished.
Those who do not flee to Christ will be forced to bear the punishment
for all of their sin. In this vision we can see His holiness in the **great
cloud**. Ezekiel sees a **whirlwind coming from the north, a great cloud
with fire flashing back and forth and brilliant light all around it**. Based
on its direction of origin, Ezekiel knows this is not a cloud of rescue but
of reckoning. Trouble generally comes from the north, as evidenced by
Gog in the distant future (38:15). In Ezekiel 1, however, Gog is not the
approaching one Israel needs to fear; God is! He is not coming to deal
with the Chaldeans primarily but with His own people.

God's holiness is also seen in the **fire**. The cloud Ezekiel is shown
has **fire flashing back and forth,** and **in the center of the fire** is **a gleam
like amber**. The prophet describes the one sitting **on the throne high
above** having from his waist upward **what looked like fire enclosing it
all around** and from His waist downward **what looked like fire. A brilliant light** surrounds **Him** as well. Scripture repeatedly describes God as
a consuming fire (Exod 19; Heb 12; Rev 1), which is never considered
good news for sinners. Paul informs the Thessalonians that Jesus will be
revealed from heaven with His mighty angels in flaming fire (2 Thess
1:7-9).

God's holiness is seen by the presence of the four living creatures
as well. Ezekiel says the form of the living creatures was like the appearance of burning coals of fire and torches. Fire was moving back and
forth between the living creatures; it was bright, with lightning coming out of it. The creatures were darting back and forth like flashes of
lightning. The living creatures are cherubim, and every time they are
mentioned in Scripture they are guardians of God's holiness (Gen 3:24;
Exod 25:18-20; 26:1; 36:8; Rev 4:6-9) (MacArthur, "Sacrifice"). From the

beginning of the vision, Ezekiel is shown God's holiness, which will be a major emphasis throughout the book.

Second, from Ezekiel's vision we are informed that *God knows everything and is everywhere*. The **wheels** and the **wheel within a wheel** demonstrate God's ability to go anywhere. He can even do so **without pivoting** or turning. With this vision God is invading Babylon and the realm of their god, Marduk. Yahweh needs no one's permission to do so, particularly not the approval of a man-made god. He is not limited to the temple. God can be anywhere He wants to be but especially wherever His people are. The rims that **were full of eyes** show He sees and knows everything. God's people may no longer be in Judah, but He can still see them just as clearly.

Third, from Ezekiel's vision we are shown that *God is sovereign and unique*. Above the great fire was an **expanse,** and **above the expanse** was **the shape of a throne,** and **there was a form with the appearance of a human on the throne high above.** God does not reign over just a little territory in the Middle East but over the entire universe. In this vision

> the absolute distinction between Yahweh and all of creation is clearly recognized. . . . Yahweh sits alone on His throne, separated from all inferior creatures. . . . God is alone above the platform, removed from all creatures, and stunning in His radiance. There is none other beside(s) Him. (Block, *Ezekiel 1–24*, 107–8)

Fourth, from Ezekiel's vision we see that *God is glorious and merciful*. Because Ezekiel lacks the vocabulary to describe all he is shown, he uses the terms "**like**," "**the appearance of**," and "**what seemed to be.**" He says, "**This was the appearance of the form of the LORD's glory.**" Block notes,

> Unlike the gods of the nations depicted on ancient seals and carvings, the glory of Yahweh defies human description, verbally or visually. And unlike the images of the heathen, which require constant attention and polishing, Yahweh's radiance emanates from His very being. (*Ezekiel 1–24*, 106)

God is indeed glorious, but He is also merciful. The Israelites have not, nor have we, done anything deserving of mercy. But in the final verse of the vision, Ezekiel describes the **brilliant light** that is around the One on the throne **like that of a rainbow in a cloud on a rainy day.** Many years later John would see a similar vision of One seated on a throne with the appearance of a rainbow all around (Rev 4:3). In thinking back to the days of Noah, the rainbow was meant to remind us not just that God would no longer cover the earth with water but that even in wrath God is merciful. Despite all the looming clouds of judgment, the beams of the bow allowed for rays of hope.

Ezekiel's Reaction and Ours

The least surprising component of the entire vision is Ezekiel's reaction. Ezekiel says, **when I saw it, I fell facedown**. No doubt! Isaiah, Peter, James, John, and Paul all had similar reactions when they were allowed to see just a glimmer of the Lord's glory. The question is not why so many in the Bible fell on the ground in the presence of the Lord but why there seems to be so little of it today. Perhaps people these days are not seeing the Lord's glory in the sermons they hear or the services they attend. Of all the feelings Ezekiel had in the first chapter, it's clear one of them is not the "Jesus is my homeboy" mentality. Dever notes Ezekiel's

> new knowledge of God did not make him feel more casual
> about God at all. He was awed by this vision of God. . . . The
> casual happiness we often regard as the height of spiritual
> intimacy with God is never pictured in the Bible. Every vision
> of God in the Bible is awesome and inspires reverence. (Dever,
> *Message*, 640)

David once told God, "So I gaze on You in the sanctuary to see Your strength and Your glory" (Ps 63:2). David's vision of God would even sustain him in the wilderness. May our people see such a vision as well.

Conclusion

What can we glean from this text? I have a few suggestions. First, if we are scared that God will ultimately abandon us in our sin, Ezekiel 1 should provide a measure of hope. Second, if we are in the middle of God's discipline, rejoice that He will use it to set us free from our selfishness and to conform us further to the image of Christ. Third, through Ezekiel, God will speak clearly to the exiles, but through Christ, God speaks most clearly to us. Fourth, we may never see God's fiery chariot roaming the landscape, but in Christ we have seen His glory (John 1:14). Fifth, we are not just to see His glory but to display it (2 Cor 3:7-18). Tim Chester asks two important questions: What impression of God would someone pick up from watching the way we live out our Christian faith? Would that impression be anything like Ezekiel's vision (Chester, *God of Glory*, 10)? Sixth, like Israel, we are in exile too (1 Pet 2:11; Heb 13:14), but we are not without a home or hope (Duguid, *Ezekiel*, 53). Seventh, there is much to be thankful for in Ezekiel 1. We can thank God that He is still the same God that Ezekiel saw in His vision (Chester, *God of Glory*, 11). We can thank God that despite the rebellion of humanity and the weakness of His people, God has preserved, and always will preserve, His people and His gospel (ibid.). We can thank God that the worst form of discipline for His people was not in Chaldea but at Calvary, and He took it upon Himself.

Reflect and Discuss

1. Why does God choose to discipline His children? Have you always seen His discipline as grace? Have you ever?
2. Have you ever felt like your sin was greater than God's grace? Why does He choose not to abandon His children, even in their rebellion?
3. When God disciplines us, what is the difference between being repentant and being regretful?
4. What consequences are your sins having on your family and faith family?
5. What is your vision of God? Is it God's vision of God?
6. If you had seen all Ezekiel was allowed to see, how do you think you would have reacted?
7. How can you help others understand that sin is still a big deal to God?
8. As glorious as the vision in Ezekiel 1 is, why is the incarnation an even greater display of God's glory?
9. In what ways are you grateful that God not only speaks but has spoken most clearly in Christ?
10. How can you avoid being caught up in the *what* of the vision in Ezekiel 1 and instead keep the focus on the *who*?

Ezekiel's Commissioning and Ours

EZEKIEL 2:1–3:27

Main Idea: God provides everything His messengers need to take His entire message to all the places and peoples to which He sends them.

I. As Ambassadors of God, We May Be Given a Difficult Ministry (2:1-7; 3:4-7).
II. As Ambassadors of God, We May Be Given a Difficult Message (2:8–3:3).
III. As Ambassadors of God, We Will Be Given Divine Means (3:8-15).
IV. As Ambassadors of God, What We Do Definitely Matters (3:16-27).
    A. The Proclamation of the Message (3:16-21)
    B. The Preparation of the Messenger (3:22-27)

We do not know many things about Titus, but one thing we do know is he was given a tough ministry assignment. Paul left Titus in Crete to set right what was left undone. He was among many rebellious people who were full of empty talk and deception and who were also liars, evil beasts, and lazy gluttons (Titus 1:5-12). Sounds delightful, doesn't it? I wonder if he wished Timothy had been given the opportunity instead? Before we throw a pity party for Titus, we should realize that few of God's messengers have been sent to receptive audiences. Isaiah, Jeremiah, and even Jesus preached God's message to those who were looking but could not see and hearing but not understanding (Luke 8:10). Ask Stephen, Peter, and Paul about how much their audiences loved to hear God's message, and they would have stories to tell you and scars to show you.

As the second chapter of Ezekiel opens, the prophet is going to be commissioned to take God's Word to God's **rebellious** people who are **obstinate, hardheaded**, and **hardhearted**. Ezekiel is **not to be afraid** though because God will provide both the message and the means to proclaim it. Ezekiel's commissioning is not that different from ours (Matt 28:18-20). Like Ezekiel we've been called to take God's Word with the promise that God will be with us. Unlike Ezekiel we've been called to take God's Word to every nation and make as many disciples in as many places as possible.

As chapter 1 in Ezekiel came to a close, we were drawn in not by what Ezekiel saw but by what he heard. He told us he **heard a voice speaking** (1:28) and then, like our favorite TV drama, the words "to be continued" flashed across the page. We now get to find out what Ezekiel heard. It was a message that left him **stunned for seven days** and changed the rest of his life. Let's turn to that message now.

As Ambassadors of God, We May Be Given a Difficult Ministry
EZEKIEL 2:1-7; 3:4-7

Discipline alone does not always guarantee repentance. How do I know? After five years in exile, God's people were still rebelling against Him. God told Ezekiel His people transgressed against Him "**to this day.**" The Israelites may have been burdened over their situation (Ps 137), but they were not yet broken over their sin. At this point we learn the vision given to Ezekiel is not just so he can have the greatest quiet time in the history of daily devotions. No, God has an assignment for him. If God's people are to be convicted of their sin, then someone is going to have to communicate God's word to them (Acts 2:37).

God's solution for His people, who are **hardheaded** and **hardhearted**, is to send His messenger with His message through His means. God informs Ezekiel, "**I am sending you to the Israelites, to the rebellious pagans who have rebelled against Me. . . . I am sending you to them, and you must say to them, 'This is what the Lord GOD says'**" (2:3-4). And again, God says, "**Son of man, go to the house of Israel and speak My words to them. . . . You are not being sent to many peoples of unintelligible speech or difficult language, whose words you cannot understand**" (3:4,6). The great news is Ezekiel is commissioned to take God's word to just one nation—his own. The bad news: they do not want to hear it.

God didn't paint a rosy picture for Ezekiel. He told the prophet his audience was a **rebellious house** and at times their **words** might cause him to be afraid and their looks would tempt him to **be discouraged.** Insert your best deacon joke here. In all seriousness, sticks and stones may break our bones, but apparently words cause our hearts to fear. What do you think those listening to the prophet would say that would tempt him to fear?

Ezekiel's audience will **not want to listen** to him because ultimately **they do not want to listen to** God (3:7). In case Ezekiel is still not grasping the difficulty, God uses the word *rebellious* six times and throws in the word *rebelled* once for good measure. If God described us seven times with one word, what would that word be? How would He characterize our desire and receptivity for His Word?

Have you ever not wanted to go to someone and share what the Lord asked you to share with him or her? I'm sure Nathan was not overly excited about the message he was asked to deliver to King David (2 Sam 12). I know Ezekiel was not initially pumped about his ministry either, since he admitted having **bitterness** and **an angry spirit** (3:14). Who can blame him? In a seemingly ordinary day God showed up and gave him an unordinary task of taking His message to people that didn't want to hear it. As God's ambassador Ezekiel did not have authority to change his assignment or his audience. Neither do we. Ministry is difficult because people are difficult. The only hope for breaking people's hardness of heart and head is the same as it was in Ezekiel's day: God's Word. Jesus' ministry audience said awful things about Him, and as His ambassadors we should not expect anything less (Matt 10:25).

What is your ministry audience like? How much do your coworkers love to hear about Christ? What about your non-Christian family members at holidays? Are they asking you to share with them the message of Christ one more time? Don't be discouraged. And don't be afraid. Overcoming minds that are hostile (Col 1:21), futile (Eph 4:17), and darkened (Eph 4:18) is what God does every day and what He did for us. We were once a difficult audience ourselves, but His grace overcame all of the hardness of our hearts (Eph 4:18). Remember how He rescued you, and run to those outside of Christ with His words of life.

As Ambassadors of God, We May Be Given a Difficult Message
EZEKIEL 2:8–3:3

Knowing that our audience does not want to hear what we are going to share with them may tempt us to change the message. But like Ezekiel we have no authority to change the message we've been given. Besides having a difficult ministry, Ezekiel was entrusted with a difficult message that included **words of lamentation, mourning, and woe** (2:10). Yay! That'll draw a crowd. The prophet's responsibility was to **listen carefully**

to all of God's **words and take them to heart** (3:10). He was then to say to the people, "**This is what the Lord GOD says**" (3:11).

Paul exhorted the church at Colossae to let God's word dwell richly in them as they were teaching and admonishing one another in wisdom (Col 3:16). Internalization of the message would not be a problem for Ezekiel. God made sure His prophet consumed His word. He fed Ezekiel the scroll with lamentations, mourning, and woe written on it, but surprisingly it was **sweet as honey** (3:3). With this action, Thomas contends, "The Lord was teaching Ezekiel that to be really effective for God in our Christian lives, His Word has to become a part of us" (Thomas, *God Strengthens*, 38).

Let's pause for a moment and ask: Is God's Word flowing out of us into our daily conversations? When others ask what we think about a topic, do we bring God's Word to bear on the situation or just our accumulated years of wisdom? Jesus told us, "The mouth speaks from the overflow of the heart" (Matt 12:34). What's our plan for internalizing the Word? Are we intentionally hiding the Word in our heart? For God's ambassadors Psalm 119:11 has to become more than just a Vacation Bible School verse. For each disciple he made, Dawson Trotman said,

> We taught him how to fill the quiver of his heart with the arrows of God's Word, so that the Spirit of God could lift an arrow from his heart and place it to the bow of his lips and pierce a heart for Christ. ("Born to Reproduce")

The best way to ensure we are taking the right message to a lost world is to consume it like Ezekiel and find it to be just as sweet.[1]

God also wanted Ezekiel to know he was not responsible for the receipt of or reaction to the message but only the delivery of it. **Whether they listen or refuse to listen**, Ezekiel's only task was to deliver God's word so that the people would **know that a prophet has been among them** (2:5). The messenger's job is to get the message to the ear of his audience, but only the Lord can get it to the heart (Acts 16:14).

Ezekiel would prove to be a faithful messenger. More than 50 times he would say, "The word of the LORD came to me," and more than 122 times he would say, "This is what the LORD says." No matter the

---

[1] If you do not have a strategy for memorizing the Word, then consider using this guide: Andrew M. Davis, *An Approach to Extended Memorization of Scripture* (Greenville, SC: Ambassador International, 2014).

audience, Ezekiel refused to change the message. God always knows what His people need to hear. Our task is not creativity but faithfulness when it comes to delivering His message.

In our day some want to change the gospel to make it more palatable. Not everyone likes the exclusivity of the gospel or the thought of an actual hell. Others are repulsed that Christ's death could be considered voluntary, much less substitutionary. Even in Christian circles some have an aversion to singing of God's wrath; people prefer to sing of His love (Stocker, "Wrath of God"). Like Ezekiel, however, we are to take all of God's words to heart. In our commissioning Jesus told us we are to teach others to observe everything He has commanded us (Matt 28:20). We do not have the authority to alter the message. My prayer is always to be able to join Paul in saying, "I am innocent of everyone's blood, for I did not shrink back from declaring to you the whole plan of God" (Acts 20:26-27).

If our confidence is anywhere besides the cross of Christ, we will be tempted to adjust the gospel message God has entrusted to us. If the approval of God we have received in Christ is not precious to us, then we may adjust the message seeking man's approval. If the love of God that we have received in Christ is not first in our mind, then we may hold back some element of the gospel hoping our audience will like us. In altering or withholding parts of the gospel, we run the risk of changing the one life-saving message into a word of death. Paul has strong words for those who want to change the message (Gal 1:8-9). May the cross of Christ free us to speak the gospel boldly, clearly, faithfully, and without compromise.

As Ambassadors of God, We Will Be Given Divine Means
EZEKIEL 3:8-15

A friend of mine once opined that 90 percent of a successful home improvement project is having the right tools. I'm a living asterisk to that folksy statistic. I often need more home improvement after I finish my projects. Graciously, God does not give His people tasks without giving the tools necessary to complete those tasks. The two greatest resources He gives are His Spirit and His Word.

Imagine for a moment that you are Ezekiel. You've just been asked to take a difficult message to a difficult group of people. Now imagine God closing His assignment by saying, "Good luck! Give it your best shot." If left to his own power, Ezekiel would have had his own Mission Impossible. Fortunately, all that God expects from us, He provides for us.

God told Ezekiel, "**I have made your face as hard as their faces and your forehead as hard as their foreheads. I have made your forehead like a diamond, harder than flint**" (3:8). God would not send Ezekiel against difficult words and discouraging looks without supplying all he needed to fulfill the mission. His very name, *Ezekiel,* means, "God strengthens" (Taylor, *Ezekiel,* 68). As hardheaded as his audience would be in rejecting the message, Ezekiel would be even more determined in delivering it. Their obstinacy was at their own peril, but his was for their eternal good.

A picture of God's empowering presence is seen in the opening description of chapter 2. Ezekiel testifies that as God spoke to him, "**the Spirit entered me and set me on my feet, and I listened to the One who was speaking to me**" (2:2). Without the Spirit's help, Ezekiel could not even obey God's command to stand in His presence.

One of my favorite parts of the movie *Facing the Giants* was when the coach challenged one of his players to carry another player on his back, all while being blindfolded. With the coach encouraging him, the young man bear-crawled the entire length of the football field. What God does for us with His Spirit, however, is not just stand on the side encouraging us, but He indwells and empowers us.

The Spirit is just as necessary in our own ministries as He was for Ezekiel. McLaughlin noted,

> General semantics, cybernetics, field theory, group dynamics
> and all other communication theories and methods may
> be likened to the sails of a ship; all of the equipment stands
> useless without the motivating winds of the Holy Spirit.
> (McLaughlin, *Communication,* 194)

The delivery of God's message is efficacious only if the Spirit attends it. In short, "everything depends on the Spirit"(Marcel, *Preaching,* 91).

Acts is full of examples of God's messengers being filled with the Spirit for the purpose of proclamation (Acts 4:8,31; 6:10; 13:9-10). The apostle Paul confessed he labored in proclaiming Christ but "with His strength that works powerfully in me" (Col 1:28). Lloyd-Jones saw the Spirit's anointing as

> an access of power. It is God giving power, and enabling,
> through the Spirit, to the teacher in order that he may do

this work in a manner that lifts it up beyond the efforts and endeavors of man to a position in which the teacher is being used by the Spirit and becomes the channel through whom the Spirit works. (Lloyd-Jones, *Preaching*, 305)

Our problem is not receiving the Spirit but relying on Him. Azurdia contends,

> The greatest impediment to the advancement of the gospel in our time is the attempt of the church of Jesus Christ to do the work of God apart from the truth and the power of the Spirit of God. (Azurdia, *Spirit Empowered Preaching*, 29)

Twice God told Ezekiel, **"Don't be afraid"** (2:6; 3:9). Realizing the magnitude of the task he'd been given would cause any heart to quiver. The Lord, however, would replace Ezekiel's fearfulness with faithfulness. He would supply all Ezekiel needed to fear disobedience to God more than he feared discouragement or death from man. If you struggle in this regard, then I cannot commend highly enough Welch's *When People Are Big and God Is Small.*

Like Ezekiel we've been given a difficult assignment. Our King has charged us to go to every nation and to make disciples. He wants us to teach them to obey everything He has commanded. We can know, however, that we will have every provision necessary because He has promised His presence (Matt 28:18-20). Our King does not wish us bon voyage and just wait to hear reports, but He goes with us every step of the way. David Livingstone found great hope in this promise (Kimbrough, *Words*, 121). May we as well. Is the Spirit's empowering evident in what you are doing and saying?

As Ambassadors of God, What We Do Definitely Matters
EZEKIEL 3:16-27

The Proclamation of the Message (3:16-21)

We are blessed in our city to have a great meteorologist. Last spring, days before a deadly storm system rolled through our area, Matt Laubhan warned our city to be vigilant and to make preparations for possible tornadoes. On the day of the storm, both Matt and the local tornado warning system sounded the alarm for us to seek refuge. Thanks to God's protection and Matt's pronouncements many lives in Tupelo were saved.

In his day Ezekiel was called to sound an alarm as well. The Lord said to him, "**Son of man, I have made you a watchman over the house of Israel. When you hear a word from My mouth, give them a warning from Me**" (33:7). Ezekiel would be held accountable for what he did with the word of the Lord.

The question for Ezekiel and us is not whether we are watchmen but whether we are good ones. Ezekiel was given the message, but it was up to him what he did with it. If he withheld the message, it meant certain peril for the people and their blood would be on his hands. If he proclaimed the message but they still failed to repent, then their blood would be on their own hands, but he would be saved.

What are we doing with the message we have been given? Do we see God as making His appeal through us (2 Cor 5:20)? Because we know those who do not seek refuge in Christ will be destroyed (Matt 7:13; Phil 3:19), why would we not warn everyone? No one will be held more accountable for the people who live in our cities during our generation than Christians. Who in your city still hasn't heard that Christ has not only come once but is also coming again (Ps 96:13)? How many moms and dads will tuck their children in bed tonight across our globe but be unable to share with their little ones the hope of Christ because they've never heard of Him? We are not responsible for someone hearing the gospel and rejecting it, but we are responsible for making sure they hear it.

The Preparation of the Messenger (3:22-27)

As the third chapter of Ezekiel draws to a close, the prophet shares how God planned to prepare him for his assignment. Does anyone else find it strange that after Ezekiel has been assigned as the watchman for his people, he is then told he will be mute and bound in his home? In fact, his muteness would last almost seven and a half years (33:21-22). Why would God choose to use this method of preparation? So that Ezekiel's peers would know he was not his own anymore, and when they saw him and heard him, it was because he had a message for them from God (Thomas, *God Strengthens*, 40).

I wonder if our friends would testify to our similarity with Ezekiel. When they see us, are we on mission for God? When they hear us, are we speaking for God? Probably not, but it's not because God wants less of us than He required of Ezekiel. It's because we do not fully grasp what it means to be Christ's slave (Eph 6:6). We often live as if we are still our own rather than living for the One who died for us (2 Cor 5:15). I want to be more like Ezekiel. Whatever God needs me to say, wherever He needs me to go, and however He needs to prepare me, I am His.

As difficult as Ezekiel's ministry and message may have been, no one has had a more difficult assignment than Christ. In reflecting on God's preparation of Ezekiel and all that he endured, Duguid has said it best:

> Our example in all of this is the self-sacrifice of Jesus Christ. Was Ezekiel confined to his house? Jesus was "despised and rejected by men, a man of sorrows, and familiar with suffering" (Isa 53:3). Was Ezekiel made dumb? Jesus was "led like a lamb to the slaughter, and as a sheep before her shearers is silent, so he did not open his mouth" (Isa 53:7). Was Ezekiel bound with ropes? Jesus was nailed to the cross and suffered there not for any transgressions of his own but for ours. The shackles of death designed for our wrists were placed on his. Thus has the greater "Son of Man" fulfilled the ministry of the earlier "son of man," giving us the good news of the gospel, which is the antidote to the bad news of our natural state. What price, then, can be too great for us to play our part in the great work of the triune God, bringing to himself a harvest of men and women from every tribe, nation, and language group, that they too might receive eternal life in Christ Jesus? (Duguid, *Ezekiel*, 86)

Reflect and Discuss

1. Is there someone with whom God has asked you to share His Word but you are hesitating? What's holding you back?
2. Is there anywhere you are hesitant to take the gospel in your city, state, or the world? Are there places you hope He sends someone else? Why?
3. Have you ever been tempted not to share with someone all that you believed God was asking you share with them?
4. Why are some people tempted to change the gospel? Why should we not change the message God has given us in Christ?
5. What's your current plan for memorizing Scripture?
6. How would you feel if God gave us the Great Commission without giving us His Spirit and His Word?
7. When was a time you truly knew the Holy Spirit was empowering you to testify about Christ?

8. How often do you think about your role as a watchman for your city? How often are you sounding the alarm and calling for people to seek refuge in Christ?
9. In what ways are you challenged by Ezekiel's willingness to do whatever God asked of him?
10. In what ways do you think people have difficulty seeing that you "completely" belong to Christ?

When God Is Against You

EZEKIEL 4:1–5:17

Main Idea: When we fail to live as children of God, we deserve every consequence of our rebellion, but even in judgment His mercy is evident.

I. **A Privileged Position (5:5-7)**
   - A. Being a child of God is something we should never take for granted (5:5).
   - B. Being a child of God brings both blessings and responsibilities (5:6-11).

II. **A Promised Persecution (5:7-17)**
   - A. Though we may not keep our word, God always keeps His, and He will not leave sin unpunished forever.
   - B. God's judgment on sin is both deserved and awful (5:7-11,16-17).
   - C. When our rebellion is public, His discipline will be as well (5:8,14-15).

III. **A Performing Prophet (4:1–5:4)**
   - A. The media of the message (4:1–5:4)
   - B. The messenger

IV. **A Planned Provision (5:13)**

When I was in fourth grade, I entered into a verbal contract with my sister. At the time we had an oscillating fan that was sitting on the floor, and I was using it as a target for my putter and golf ball. Unsolicited on her part, I offered an agreement: if I missed the fan on my next putt, then for the next year she could call me "Mud." I can't remember where I got the idea, but I had confidence it would not matter. It mattered! On my next attempt I calculated and then fired away—missing badly. My sister immediately said, "Good shot, Mud!" Was I upset? You bet. How could she have the audacity to keep her end of the bargain I had arranged? I immediately tattled to my mother.

How many commitments have we made to God? Maybe we made a commitment at a youth camp or marriage conference or even after choosing a besetting sin one more time. I wonder how many of those commitments we've kept? I learned early on that one must be cautious when entering into a contract or agreement. As the book of Ezekiel will often remind us, God and Israel had an agreement. It was called a covenant. God always keeps His commitments. We, however, do not. In Ezekiel 4 and 5 God is keeping His end of the agreement, just not in the way Israel wanted.

A Privileged Position
EZEKIEL 5:5-7

Being a Child of God Is Something We Should Never Take for Granted (5:5)

God does not owe us anything but what the wrath our rebellion has merited. His grace and mercy are not birthrights of our national citizenship. He could remain cold and distant and still be holy and right. But according to His own counsel, He has chosen to make Himself known and to have a people to the praise of His glory (Eph 1:14). For Israel this meant that out of all peoples on earth, He chose them to be holy to Himself (Deut 6:6-8). He even reminded Ezekiel that He set Jerusalem in the **center of the nations** (Ezek 5:5; 38:12). What an amazing blessing! They above all others had a unique relationship with Yahweh.

For those of us who have been grafted in by Christ, God's special relationship with His people continues. All who are in Christ have the privilege of knowing God not just as the Creator but also as their Father (Eph 1:4-5; Gal 4:6-7). Have we become desensitized to such an unmerited blessing? Packer noted, "If you want to judge how well a person understands Christianity, find out how much he makes of the thought of being God's child, and having God as his father" (Packer, *Knowing God*, 201). As we consider Ezekiel 4–5, I'm not sure which is the greater mystery: why God chose to have a people for His name's sake or why His people have so often failed to appreciate their privileged position. Without doubt He had a special relationship with Israel, but they failed to demonstrate gratitude for such a gift.

Being a Child of God Brings Both Blessings and Responsibilities (5:6-11)

God did not just choose to have a people but to have a people for His name's sake (Pss 23:3; 106:8; 1 John 2:12). Reconciliation brings with it responsibilities (Luke 12:48), and God's plan has always been for His people to be a light to the nations (Deut 4:5-8; Isa 49:6; Matt 5:14; Phil 2:14-16). Israel, however, failed miserably at shining His light. They rebelled against His **ordinances with more wickedness than the nations** and against His **statutes more than the countries** that surrounded them (Ezek 5:6; cf. 16:27). If sinning were an Olympic sport, then Israel "won the international contest in wickedness" (Block, *Ezekiel 1–24*, 107–8). In failing to live up to not just God's standards but even those of the pagan nations around them, Israel led those who most needed to see the light further into darkness (Duguid, *Ezekiel*, 100).

Because of Israel's failure Ezekiel's first message from God for His people was, "**I am against you . . . I will execute judgments within you . . . I am going to cut you off**" (5:8,11). How sad. Moses's worst nightmare comes true (Exod 33:15-16). If you were Ezekiel, how would you like the message of God's judgment and withdrawal to be your first sermon? I often joke that my first sermon was awful and the rest have steadily gotten worse. But thankfully my first sermon was not the same as Ezekiel's. To be sure, nothing was lost in translation with the prophet because God would repeat the same message at least 11 more times throughout the book: **I am against you**.

Israel had likely complained to God that they wanted justice, and they defined justice as God's judgment against their Babylonian captors. According to the first vision Ezekiel received, God was definitely coming to enact judgment, just not on the Babylonians (at least not yet). For many generations Israel enjoyed covenant blessings without honoring their covenant responsibilities. They wanted God's protection and provision but withheld their devotion and obedience. Sound like anyone we know?

A Promised Persecution
EZEKIEL 5:7-17

Though We May Not Keep Our Word, God Always Keeps His, and He Will Not Leave Sin Unpunished Forever

In formulating a defense against God's judgment, Israel may have considered many options, but ignorance was not one of them. In Leviticus 26 the blessings for obedience and the punishment for disobedience were clearly communicated when God and Israel covenanted together.

God's people knew what they were supposed to do; they just chose not to do it. Israel would find out "those who claim to be his people may not exchange him for another god without cost to themselves" (Block, *Ezekiel 1–24*, 217). What's tragic is that Israel seemed more upset at God's keeping His word than at their failure to keep theirs.

God's Judgment on Sin Is Both Deserved and Awful (5:7-11,16-17)

I do not know any healthy parents who love disciplining their children. I know I am grieved each time my children choose rebellion and I have to administer correction. God is indeed slow to anger, but when He arrives there, it is awful. Because of their **detestable practices and abominations,** God would do to Israel what He had **never done before** and would **never do again.** He would consume a third of His people **by plague** and by **famine.** The famine would be so devastating that cannibalism would occur in Jerusalem (5:10) and **dangerous animals** would consume what children were left. Another third of Ezekiel's peers would **fall by the sword.** The final third would be scattered in **every direction of the wind,** and God would draw **a sword to chase after them.** This may sound harsh, but those who believe the judgments of God are too severe have "not seen sin as God sees it" (Thomas, *God Strengthens*, 50).

When Our Rebellion Is Public, His Discipline Will Be as Well (5:8,14-15)

On top of the severity of God's judgment would be the public shame that accompanied it. Israel's rebellion toward God had not been hidden but was in plain sight. Likewise, God would do His work **in the sight of the nations.** He would make Israel a **ruin** and **disgrace among the nations** and **in the sight of everyone who passes by.** Why? Why would God do this to His people? Because He wanted Israel to be a **warning and a horror to the nations** as they witnessed God's **anger, wrath, and furious rebukes.**

God never intended our relationship with Him to be just a private matter. In placing Jerusalem at the center of the nations God

> staked his reputation on her. Since she has failed publicly, she must also bear her humiliation before the eyes of the world. Through her experience the nations will learn who God is: he is not only gracious but also passionate, demanding absolute and exclusive allegiance. (Thomas, *God Strengthens*, 50)

One Sunday morning just before a worship service was to begin, two families had a verbal disagreement on the front sidewalk by the main doors of our building. I did not find out about it until after the service, but many of our people witnessed what took place. I immediately contacted the parties involved and arranged a meeting. The Lord graciously provided reconciliation and forgiveness between the parties. On the following Sunday we asked all who were involved to seek the forgiveness of the congregation as well. Some feared utilizing a public form of restoration, but their disagreement had been in plain sight, and there was no way reconciliation could occur privately with each one who witnessed what transpired.

Two noticeable results came from the incident mentioned above. First, a guest in our service sent a comment card to our church office the following week. This person said, by our following through with the public restoration, they knew God and His Word were important to us. The second result was with one of the parties involved. From the point of restoration forward, the wife repeatedly would say, "I'm not doing (whatever the temptation of the day was) because I might have to stand up in front of the whole church again and apologize." She would share this in humor, but it also proved to be a deterrent for her and for many others. God's public shaming of Israel because of their public sins was meant to be a deterrent for everyone watching them as well.

A Performing Prophet
EZEKIEL 4:1–5:4

The Media of the Message (4:1–5:4)

Few messengers of God have been asked to do more and give more in communicating God's message than Ezekiel (see 24:15-18). God not only had a specific message for His people but also specific media through which His message would be communicated. Preaching for Ezekiel would include laying **siege** to a model city, lying on his **left side** and then **right side** for a specific set of days, having a certain sustenance, and using a **sword** to shave his **head and beard**. I wonder what grade he would have received from his peers at seminary in a sermon delivery course.

Why go to such great lengths? Couldn't three points and a poem suffice to let God's people know what He was going to do in light of all their idolatry and rebellion? Unfortunately, one of the most difficult tasks in every generation is convincing people they are sinners. We also rarely learn a truth the first time we see it. God knows not only what His people need to hear but also the exact way we need to both hear and see the message. The fact any message of His is offered more than once is nothing but grace.

Ezekiel's first sermon would make any Lego enthusiast jealous. Utilizing a **brick**, dirt, and sticks, the prophet created a model of a **siege** that would come against Jerusalem. Like insult being added to injury, this message would have been grievous news to Ezekiel's audience in Babylon. The worst aspect of the model was the **iron plate** that was to be **an iron wall between** Ezekiel **and the city**. The first way God demonstrated to His people that He was against them was to reveal the "cutting off of relationships" between Him and His people (Duguid, *Ezekiel*, 88).

Lest Israel think God is reacting rashly to something insignificant, Ezekiel's second sign act was to lie on his **left side** for **390 days** and then on his **right side** for **40 days**. Ezekiel was to be a visible reminder of how long the Lord endured His people's rebellion and how grievous the burden of their sin was. God would have **cords** placed on Ezekiel so that he could not **turn side to side** and he would **bear their iniquity**. There is much debate about whether he did this continually or only for certain portions of each day. What is not debated is that, unlike Christ, Ezekiel's bearing the iniquity of his people was no substitutionary atonement that would prevent the impending judgment (Duguid, *Ezekiel*, 90). Ezekiel's suffering would not prevent Israel's.

While on his side, Ezekiel was prescribed a specific diet. God instructed him to **take wheat, barley, beans, lentils, millet, and spelt** to make bread. He also gave the prophet a specific **weight** of **eight ounces** of food and **a sixth of a gallon** of water per day. The meager rations were meant to communicate the impending famine when God would **cut off the supply of bread in Jerusalem**. Those in Jerusalem would **lack bread and water** and **be devastated and waste away because of their iniquity**. The judgment of famine would be awful, but as Thomas notes, "The real famine was a spiritual one. The famine was a reminder of their spiritual starvation. They had forgotten God" (*God Strengthens*, 48). Interestingly, Ezekiel's only protestation in the entire book was over which type of **dung** to cook the bread.

Ezekiel's final sign act in this set of messages was to **shave** his **head and beard** with a **sharp sword**. He was to **take a set of scales and divide**

the hair. Some of the hairs were to be burned, some of the hairs were to be slashed, and some were to be scattered in the wind, all of which represented the variety of methods God would use to judge His people. From this judgment **a fire** would **spread** to **the whole house of Israel**.

Let's pause for a moment and take this all in. From time to time I've seen pastors use unique illustrations to drive home a point. Once I put my head in a bucket of water during a sermon to demonstrate longing for God as we long for our next breath. So why did God ask Ezekiel to do such outlandish acts? He did so because He was not just aiming at eyes and ears but at the hearts of His people. Ezekiel's sermons were "not merely to help people see the truth, but to feel the truth" (Duguid, *Ezekiel*, 93).

As we consider Ezekiel's visible sermons, we would be remiss if we did not note the greatest sign act ever: the cross of Christ. In the cross of Christ, God communicated in a visual way His deep hatred for sin and His overwhelming love for His people. As we ponder the cross, we not only hear what God is preaching, but we also see and feel the weight of our sin and His commitment to die for us rather than "let us go" (Duguid, *Ezekiel*, 95).

The Messenger

Hundreds of years after Ezekiel's day, Paul asked, "How can they hear without a preacher?" (Rom 10:14). Amazingly, Scripture never indicates that Ezekiel was tempted to ask, "Can they hear it from a different preacher?" One of the benefits of studying this Bible book is being challenged by the prophet's faithfulness to the message given to him and willingness to make whatever sacrifice was necessary to communicate the message. His own reputation was not his highest treasure, which is good since some refuse to celebrate his obedience but believe Ezekiel was psychotic and schizophrenic (LaSor, Hubbard, and Bush, *Old Testament Survey*, 357).

If we were brutally honest, few of us would want to do what Ezekiel was asked to do and even fewer of us would do it. And whatever we did, we would complain about it loudly. If what the audience thinks is most important, then we might be tempted to change the message. Ezekiel didn't. If our comfort, ease, and safety are priorities, then we might not take God's Word to difficult places or endure difficult circumstances to proclaim it. Ezekiel did. As we walk through Ezekiel 4–5, don't miss the message that is being preached with Ezekiel's life. Let us pause and consider what our lives are communicating about the message we've been given.

A Planned Provision

EZEKIEL 5:13

After hearing the severity of the judgments God was bringing on His people and seeing all that Ezekiel was asked to do, you may have a few questions. For instance, "Are God's judgments too severe?" Or in modern language, "Does the punishment fit the crime?" First of all, we should remember God's wrath is not out of control but is His focused and disciplined response to sin. Though He intensely hates all sin, He never loses control of His temper (Grudem, *Systematic Theology*, 206). He warned His people for generations (2 Chr 36:11-16). Second, the only innocent person that has ever been punished was Christ (Rom 3:23). God is the One who put Jesus forward as a propitiation for our sin (Rom 3:25). Third, those who see God's judgment as harsh are also those who tend to trivialize sin. Bridges exhorts, "We may trifle with our sins or excuse them, but God hates them" (Bridges, *Holiness*, 28). One of our greatest struggles is that we tend not to see sin as God sees it (Thomas, *God Strengthens*, 50).

Another question you may be asking is, "Where is the grace in this passage?" or "Is there any ray of hope?" The answer to these questions is found in 5:13 when God says, "**When my anger is spent and I have vented my wrath on them, I will be appeased.**" There will be an end to God's judgment on His people. Of course, they should have known this because God made it clear in the very covenant they broke that He would not withdraw from them forever. A time was coming when God would no longer hide His face from them (39:29).

In Leviticus 26:44-45 God said,

> *Yet in spite of this, while they are in the land of their enemies, I will not reject or abhor them so as to destroy them and break My covenant with them, since I am Yahweh their God. For their sake I will remember the covenant with their fathers, whom I brought out of the land of Egypt in the sight of the nations to be their God; I am Yahweh.*

The promise from Leviticus 26 and Ezekiel 5 is "that the Lord's anger will reach an end before Israel will" (Duguid, *Ezekiel*, 100). Because God does not change, His people are not consumed (Mal 3:6).

The grace in this passage is that God loves us enough not to leave us in our sin. He may leave us in the consequences of our sin but not the condemnation of it. For believers the end of God's judgment is heard in the cry of Christ—"It is finished!" Many in Ezekiel's generation would pass away, but God would return their children and grandchildren to Jerusalem. I don't know about you, but I don't want to be a part of a generation for which God is waiting to die so that He can do something with the next one.

Reflect and Discuss

1. When was a time you made a commitment to God but did not keep it?
2. Why are we so prone to rely on ourselves in seeking to honor our commitments to God rather than relying on Him?
3. As children of God, why are we so prone not to appreciate fully this special position?
4. What can we do to minimize the times in our lives we take for granted being able to call God "Our Father"?
5. Why is God judging His people? What would you say to someone who looked at the judgments of God in this passage and considered them to be too severe?
6. Which of Ezekiel's sign acts would you have least wanted to do? Has there ever been a time when you felt God wanted you to communicate a message in a way that seemed a little different?
7. As messengers of God, are we willing to say whatever God wants us to say in whatever manner He wants us to say it? What hesitations do you have?
8. We know God's judgment is coming once again (Ps 96:13; Rev 20:11-14). In what ways is our message similar to Ezekiel's, and in what ways is it dissimilar?
9. How should we think about God's judgment on this side of the cross?
10. In what ways does Ezekiel 4–5 cause you to be grateful for the cross of Christ?

When Our Promiscuous Hearts Grieve God's Heart

EZEKIEL 6:1–7:27

Main Idea: When our promiscuous hearts grieve God, He steps in to remind us who He is and that whatever we choose in His place is not worth what it costs us.

I. One Truth We Should Always Remember: God Is Yahweh (6:7,10,13-14; 7:4,9,27).
II. Though We May Not See Our Sin as Adultery or Idolatry, God Does and Is Grieved by Us (6:1-14).
III. A Day Is Coming When Repentance Will No Longer Be an Option (7:1-27).
IV. Even in Judgment, God Remembers His Mercy (6:8-9).

When I was a child, my father was not a Christian. He would come to church with us occasionally, but most often he would stay home and watch TV. One Sunday morning I decided I would stay home with dad and watch wrestling (and on a side note, I was more crushed to learn the truth about wrestling than Santa Claus). My mom begged me to get dressed and come with her to the morning worship service, but I resisted. As she walked out the door, she turned around with tears and said to me, "Please don't turn out like your father." Immediately, I was cut to the heart. I wanted to throw on my clothes and go with my mom, but it was too late. The thought of her broken heart crushed my calloused heart as I watched her pull out of our driveway.

In Ezekiel 6–7 God reveals to His prophet that His people have **crushed** His heart (6:9) by turning away from Him and worshiping idols. He lets them know the discipline they are receiving is not random but deserved (6:10; 7:3,27) since they have repeatedly committed adultery by having other gods besides Him. He will destroy the places where His people have worshiped other gods and **lay the corpses of the Israelites in front of their idols** (6:4), which leads us to an important question: Is what we worship worth our lives? If we worship anything or anyone besides the Lord God, then it will cost us more than it's worth.

Israel will learn a painful lesson in the chapters we are about to examine. For many, it will be the last lesson they learn (6:13). But even in judgment, God will be merciful and will preserve a remnant of His people—not because they have been faithful but because He is.

One Truth We Should Always Remember: God Is Yahweh
EZEKIEL 6:7,10,13-14; 7:4,9,27

I rarely learn how to do something the first time I'm introduced to it. For instance, I didn't learn how to tie my shoes until fourth grade (but I was still in the gifted program in Louisiana—go figure). The first day I had a vehicle with a standard transmission, I reversed down countless hills because I could not find the "magic spot" in the clutch. One of my worst failures in learning how to do something the first time I tried it was snow skiing. I'll spare you the details, but by the end of the day, I was worried that I had broken the hip of the person "instructing" me, and I also had a huge rip down the back of my ski bibs.

For whatever reason God's people forgot one of the most basic lessons of Covenant 101: God is **Yahweh**. Doesn't it seem strange that God's people could forget who God was? Of course, these are the same people who once lost His book (2 Kgs 22:8), so they do not have a great track record of keeping up with important matters. But if there was ever a lesson that is taught once and should be grasped immediately it is that God is the Lord. If Israel knew this to be true, they had not lived like it. So Yahweh reveals seven times that one of His main reasons for disciplining His people is that they **will know** He is **Yahweh** (6:7,10,13-14; 7:4,9,27). Over and over and over He tells Ezekiel they **will know that I am Yahweh.** Just because His people have forgotten who He is does not mean He has forgotten them.

So what has Israel done that warrants God's educating them again on basics? In plainest terms they have forgotten who He is, and they have broken the first two commandments (Exod 20:2-4). They have suffered from ignorance and idolatry or amnesia and adultery. God's people somehow forgot what God had done for them, and they chased after gods that do not even exist. Despite all the raising of Ebenezers—stones of remembering—Israel forgot who they were when God found them (Ezek 16:4-5), and they trusted more in what they had been made into than in the One who had transformed them (Ezek 16:15). May the same not be true of us (Col 1:21; Eph 2:1-3; 1 Cor 1:26-31).

In describing Israel's **idols**, God does not mince words. He uses some of the most graphic language to let Israel know what He really thinks of their gods (Block, *Ezekiel 1–24*, 226). Foolishly, Israel has pursued gods that cannot see or hear them, and they've forsaken the one true God who actually can do those things. God will expose the idols as the frauds they are and show His people that He is living and active. Sadly, many of God's people will lose their lives next to their lifeless idols. We should look and learn at this point: if what/who we worship cannot hear us, see us, move itself, or even save itself, then it probably cannot do anything for us either, and it is not worthy of worship.

What will be God's method for reminding His people He is Yahweh? Will He demonstrate that He is the Lord who provides, the Lord who heals, or the Lord who saves? No, they will know that He is Yahweh **who strikes** (7:9). For a people in captivity, the Lord who strikes is exactly what they wanted to hear, except that the blow was not aimed at their enemies but at them. He was going to **stretch out** His **hand against** His people (6:14). At this point I'm sure someone in Ezekiel's crowd asked out loud, "Wait, what?"

God will **bring a sword against** the **high places** and against those who worshiped there (6:3-4). The lesson He wants to teach will be learned. A remnant of survivors will remember Him **among the nations where they are taken captive** (v. 9). They will remember how their promiscuous hearts crushed Him, and they will **loathe themselves because of the evil things they did, their detestable practices of every kind** (v. 9). What God is doing in Ezekiel 6–7 is making sure His people and the nations know who He is and they remember it.

What about us? Do we ever act as if God is not Yahweh? Do we live at times as if we have forgotten who He is and what He has done for us? When we see what these chapters reveal of the length to which God goes to remind His people, may we be stirred to do whatever is necessary never to forget He is the one, true, living God and He alone is worthy of our worship.

Though We May Not See Our Sin as Adultery or Idolatry, God Does and Is Grieved by Us
EZEKIEL 6:1-14

All Sin Is Idolatry and It Grieves God (6:9)

One of the most gripping verses in the passage is 6:9, where God confesses He was **crushed by their promiscuous hearts that turned away**

from Him **and by their eyes that lusted after their idols.** The word translated "crushed" can also be rendered "broken in pieces," "rent violently," "wrecked," or "quenched." The word *devastated* has been used as well to convey what God was feeling (*MSG*). Love makes us vulnerable. In 6:9 God is completely transparent about how grieved He is over the actions of His people. My immediate question is, How can I avoid making God feel this way, or how can I at least try to minimize the times I make Him feel like this? Even on this side of the cross, the potential for grieving Him still exists (Eph 4:30).

The best way not to repeat Israel's failures is to identify what they were and avoid them at all costs. What was particularly grieving to God was that **their promiscuous hearts turned away from** Him and **their eyes lusted after their idols** (6:9). They took **His beautiful ornaments** He had **appointed for majesty** and **made abhorrent images from them, their detestable things** (7:20). And what's worse, they were not the least bit secretive or shameful with their sin; instead they engaged in rampant adultery on **every high hill, on all the mountaintops, and under every green tree and every leafy oak** (6:13).

How deeply wounding it must have been for God to watch His bride use the gifts He had given her to create and worship gods that didn't exist and to know His people were not even remorseful. In fact, they were arrogant and prideful (7:10,24). The blueprint for idolatry then is to set our affections and our eyes on something other than God and to place confidence in us rather than in Him. Lest we view the example of promiscuous hearts in Ezekiel as an isolated incident, we should remember that heart promiscuity is a struggle for every generation (Isa 29:13; Matt 15:8).

We should also understand that all sin is idolatry. We can look at what's happening in Ezekiel and consider it irrelevant because we're not bowing down to images or carvings on top of mountains. But the Bible

> does not consider idolatry to be one sin among many (and
> a rare sin found only among primitive people). Rather, all
> our failures to trust God wholly or to live rightly are at root
> idolatry—something we make more important than God.
> (Keller, "Idolatry")

Similarly, Wilson has contended, "All sin is idolatry because every sin is an exercise in trust of something or someone other than the one true God to satisfy, fulfill, or bless" (Wilson, "The Church and Idolatry"). We may not be on the hills of Israel, but if we continually offer our worship to and seek security in something other than God, then we are just as guilty as Ezekiel's generation, and God is just as grieved.

God Is Not Interested in a Portion of My Heart but All of It

Considering Israel's adulterous heart and God's desire to own it completely could lead us to some important questions. How much of our spouses' hearts do we desire? Are we happy with half? Are we happy with a tenth? Are we happy when they only want to give us their hearts because they want something from us in return? How long would we tolerate adultery in our marriage? How many affairs would we be happy with our spouses participating in right in front of our eyes? Do we see our sin in the same way God sees it? Are we grieved that we grieve Him?

Though God certainly is jealous for our affections (Exod 20:5; 34:14), His jealousy is always for our best. God's desire for all of our heart (Deut 6:5) is so we will not give portions of our heart to unworthy lovers. The world, the flesh, and the Devil never have our best interests in mind but only want to shred our hearts to pieces. When we pursue sin, we are like a girl in high school who continues to give her affections to a boyfriend who has never once cared about what was best for her. God alone is always trustworthy with our hearts. Our problem is that we do not believe Him and continue to think there are other paths to satisfaction and joy.

Another problem is that we may be talking about the wrong things as we make disciples. Thune contends that in discipleship,

> we spend all sorts of time talking about petty sins and surface issues, when the real battle is going on in the heart. You can talk about behavior and external circumstances all day, but unless you drag some heart idols out on the table, you're just putting a Band-Aid on the problem. . . . The real question is not what we're doing, but what god we're worshiping. That's why what your disciples want is much more important than what they know. (Thune, "How to Disciple")

Likewise, Wilson exhorts, "The hottest 'worship war' going is the one taking place daily in the sanctuary of our own hearts (Wilson, "The Church and Idolatry").

What God's people did in Ezekiel's day and we do in ours is because of what drives our affections. Like Ezekiel's peers, we foolishly turn from the God who loved us in our worst state (Eph 2:1-4) to gods who are incapable of loving us at all. Why do we set our affections in such low places, and what can we do about it?

God Knows We Have Short-Term Memories of His Goodness Toward Us and the Wretchedness from Which He Brought Us

In order to minimize promiscuity in our hearts, we must find ways to remember who God is and what He has done for us. The Lord knows us better than we know ourselves, and He knows we are prone to forgetfulness (Deut 9:4-5; 10:12-22; 11:11-17). In fact, God made a provision so Israel could avoid the sins they are being disciplined for in this text. In Numbers 15:37-41,

> The LORD said to Moses, "Speak to the Israelites and tell them that throughout their generations they are to make tassels for the corners of their garments, and put a blue cord on the tassel at each corner. These will serve as tassels for you to look at, so that you may remember all the LORD's commands and obey them and not become unfaithful by following your own heart and your own eyes. This way you will remember and obey all My commands and be holy to your God. I am Yahweh your God who brought you out of the land of Egypt to be your God; I am Yahweh your God."

God knew His people's hearts and eyes would constantly be tempted to wander. The tassels were to be a reminder and protection for His people so they would follow God's commands instead of their inclinations (Bloom, "No More Whoring"). The Israelites failed because they did not heed His warnings, and we are just as susceptible. What intentional reminders do we need to set in place so that we will not be easily led toward sin?

Though He Never Takes His Eyes Off of Us, God Knows We Frequently Set Our Gaze Somewhere Besides Him

A strong link exists between looking and coveting. The Israelites had **eyes that lusted after their idols**. The desire of the eyes has long been a source of trouble for God's people. Consider what looking and coveting cost Eve (Gen 3:6), Achan (Jos 7:21), and David (2 Sam 11:2). We are not exempt ourselves (1 John 2:16). The question, however, is not if we will wander from God, but why we set our gaze anywhere else. Where we look is reflective of what we want.

In order for us to join the psalmist in his commitment not to set anything worthless before his eyes (Ps 101:3), we should pray Appleton's prayer:

> O God, I know that if I do not love You with all my heart, with all my mind, with all my soul and with all my strength, I shall love something else with all my heart and mind and soul and strength. Grant that putting You first in all my lovings I may be liberated from all lesser loves and loyalties, and have You as my first love, my chief good and my final joy. (Appleton, quoted in Boa, *Conformed to His Image*, 196)

We no longer have tassels, but we do have a cross. Bloom encourages us to set our eyes on the cross because "it reminds us not only of God's holy commandments, but also how he perfectly fulfilled them all on our behalf" (Bloom, "No More Whoring"). How often do we struggle with sin because we are not keeping our eyes on Jesus (Heb 12:3)?

Though We May Refuse to Put Away Those Things That Lead Us Away from God, He Will Not Suffer Them Forever

One of the reasons Israel struggled continuously is because they did not put away what often drew them away from God. As Ezekiel 6 opens, the prophet is told to say,

> *Mountains of Israel, hear the word of the Lord God! This is what the Lord God says to the mountains and the hills, to the ravines and the valleys: I am about to bring a sword against you, and I will destroy your high places.* (v. 3)

A good question might be to ask why Ezekiel was preaching to the high places of Israel, but a better question would be to ask why the high places were still there.

In between the time of the tabernacle and the temple, the Israelites offered sacrifices to the Lord at specific locations known as **high places** (1 Kgs 3:2). After the temple was built, God's people were supposed to worship and offer sacrifices in Jerusalem. They should have destroyed the high places, but, to their detriment, they retained them. Throughout the generations they used the high places for worship of pagan gods. Nothing good can be gained by holding on to what leads us away from God.

Are there any "high places" in our lives? Are our eyes and hearts being drawn toward God or away from God by what we allow to have influence in our lives? Are we assigning value to anything that lacks it intrinsically? Let us put away anything that draws us away from the Lord, for it will end up costing us far more than it is worth.

A Day Is Coming When Repentance Will No Longer Be an Option
EZEKIEL 7:1-27

For those who use credit cards, there is a reckoning every month. Every swipe of the card has been recorded, and a debt has been accumulated. Not a cent is unaccounted. If God's people thought God was not watching or did not care about all their rebellion, they are about to find out they were dead wrong. For Jerusalem **the time has come; the day has arrived** (7:12). Through Ezekiel, God declared to His people five times: **the end has come** (vv. 2,3,6).

God is going to **pour out** His wrath on His people and **punish** them for all their **detestable practices** (vv. 8-9). **Doom has come on** them (vv. 7,10), and **one disaster after another is coming** (vv. 5,26). God's people will **seek a vision from a prophet, but instruction will perish from the priests and counsel from the elders** (v. 26). In **anguish** God's people **will seek peace, but there will be none** (v. 25). Their disobedience will not only cost many of them their lives but will also cost the next generation their land (vv. 21-24). They will not be able to buy their way out of the judgment (v. 19), and no one will be exempted (vv. 11,15). God's wrath will be in exact proportion to the sin His people have committed (Thomas, *God Strengthens*, 60). If we think differently, then we lack an accurate view of His holiness and our wretchedness.

For Jerusalem the time for repentance had passed. However secure they felt in their wealth or in their worship of idols, they found their refuge to be wanting. Many in our day are seeking refuge in similar places. They are putting their confidence in what they have accumulated or what they have achieved. The judgment in Ezekiel 7 does not compare with the judgment that is coming (Ps 96:13; Matt 26:41; Rev 20:11-15). But unlike Ezekiel's generation our peers still have an opportunity to repent and believe. Of all the things our friends and coworkers need from us today, silence with the gospel is not one of them.

Against the backdrop of Ezekiel 7, can the cross of Christ be more glorious? We are just as guilty of idolatry as Ezekiel's generation, and we deserve every bit of the punishment they received, but Christ has taken our place. Upon Him has been laid every act of our rebellion toward God. Christ has been treated as if He were the one who sought security somewhere besides the Father. His atonement has covered every adulterous tryst we've committed against God with our eyes and hearts.

Plead with those around you to be reconciled to God (2 Cor 5:20). Don't let them consider Ezekiel 7 and think that God will treat them any differently. Exhort them to run to the One who has borne their judgment; otherwise they will pay the price for their sin themselves. There is nowhere to find refuge from the wrath of God except for the cross of Christ.

Even in Judgment, God Remembers His Mercy
EZEKIEL 6:8-9

Even in His wrath God is merciful. He told Ezekiel He would **leave a remnant. Scattered among the nations** would be some who **will escape the sword**. The remnant will not survive because they are smart, strong, or good at hiding. The remnant certainly will not survive because they are faithful to the Lord. As a matter of fact, they will **loathe themselves because of the evil things they did** and **their detestable practices of every kind**. There will be a remnant solely because God is faithful. Even in discipline He will not fully destroy His people (Deut 30:1-6). They will know that He is the Lord.

Reflect and Discuss

1. When you read that God was crushed by the actions of His people, what are your thoughts? How can we minimize causing Him to feel the same about us?
2. What lessons or truth have you failed to learn the first time God tried to teach it to you? Are we as patient in teaching others as He is with us?
3. Though we want all of His affection and attention, why are we prone to give God only portions of ours?
4. Why do we fail to see that sin never provides what it promises and always costs us more than its worth?
5. Is there evidence in our lives that God is Yahweh? In what ways would people struggle to know He is the Lord by watching you?
6. In what ways are we guilty of idolatry in our generation?

7. How can we continually set our eyes on Christ? Why don't we do this?
8. Are you currently holding on to something or someone that is leading you away from Christ? Why? What will you do about it?
9. How do you feel about God's judgment in Ezekiel 7? In what ways does our disobedience have consequences for others?
10. What can we learn from God's preserving of a remnant?

Ichabod: When Elvis Is Not the Only One to Leave the Building

EZEKIEL 8:1–11:25

Main Idea: To be in the midst of discipline with the Lord is better than being in the middle of disobedience without Him.

I. **Both in Public and in Private, God Knows Whether We Treasure His Presence (8:1-18).**
   A. God's vision
   B. God's verdict
II. **God Disciplines Those Who Practice What Is Detestable, but He Delivers Those Who Protest It (9:1-11).**
   A. God's discipline
   B. God's deliverance
   C. God's departure
III. **Our God Is a Consuming Fire (10:1-22).**
   A. The removal of His glory (10:18-22)
   B. The refining of His glory (10:1-8)
   C. The reminder of His glory (10:9-17)
IV. **To Be in the Midst of Discipline with the Lord Is Better Than Being in the Middle of Disobedience Without Him (11:1-25).**
   A. God's declaration to the deceitful (11:1-13)
   B. God's deliverance of the deported (11:15-25)

I believe one of the saddest verses in the Bible is Judges 16:20. There's much in the verse that could produce grief, such as Samson's constant following of his cravings and his ill-advised trust in a deceitful woman. But the saddest component of the verse is when Samson awakes to fight the Philistines once again, but "he did not know that the LORD had left him." He was somehow unaware of the departure of the Lord's presence.

Moses so treasured the Lord's presence that he did not want to move forward with the Israelites if God would not go with them. Moses understood that the Lord's presence made His people distinct among all others. Moses pleaded,

If Your presence does not go, . . . don't make us go up from here. How
will it be known that I and Your people have found favor in Your sight
unless You go with us? I and Your people will be distinguished by this
from all the other people on the face of the earth. (Exod 33:15-16)

When Eli's pregnant daughter-in-law heard that the ark of the covenant had been captured by the Philistines, she was so grieved by the news
that she went into labor and gave birth. She named her son, "Ichabod,"
meaning, "where is the glory?" since she perceived that God's glory had
departed from Israel (1 Sam 4:19-22). God's people are identified by
God's presence (Wiersbe, *Be Reverent,* 49).

Ezekiel 8–11 is a single vision Ezekiel receives about 14 months after
his first vision of the Lord. He either has just completed his assignments
from Ezekiel 4–6 or is just about to do so. The Lord gives Ezekiel and
the elders in exile a vision of Jerusalem, and it's not good. There is rampant disobedience, debauchery, and defilement that will ultimately lead
to the people's destruction and the Lord's departure. By the end of the
vision, the real wonder is not that God's glory departs the temple, but
why He let it remain for so long.

What about us? How much do we value the Lord's presence (Matt
28:20)? Does His presence make us distinct in our cities and in our worship gatherings? If God were to remove His presence, would we be devastated? Would we even notice? Are we like Asaph and desire God above
all things (Ps 73:25)? Are we like David and earnestly seek the Lord
because His love is better than life (Ps 63:1,3)? The worst part of hell will
not be the fire but the forsakenness. The departure in Ezekiel 8–11 of
the Lord's presence will not happen to Christians because it happened
to Christ on the cross. God forsook His Son so that He would never
depart from us. On this side of the cross and Pentecost, however, are we
any more appreciative of the Lord's dwelling with us than the Israelites
were in Ezekiel 8–11? I pray we are.

Both in Public and in Private, God Knows Whether We Treasure His Presence
EZEKIEL 8:1-18

God's Vision

If you have watched a college or pro football game in the past few seasons, you might have seen a player wave his hand back and forth in front

of his face after making a big play. The motion has been adapted from pop culture and carries the meaning of, "You can't see me." In a sense a player is saying, "You can't stop me because you can't see me." The Israelites were making the same accusations of God.

As they practiced their idolatry in the temple, the **elders** in Jerusalem were saying, "**The LORD does not see us**" (8:12), and they were acting as if He was not going to stop them. Thinking the Lord cannot see you is one thing, but not caring if He does is another. The people in Jerusalem were wrong. Dead wrong. The Lord could see all they were doing, and He was going to stop them. David once declared, "If I say, 'Surely the darkness will hide me, and the light around me will be night'—even the darkness is not dark to You. The night shines like the day; darkness and light are alike to You" (Ps 139:11-12). As chapter 8 unfolds, it becomes apparent that God sees clearly, and He wants Ezekiel and the exilic elders to see what is happening in Jerusalem as well.

In the sixth year (of the exile), **in the sixth month, on the fifth day of the month**, while the **elders of Judah** were **sitting in front** of Ezekiel in his **house**, he received another vision from the Lord. In this **vision** God's **Spirit lifted** Ezekiel and carried him to **Jerusalem, to the entrance of the inner gate that faces north**. Ezekiel **saw the glory of the God of Israel there, like the vision** he **had seen in the plain**. But that's not all he would see.

The Lord said to Ezekiel, "**Son of man, look toward the north.**" When he **looked to the north**, Ezekiel saw an **offensive statue north of the altar gate, at the entrance**. The Lord asked Ezekiel, "**Do you see what they are doing here?**" and then told him, "**You will see even more detestable things.**" As the vision in Ezekiel 8 unfolds, the Lord takes Ezekiel from outside the temple gates to inside the temple itself (8:5,7,14,16). As he is drawn closer and closer to the most holy place, Ezekiel is shown detestable acts that increase in wickedness (vv. 6,13,15). Worship is being offered by men and women, leaders and laypeople, but none of it to Yahweh. Who would have ever thought the people of God in the place of God would worship every other god but their own?

Duguid offers a helpful summary:

> In four brief scenes, then, Ezekiel has been shown the comprehensive nature of the sins of Jerusalem. Their sin extends from outside the city gate to the inner courtyard of the temple itself. It involves both men and women, even the seventy elders, symbolic of the leadership of the whole people.

It includes idolatry imported from all sorts of surrounding nations (Canaan, Egypt, and Babylon) and involving all kinds of gods (male and female human figures, animal figures, and stellar bodies). This is a unified, universalized religion, the ultimate multifaith worship service. From the Lord's perspective, however, the picture is one of abomination piled on abomination. (Duguid, *Ezekiel,* 133)

One would think seeing a large number of your population carried away to another land would have a profound impact on those who were left behind. Hopefully, remaining would lead to repentance. It did not. For those not taken to Babylon, their understanding was, "**The LORD has abandoned the land**" (8:12; 9:9). So those in Jerusalem sought protection from other gods (8:3,5), they offered incense to every god they could draw or think of (vv. 9-11), they mourned the nondeath of a nongod (v. 14), and they turned **their backs to the Lord's temple and their faces** to the **east** and bowed down to worship the sun (v. 16). On top of all this, they even filled **the land with violence** (v. 17). The people in Jerusalem did as they pleased with no fear of the Lord or of consequences.

The vision shared from Jerusalem had to be devastating to Ezekiel and the leaders in exile with him. Particularly disappointing would be hearing what the 70 elders and **Jaazaniah son of Shaphan** were doing. Instead of leading the people to repentance and restoration with God, they were leading the people away from Him. Instead of questioning their own faithfulness, they questioned God's. **Jaazaniah** was part of a great family (2 Kgs 22:3; Jer 26:24), but familial obedience does not always guarantee individual obedience.

God's Verdict

God not only shared His vision of Jerusalem with Ezekiel but also His verdict on their actions. He confessed that His people's sin **repeatedly** provoked Him to **anger** (8:17) and **jealousy** (v. 3). **Therefore**, the Lord would **respond with wrath** (v. 18). He would **not show pity or spare** His people in Jerusalem. **Though they cry out** to Him **with a loud voice**, He will **not listen to them** (v. 18). He is going to **depart from** His **sanctuary** (v. 6).

God's verdict would have been devastating to David. He once prayed, "Do not banish me from Your presence or take Your Holy Spirit from me" (Ps 51:11). What is ironic is that no matter how many times we go away from God, we do not want Him to go away from us. We expect

Him to suffer our turning our backs toward Him and our faces from Him but never want Him to respond in like manner.

Sometimes those closest to us can wound us the deepest. It would be understandable for those who did not know God to repeatedly provoke Him to anger with their sinful actions. But it is unfathomable that God's people who dwelled in God's place with God's presence would repeatedly crush His heart (6:9). All this leads to an important question: What does it really mean to be the people of God? For Israel it meant God's presence, protection, and provision. Based on Ezekiel 8, however, those in Jerusalem seem to be His people in name only and not in function. There was no appreciation for their privileged position. They look more like the pagans around them than the God who formed them. And God had had enough. The time for repentance had passed, and the time for judgment had come.

What About Us?

Before moving to the next chapter, we should pause and ask a few questions: Are we living as if God cannot see us or, worse, not caring whether He does? Is there anything in our lives that would provoke God to jealousy? If the real story of our worship was revealed as it was for those in Jerusalem, what would others see? Have we added to or taken away from true reliance on Him? Are we leading others toward God or away from Him? Are we seeking security in God alone, or are we looking for other places of refuge? Is God's presence precious to us? Is it evident we are His people who know Him or do our lives look more like pagans who do not?

God Disciplines Those Who Practice What Is Detestable, but He Delivers Those Who Protest It
EZEKIEL 9:1-11

God's Discipline

Many years after Ezekiel's time Paul would write, "For whatever was written in the past was written for our instruction" (Rom 15:4). He would also write, "For the wages of sin is death" (Rom 6:23). Ezekiel 9 is a passage that combines the essence of both of Paul's statements. What Ezekiel is allowed to see and hear is a word for every generation that the cost of sin is death.

The worst punishment anyone can receive from God is eternal wrath. The cry from the cross, "It is finished," will never be shouted in hell. The cost of forsaking God in this life will be an eternity of being forsaken by God in the next one. God's judgment of those outside of Christ will be awful and eternal but also deserved.

For God's children the severest discipline He enacts is physical death. Lest we think this judgment is only a precross discipline, we might want to review Acts 5:1-11. When word spread throughout the first church of the deaths of Ananias and Sapphira, Luke records that "great fear came on the whole church" (Acts 5:11). You think?

A passage like Ezekiel 9 is probably not among the most popular in sermon podcast downloads, but there is much to be gleaned from this type of lesson. First, God can use Ezekiel 9 to bring us back to the beginning of knowledge, which is fear of Him (Prov 1:9). In the era of "Jesus is my homeboy" theology, familiarity with God has been to the detriment of fear of God. The most calloused heart cannot see the judgment of God in Ezekiel 9 and fail to experience at least the slightest of quivers. Second, God can use Ezekiel 9 to move us to gratitude for and proclamation of the gospel. When we see the severity of His discipline, we are moved to gratitude for "Jesus, who rescues us from the coming wrath" (1 Thess 1:10) and want to proclaim His name that all might run to Him for refuge. Third, God can use Ezekiel 9 to mature us as we are forced to deal with a difficult passage that includes elderly women and little children being put to death. Even these details have been recorded for our good and God's glory.

The prophet is not left wondering how God will discipline His people in Jerusalem. He hears God call in a loud voice, "**Come near, executioners of the city, each of you with a destructive weapon in his hand**" (9:1). The prophet then sees **six men coming from the direction of the Upper Gate, which faces north, each with a war club in his hand. They came and stood beside the bronze altar**. God instructed the men to "**pass through the city . . . and start killing; do not show pity or spare them! Slaughter the old men, the young men and women, as well as the older women and little children.**" They were to begin at His **sanctuary** and **with the elders who were in front of the temple**. The Lord told the executioners to "**defile the temple and fill the courts with the slain. Go!" So they went out killing people in the city**.

In Ezekiel 9 we are taught afresh that God will not let sin go unpunished forever. Most likely what Ezekiel saw in the vision as "six men" would be invading countries in reality—Babylon in particular. God disciplines those who do what is detestable in His sight. But we are left wondering, what about the **older women and little children**? And the answer is that God never punishes an innocent person. Jerusalem was not full of victims but sinners (12:19).

God informed Ezekiel,

> The iniquity of the house of Israel and Judah is extremely great; the land is full of bloodshed, and the city full of perversity. For they say, "The LORD has abandoned the land; He does not see." But as for Me, I will not show pity or spare them. I will bring their actions down on their own heads. (9:9-10)

God is not doing something strange. He is doing what He told them He would do (Lev 26:14-33). He is punishing sin. It is a sad day when God's judgment is more surprising than His grace. God is exercising His sovereign right to withhold mercy and instead to repay His people's rebellion with His wrath.

All of God's enemies will ultimately be destroyed (Phil 3:19; Matt 7:13; Rev 20:13-15). When we think of the Devil and death, then we rejoice in their destruction and the Lord's triumph. We affirm the repayment of their wrongs. But when we think of our loved ones, our friends, our neighbors, and our coworkers who have never yielded their lives to Christ, then celebrating the judgment of God is a little more difficult. When we think of people groups who have never heard the gospel, we know they will be without excuse before the Father, but we are broken that many of them are perishing without ever hearing of Christ. Neither ignorance nor innocence will be an acceptable plea before the Lord's throne. All will receive what is fair—the punishment of their sin.

It would be a mistake to consider God's judgment in this passage and think we deserve any less. Even more tragic would be to see the events of the chapter and to sit silent with the gospel. The wonder in this passage is not that so many are being disciplined but that any would be delivered. Yet God will have His remnant.

God's Deliverance

In his day Moses once stood at the entrance of the camp of God's people and said, "Whoever is for the LORD, come to me," and we are told that all the Levites gathered around him (Exod 32:26). Based on all that has been revealed so far in Ezekiel 1–9, if Ezekiel stood at the gates of Jerusalem and asked the same question, we might doubt any would gather around the prophet. But we would be wrong.

God's judgment is so severe in Jerusalem that Ezekiel is left wondering, "**Oh, Lord God! Are You going to destroy the entire remnant of Israel when You pour out Your wrath on Jerusalem?**" (9:8). But the Lord knows those who are His (2 Tim 2:19). When God called the executioners of the city, **there was another man among them, clothed in linen, with writing equipment at his side**. God told this man to "**pass throughout the city of Jerusalem . . . and put a mark on the foreheads of the men who sigh and groan over all the detestable practices committed in it.**" He also told the executioners, "**Do not come near anyone who has the mark.**" **The man clothed in linen with the writing equipment at his side reported back, "I have done as You commanded me.**"

Apparently all is not lost in Jerusalem. Or more correctly, apparently all *are* not lost in Jerusalem. Despite rampant idolatry and depravity, God still had those who shone like stars in the midst of a crooked and perverted generation (Phil 2:15). There were some who, rather than joining the sin that surrounded them, grieved it. Perhaps some of these were the Levitical priests descended from Zadok (44:15). Ezekiel is not told the exact number in the group that will be preserved, only that the **man clothed in linen with the writing equipment at his side** had done his job. If the events of Ezekiel 9 were to take place today, how many of us would be in the group that was sighing, and how many of us would be in the group that was sinning? Are we grieved when those around us go away from God or act as if He does not see them? Or are we joining them?

As God's children, we should never be content with sin in our lives or the lives of those around us. We should not lead others to sin, nor should we sit silent, like Adam, when they head toward it themselves. Doing and saying nothing while others engage in rebellion toward God is never a loving action. The best way, of course, to feel the same way God does toward sin is to ask Him. We should pray and ask God to put distaste for sin in our lives and to break our hearts for what breaks His.[2] I pray it will be clear in our cities that we are on the side of our Savior and not the side of sin.

---

[2] *The Valley of Vision* is a helpful resource for praying along these lines. Arthur Bennett, ed., *The Valley of Vision: A Collection of Puritan Prayers and Devotions* (Edinburgh: The Banner of Truth Trust, 2009).

Though we may not have a physical sign on our forehead, as God's children we too have been marked. We who are in Christ have been "sealed with the promised Holy Spirit. He is the down payment of our inheritance, for the redemption of the possession, to the praise of His glory" (Eph 1:13-14). We are both preserved and persevere because of His presence in our lives. As He leads us to obey, one of the clearest ways we can identify as being on the Lord's side is with our baptism. If the Spirit is our seal, then baptism is our sign. We profess to all that we are no longer our own but have been purchased by Christ. Our lives are now yielded to His purposes and no longer to just our cravings.

God's Departure

Though more dramatic moves of the glory of the Lord will be revealed in the next two chapters, one can already see the beginning of the Lord's departure from Jerusalem in Ezekiel 9. Ezekiel saw **the glory of the God of Israel** rise **from above the cherub, where it had been, to the threshold of the temple.** As severe as the Lord's discipline is, nothing is more tragic than His departure. In Ezekiel 9 the Lord begins to move His glory away from those who had moved away from Him.

Our God Is a Consuming Fire
EZEKIEL 10:1-22

The Removal of His Glory (10:18-22)

If a contemporary idiom were used to describe God's actions in Ezekiel 10, it would be "going out in a blaze of glory." God is clearly on the move. This is why Ezekiel is given another vision of God's throne chariot (10:1). The prophet will see God's glory fill the temple and the court (v. 4) and then move from the **threshold of the temple** to the **entrance to the eastern gate of the Lord's house** (vv. 18-20). Ultimately God's glory will leave the city (11:23).

God's presence is a blessing. Stuart notes, "The presence of God is a sign of His favor (Deut 4:29,31) whereas the absence of God is a sign of His rejection (Deut 31:17,18)" (Stuart, *Preacher's Commentary*, 92). God has been patient with those in Jerusalem; yet they never wavered in their rebellion. His patience has run out, and His punishment is beginning with the most severe consequence—not their death but His departure.

The Refining of His Glory (10:1-8)

Before leaving town, God has one more assignment for the **man clothed in linen**. In the previous chapter he passed through Jerusalem and marked those who sighed and groaned **over all the detestable practices committed in it** (9:4). His next assignment from the **Lord** is to **go inside the wheelwork beneath the cherubim, fill** his **hands with hot coals from among the cherubim and scatter them over the city.** While Ezekiel **watched**, the man **went in** and **stood beside a wheel. A cherub reached out his hand to the fire that was among** the cherubim. **He took some, and put it into the hands of the man clothed in linen, who took it and went out.**

With hands full of coals that originated from the blazing glory of God, the man will rain down God's punishment on Jerusalem. As much as the residents of Jerusalem might have hoped for an experience like Isaiah had with God's coals (Isa 6:6-7), they were going to get an experience more consistent with Sodom and Gomorrah (Gen 19:1-29). With their destruction and God's departure, the people of Jerusalem will know firsthand what it means for God to be a consuming fire (Heb 12:29).

The Reminder of His Glory (10:9-17)

Why is Ezekiel given the privilege of seeing God's throne chariot for a second time? I believe one reason is so he will be humbled again by God's glory. Who can see what Ezekiel saw and not be led to humility, worship, and appreciation for how awesome the Lord's presence is? I think a second reason Ezekiel is shown **the wheelwork** again is to be reminded God is free to go wherever He wants to go. The temple is not a prison for God but a protection for His people so He can dwell with them and not destroy them. He is done with His people in Jerusalem, but He is not done with His people in exile. Though they cannot come to His sanctuary, He will go to them and be theirs (11:16).

To Be in the Midst of Discipline with the Lord Is Better Than Being in the Middle of Disobedience Without Him
EZEKIEL 11:1-25

God's Declaration to the Deceitful (11:1-13)

To be self-deceived is one thing; to spread those delusions and contribute to the destruction and death of others is another. On His way out of town, God stops at the **eastern gate of the Lord's house. Lifted by the Spirit**, Ezekiel joins Him there and sees **25 men**, among whom are **Jaazaniah son of Azzur** (not the same man from 8:11) **and Pelatiah son of Benaiah, leaders of the people.** We do not know anything about these men except they had risen to a position of influence over others in Jerusalem.

Considering that the best and brightest leaders of God's people had already been carried to Babylon, those who remained in Jerusalem should have been careful whom they chose to be their leaders. Tragically, they picked men **who** planned **evil and** gave **wicked advice** in Jerusalem. Jaazaniah and Pelatiah would say to the people, "**Isn't the time near to build houses? The city is the pot, and we are the meat.**" In case you do not use this phrase too often, the leaders were saying, "We are the chosen ones, and just like the meat goes in the pot and the entrails are discarded, we've been kept in the city and the others taken away." They were encouraging the people to build houses because they believed the land had been given to them **as a possession** (11:15). Their inflated view of themselves had to be based on their location because it was certainly not based on their sanctification. "We are in Jerusalem. We have the temple. Nothing is going to harm us. Let's settle down again and build homes. We are safe." Sadly, nothing could have been further from the truth.

After seeing the leaders and hearing what they were saying, Ezekiel is informed that he is to **prophesy against them. The Spirit of the Lord came on** the prophet and he told them, **I know the thoughts that arise in your mind. You have multiplied your slain in this city, filling its streets with the dead.** Their distorted thinking led to disobedient living. They failed to follow Yahweh's statutes and practice His ordinances, choosing instead to act according to the nations around them (11:12). God would not tolerate their evil leadership anymore; instead He would **bring their actions down on their own heads** (v. 21).

Humbling those with inflated egos has never been a problem for God (Dan 4:28-33; Luke 12:13-21; Acts 12:20-25). Since the leaders in Jerusalem lacked proper perspective, God would provide it for them through His prophet. Ezekiel was told to say,

> *The slain you have put within it are the meat, and the city is the pot, but I will remove you from it. You fear the sword, so I will bring the sword against you. . . . I will bring you out of the city and hand you over to foreigners; I will execute judgments against you. You will fall*

by the sword, and I will judge you at the border of Israel. Then you will know that I am Yahweh. (11:7-11)

The myth of their favored position came crashing down quickly, especially when **Pelatiah son of Benaiah died** while Ezekiel was prophesying. Were it not for God's grace, we would be no different than Jaazaniah and Pelatiah. We would be full of ourselves, full of confidence, and full of sin. We would make wrong assessments based on our own wisdom and all the while spew religious speech from our mouths. We would not only be self-deceived but also lead others in our deceit. Thankfully, God rescues us from ourselves. In seeing Him rightly we see everything else more clearly, including ourselves.

We should not move beyond the first part of Ezekiel 11 without considering those we follow. Who has influence over us? Are they giving us a true message from the Lord or just a message from themselves? Are they considering our circumstances through the Lord's lens or their own? The best way to know if we can trust those who lead us is how they handle God's Word and how they live it (Heb 13:7). Do they practice what they preach, and are they progressing in Christ (1 Tim 4:15)? Do those we follow look more like Jesus this year than they did last year, and are they helping us do the same? If so, then they are worthy of our trust.

God's Deliverance of the Deported (11:15-25)

As overwhelmed as the exilic leaders in Babylon must have been due to all the Lord had revealed to them, I believe the final portion of the vision surprised them the most. Up to this point in Ezekiel 8–11, God's actions were driven by His holiness, but what comes next is entirely because He is gracious. Ezekiel was told to speak for the Lord and say,

> *Though I sent them far away among the nations and scattered them among the countries, yet for a little while I have been a sanctuary for them in the countries where they have gone.* (11:16)

As unlikely as they thought it was, even in Babylon God was Jehovah-Shammah ("Yahweh is there"; 48:35). God left His temple to be their sanctuary.

They had not been deported because God was asleep or because He was weak. God had not been overpowered by another god and proven incapable of protecting His people. In fact, the opposite was true. He *sent* and He *scattered*, but He will also be the One who *sustains*. Those with Ezekiel will come to understand being in the midst of discipline with the Lord is better than being in the middle of disobedience without Him.

The Lord had more good news to share through Ezekiel. He would not leave His people in foreign lands forever but would **gather** them and **give** them **the land of Israel**. For God's people exile is always an opportunity for exodus. Because of His mercy the time of discipline would come to an end, and He would deliver His people again.

Once home God's people will remove **all** the **detestable things and practices from it**. The punishment will not be without purpose. Those who were sent away will one day return to Jerusalem and put away all that previously led them away from the Lord. For those of us in Christ, are we doing the same? Are we putting sin to death by the power of the Spirit (Rom 8:13)? Are we putting away what belonged to our worldly nature (Col 3:5)? Israel could never seem to remove fully the detestable things from their land. What will be different this time? Will it be because God's people make strong resolutions and commitments within themselves to live differently? No, they will change their homeland because God will change their hearts.

God is going to **give them one heart and put a new spirit within them**. He will **remove their heart of stone from their bodies and give them a heart of flesh**. The result will be that God's people will follow His **statutes** and **keep** His **ordinances**. He will not only empower them to *do* His will but also to *desire* it (Phil 2:13). After all this occurs, God says, "**Then they will be My people, and I will be their God**" (11:20). This, of course, was the whole point of the first exodus.

As glorious as the news was for the exiles in Babylon, we have received even greater blessings. For us God is not only Jehovah-Shammah but also Emmanuel. Jesus is God dwelling with us. In Christ, God lived among His people like never before. But in the gift of His Spirit, He is now the God who dwells in us. What both Ezekiel and Jeremiah prophesied (Jer 31:31-34) we know in reality. Instead of *going* to the sanctuary, we have *become* it (1 Cor 6:19; Eph 2:18-22).

Even in exile God's people were incapable of cleansing themselves or changing their ways. If God had waited on His people to realize the gravity of their rebellion on their own, they would have never repented. Even though they had gone away from Him, God chose still to pursue them and meet them in their worst state. He did all that was necessary to forever change them and us (Eph 2:1-10). The gospel is not a message of cleaning yourself up and doing something to get God's attention.

The gospel is not about working our way to heaven. The gospel is the news that Christ left heaven to live among, atone for, and rescue the exiles. All that God expects from us, He provides for us in Christ. This was great news for those sitting with Ezekiel in **Chaldea** and for wherever you are sitting today.

Reflect and Discuss

1. On this side of the cross and Pentecost, do you think we are any more appreciative of the Lord's dwelling with us than the Israelites were in Ezekiel 8–11? How can we demonstrate our appreciation?
2. How does God's presence make His people distinct? In what ways can people in your city see that God dwells with your faith family?
3. Is there anything in your life that would provoke God to jealousy? Is there anything you are looking to for satisfaction and security more than Him?
4. If the real story of our worship was revealed like it was for those in Jerusalem, what would others see?
5. In what ways are you leading others toward God, and in what ways are you leading people away from Him?
6. If God were to discipline someone in your church like He did Ananias and Sapphira, how do you think your faith family would react? How would you react?
7. How has familiarity with God in some ways been to the detriment of the fear of God?
8. In what ways are you burdened by the sins of others around you? What are you doing about it?
9. What are some consequences that occur when God's people have evil leaders? How can we recognize godly leaders today?
10. What truths from Ezekiel 8–11 have impacted you the most?

Our Response to God and His Word

EZEKIEL 12:1–13:23

Main Idea: Some may disbelieve, deny, disregard, or distort God's Word, but we should deliver His message and desire to obey Him no matter the cost.

I. Will We Disbelieve and Deny God and His Word (12:1-25)?
II. Will We Disregard and Delay Responding to God and His Word (12:26-28)?
III. Will We Distort God's Word (13:1-23)?
IV. Will We Deliver God's Word and Desire to Obey Him No Matter the Cost (12:7)?
V. Will We Delight in the Greatest Word God Has Spoken to Us— Christ (Heb 1:2)?

On several occasions I have had the privilege to visit the Bugiri Baptist Church in Uganda. Once when I was there, a man stood up and began to tell the congregation, "As petro is for the car, so God's Word is fuel for us. As food is for the stomach, so the Word is necessary for us." While I was rejoicing in and affirming his declarations, the missionary I was with leaned over and said, "The Word has not always been a priority in this man's life." He went on to tell me how this man became a student at the Uganda Baptist Seminary and while there had become convinced of the importance of God's Word for life and ministry. Now everywhere this student goes he wants everyone to treasure and follow God's Word.

God is a communicator. In fact, He is the original communicator. By speaking, He brought all things into existence. His word is effectual. Though we do not know or understand everything about Him, what we do know is because He has chosen to make Himself known. Everything He has revealed about Himself is a grace to us.

What we know specifically about God is recorded in His Word. The contents of the Bible are not all there is to know about God but all He wants us to know now. To have the Word in our language and to have His Spirit to illuminate it are two of the greatest gifts God can give His children.

But just because God communicates does not mean that all are eager to hear and receive His Word. Some respond to God's Word like the rich, young ruler did, by rejecting it and walking away (Mark 10:17-22). Other responses to what God says are similar to Felix, who did not want to deal with what he heard and assumed he would have another opportunity to respond (Acts 24:24-26). Ideally our response to God and His Word would be in belief and acceptance like Mary, when she said, "May it be done to me according to your word" (Luke 1:38).

In Ezekiel 12–13 **the word of the Lord** will come to His prophet six times. The responses to the message of the Lord will include disbelief, denial, disregard, and distortion. Ezekiel, however, will faithfully deliver the message that is entrusted to him. How we respond to God and His word is eternally significant. Rejection of His message is ultimately rejection of God, and obedience to His Word is obedience to Him.

Let us consider Ezekiel 12–13 by asking how we are responding to God's Word. Can others see that God's Word is a priority in our lives? Is our joyful submission to what He says evident? Are there any ways we are denying, disregarding, distorting, or even disbelieving His Word? May the Lord grant every desire in us to obey His message and in particular to delight in the greatest Word He has spoken to us—Christ.

Will We Disbelieve and Deny God and His Word?
EZEKIEL 12:1-25

If a soundtrack were set to Ezekiel 12, the opening lines would be, "All my bags are packed, I'm ready to go"—except the people in Jerusalem would not be leaving on a jet plane, nor would they want to go. Ezekiel is asked by the Lord to perform two more sign acts. In the first one he will symbolize the coming exile of Jerusalem (12:3-7). In the second act he will symbolize the anxiety that will come on the residents of Jerusalem (12:17-20). Ezekiel faithfully portrays both.

In obedience to the Lord, Ezekiel **brought out** his **bags like an exile's bags. In the evening** he **dug through the wall by hand.** After pushing his bags through the hole in the wall, he carried them on his shoulder in the sight of the people. Eventually some who were watching asked him, **"What are you doing?"** The response the Lord told him to give to the people was,

This oracle is about the prince in Jerusalem and all the house of Israel
who are living there. . . . Just as I have done, so it will be done to
them; they will go into exile, into captivity. (12:10-11)

The Lord had a specific message for Zedekiah, the "prince" in
Jerusalem. Along with the others he would **lift his bags to his shoulder
in the dark and go out. They will dig through the wall to bring him out
through it. He will cover his face so he cannot see the land with his
eyes.** But the Lord is going to **spread His net over him, and he** will **be
caught in** the Lord's **snare.** Zedekiah will be brought to **Babylon, the
land of the Chaldeans,** but **he** will **not see it.** His deportation will lead
to his death.

Zedekiah's **attendants** and **troops** that surround him will not fare
any better. God is going to **scatter** them **to every direction of the wind,**
and He will **draw a sword to chase after them.** Just as with previous
visions, the purpose remains the same, those who are dispersed and
scattered **among the nations** will **know that** He is **Yahweh.** A **few,** however, will be spared **from the sword, famine, and plague so they** can **tell
about all their detestable practices among the nations** where they will
go. Both the nations and Zedekiah's entourage will **know** He is **Yahweh.**

Ezekiel's sign act moves beyond Zedekiah and his supporters to the
other **residents of Jerusalem in the land of Israel.** The prophet is told
to **eat** his **bread with trembling and drink** his **water with shaking and
anxiety.** This will be a sign to Jerusalem's residents that they will **eat their
bread with anxiety and drink their water in dread, for their land** will **be
stripped of everything in it because of the violence of all who** live **there.
The inhabited cities** will **be destroyed, and the land** will **become a deso-
lation.** Then, like Zedekiah and his crew, the residents of Jerusalem will
know God is **Yahweh.**

So how do you think Ezekiel's audience received his messages? For
the first time in the book, we actually get to hear some of the responses
of Ezekiel's peers, and they were not great (12:22,27). Of course, this
should have come as no surprise to Ezekiel because the Lord told him,
**"Son of man, you are living among a rebellious house. They have eyes
to see but do not see, and ears to hear but do not hear, for they are a
rebellious house"** (12:2).

Despite Ezekiel's faithfulness to proclaim and portray every message the Lord gave him, his audience did not believe what they saw and
heard. As a matter of fact, **they** had a **proverb about the land of Israel,**

which said, **"The days keep passing by, and every vision fails."** They did not believe what Ezekiel was saying because up to that point they had seen no evidence to validate his claims. Much like Thomas, they needed proof before they would believe (John 20:24-29). They rejected Ezekiel's messages as the crazy talk of a deranged man who acted weird in public. Of course, not believing God's message through His messenger is the same as not believing God.

Zedekiah in Jerusalem was no different from those who were with Ezekiel in Babylon. He didn't believe the word of the Lord given through Jeremiah (Jer 27:1-22; 38:14-28). If he had trusted the word of the Lord instead of listening to false prophets, then his life would have been spared, the city would not have been burned, and those who were in Jerusalem could have remained there and worked their own land (Jer 27:11; 38:17). But Zedekiah refused to believe the word of the Lord, and it would be at his own peril and the destruction of many others.

God had suffered the disbelief of His people for long enough. God told Ezekiel He will **put a stop to** the exiles' proverb and the people will never **use it again in Israel**. The time has come. **The days** are drawing **near, as well as the fulfillment of every vision. There** will **no longer be any false vision or flattering divination within the house of Israel. Whatever message** Yahweh speaks will **be done. It** will **no longer be delayed**. To Ezekiel's peers the Lord declares, **"For in your days, rebellious house, I will speak a message and bring it to pass."** And He did.

The Lord brought everything to pass just as He said it would happen (2 Kgs 25:1-21). Zedekiah's army was scattered and he was seized. The last thing he would see before he was blinded was the slaughtering of his sons. He would be taken to Babylon, but he would never see it, just as Ezekiel foretold (Ezek 12:13). Judah would indeed go "into exile from its land" (2 Kgs 25:21). Sadly it could have all been avoided. If Zedekiah and the others had simply believed the word of the Lord, then they would have been spared. Disbelief cost them everything, even their lives.

Ultimately, every denial and disbelief of God's word can trace its roots back to one source. The first denial of the Lord's word was in the garden of Eden. There the serpent hissed to Eve, "No! You will not die" (Gen 3:4). We never look more like the Devil than when we deny and disbelieve God.

True folly is thinking things will turn out differently from what the Lord declares. Do we think He does not know what He is talking about? Is He not trustworthy? Has His Word not been proven right time and time again? Of course, God does not just know what is going to happen, but He is also decreeing and accomplishing it.

True folly is also not believing that God's plan is best. I'm sure some of the exiles in Babylon were thinking, "Why am I here and not in Jerusalem? I bet Jerusalem is so awesome right now." Of course, they were wrong. God's discipline of His people was a plan both to preserve and to purify them, and it was for their best. As a matter of fact, the Lord would lead Jeremiah to send a letter from Jerusalem to the elders of the exiles in Babylon (Jer 29:1-29). In the letter Jeremiah assured the exiles that God's plan was best and that He had plans to give them "a future and a hope" (Jer 29:11). Seeing those words in their proper context is even more powerful knowing it was spoken to a people He was disciplining but not destroying.

Just because God seems delayed to us does not mean He is. When Habakkuk was in a period of waiting, he received this response from the Lord: "The vision is yet for the appointed time; it testifies about the end and will not lie. Though it delays, wait for it, since it will certainly come and not be late" (Hab 2:3). For years Israel waited for their Messiah, but He was sent "when the time came to completion" (Gal 4:4). In our own generation there will be those who say, "Where is the promise of His coming? Ever since the fathers fell asleep, all things continue as they have been since the beginning of creation" (2 Pet 3:4). But "with the Lord one day is like a thousand years, and a thousand years like one day" (2 Pet 3:8). What seems like "delay" to us is not and should never be used to fuel disbelief. The Lord is on time every time and keeps every promise He makes.

If we choose to disbelieve God and refuse every offer of His grace, then His discipline should not take us by surprise. God did not have to warn Zedekiah, but in His graciousness He did. Repeatedly, Zedekiah refused to heed the word of the Lord; and, as was noted previously, his disbelief led to his death and the destruction of Jerusalem. All of this should lead us now to pause and ask, Is there any word of the Lord that we do not believe? Is there something He has said that we are struggling to receive? Is there anyone who is being impacted by our disbelief? Hopefully, others are being blessed by our belief and not burdened by our disbelief.

Will We Disregard and Delay Responding to God and His Word?

EZEKIEL 12:26-28

In a sermon on Ezekiel 12 Spurgeon said,

> Men display great ingenuity in making excuses for rejecting the message of God's love. They display marvelous skill, not in seeking salvation, but in fashioning reasons for refusing it. They are dexterous in avoiding Divine Grace and in securing their own ruin. They hold up first this shield and then the other to ward off the gracious arrows of the gospel of Jesus Christ, which are only meant to slay the deadly sins which lurk in their bosoms. The evil argument which is mentioned in the text has been used from Ezekiel's day right down to the present moment, and it has served Satan's turn in tens of thousands of cases. By its means men have delayed themselves into Hell. ("A Sermon for Young Men and Women")

For some, disbelief of God's Word is not their primary struggle but disregarding it and delaying their obedience. In Ezekiel's day some in **the house of Israel** were **saying, "The vision that he sees concerns many years from now; he prophesies about distant times."** The Lord's response to them is, **"None of My words will be delayed any longer. The message I speak will be fulfilled."**

The act of delaying our obedience indicates we believe we will have additional time and opportunities to obey whatever the Lord is telling us. Nobody can be certain of further occasions for obedience, nor are they deserved. James exhorts his readers,

> *Come now, you who say, "Today or tomorrow we will travel to such and such a city and spend a year there and do business and make a profit." You don't even know what tomorrow will bring—what your life will be! For you are like smoke that appears for a little while, then vanishes.* (Jas 4:13-14)

One of the worst examples of being a day late in obedience is recorded in Numbers 14. God was ready to take His people into the promised land, but they doubted His protection and provision, so they refused to enter Canaan. After God judged them for their disobedience and disbelief and informed them they would die in the wilderness, the Israelites decided they would enter the land. It was a disaster! Neither Moses nor the Lord went with them, and they were routed. Their obedience was a day late. Had they not disregarded His instructions and not delayed their obedience, then they would not have died in discipline.

What can we learn? First of all, *God does not just have a word for yesterday or tomorrow but for today.* The psalmist has warned us, "Today if you hear His voice: Do not harden your hearts" (Ps 95:7-8). Citing this psalm, the author of Hebrews tells us to "encourage each other daily . . . so that none of you is hardened by sin's deception" (Heb 3:13). Delayed obedience is disobedience. One of the best ways we can serve others in our faith family is by encouraging them to obey the Lord the first time they are called to obedience and every time they are so called.

Second, we must be careful not to be quick to discern a word for others and miss the word for us. Ezekiel's audience claimed his message was for people years down the road and in essence did not have anything to do with them. *God does not just have a word for others but for us.* If you find yourself thinking often about how someone you know needs to hear the sermon you are listening to, then you might just be the "someone." When we hear a word from the Lord, there is a reason we have been given the opportunity. It may indeed be that the Lord wants us to pass the message on to others, but that should only be after it has done its work in our own lives.

Like Moses, we should pray, "Teach us to number our days carefully so that we may develop wisdom in our hearts" (Ps 90:12). All of our days were written in the Lord's book and "planned before a single one of them began," but only the Lord knows their total and where we are in the count (Ps 139:16). So many worry if these are the "last days," and in one sense the answer to this is yes (Heb 1:2). I encourage the people I shepherd, however, not to think of them as the last days but as our only days. Now is the time for obedience. Any delay or disregard of the Lord's Word on our part is an arrogant presumption and a waste of time. At what point has delaying obedience ever been for our best or for the best of those around us? Our delay and disregard reveal that someone else's word (perhaps our own) is more important to us than the Lord's.

Will We Distort God's Word?

EZEKIEL 13:1-23

When I was a student in seminary, I would often eat in the French Quarter in New Orleans. When I was leaving a parking area one night, I saw a woman who seemed to have a problem with her car. I stopped and asked if I could help. It turned out it was just a car battery that needed to be jumped, so my limited auto skills could be used. What was funny to me is the woman was a fortune-teller. She and others like her would set their tables and chairs up in Jackson Square and claim to know everyone's future. I could not help but laugh when I asked her, "You didn't see this coming, huh?"

In Ezekiel's day there were not only those who disbelieved or disregarded God's word, but tragically, there were also those who distorted it. Nothing is worse than someone who claims to have a word from the Lord but really speaks for himself. In Ezekiel's day false prophets and false prophetesses alike were offering divinations, deceit, and distortions. The Lord, however, had a true word for both groups.

Ezekiel was told to **prophesy against the prophets of Israel**. The Lord was angry with this group because they prophesied **out of their own imagination** and followed **their own spirit** since they had **seen nothing** and they were **like jackals among ruins**. If we learned anything about jackals from the movie *The Lion King* (1994), they are selfish and opportunistic, seeking only their own good.

The false prophets **did not go up to the gaps or restore the wall around the house of Israel so that it might stand in battle on the day of the Lord**. They had seen **false visions** and spoken **a lying divination** when they proclaimed, "**This is the Lord's declaration**," even though He had not spoken. Finally, the false prophets **led** God's **people astray** when they said, "**Peace**," **when there** was **no peace**. They were like those who **plaster** a wall **with whitewash**.

The prophetesses were no better. Like the men the women prophesied **out of their own imagination**. They had sewn **magic bands on the wrist of every hand** and made **veils for the heads of people of every height in order to ensnare lives**. The prophetesses had **disheartened the righteous person with lies, even though** Yahweh **had not caused him grief**. They also **encouraged the wicked person not to turn from his evil way to save his life**. With their lies the women killed **those who should**

not die and spared **those who should not live.** And they had done all of these things merely **for handfuls of barley and scraps of bread.**

God's people were already struggling to believe and obey His true messages, and the proliferation of false messages did nothing to help the situation. God would no longer tolerate the false prophets and prophetesses. He would put them out of business. They had given His people false hope, so God would give these dispensers of deceit no hope. **Because** the false prophets and prophetesses spoke **falsely and had lying visions,** God was **against** them (13:8).

The punishment for their pretense was severe. The false teachers would **not be present in the fellowship of** His **people or be recorded in the register of the house of Israel.** They would also not be allowed **to enter the land of Israel.** The false prophets would **be destroyed** with their whitewashed wall in the city (cf. Jer 28:1-17). For the women God was going to **tear** the magic bands from their arms and **tear** the veils from their heads. He would **free the people** the women ensnared in their lies, and He would **deliver** His people from the predators' hands. He would also stop **false visions** (13:23) and **flattering divination within the house of Israel** (12:24). Why would He do all of this? For the same reason repeated throughout the book—so they will know He is **the Lord Yahweh** (13:9).

What can we learn from the presence and then the punishment of the false prophets and prophetesses in Ezekiel 13? First of all, *not everyone who claims to speak for the Lord really does.* Competing voices are not new. So how can we recognize who is giving us God's message today? Duguid is helpful here: "The contrast in our day between 'true prophet' and 'false prophet' is not so much as to who has really received the word of God, but rather who is rightly handling the Word of God" (Duguid, *Ezekiel,* 177). To know the difference, we should be like the Bereans who "examined the Scriptures daily to see if" what Paul and Silas shared with them was based in God's Word (Acts 17:11).

My mentor, Jim Shaddix, exhorted us young pastors to make sure the biblical text was not just a diving board for our oral presentation but the pool in which our sermon swam (Vines and Shaddix, *Power in the Pulpit,* 204). He would tell us our job as preachers is not to present good stuff but to present God stuff, which is done best by biblical exposition. I once listened to a preacher reference the text where Jesus says, "Among those born of women no one greater than John the Baptist has appeared" (Matt 11:11). The preacher then proceeded to give us five ways we could be great and six ways not to be great. After listening for a little while, I closed my Bible. Apparently it was a bit dramatic because my wife elbowed me. I turned to her and said, "He's not preaching from here anymore, so I don't need to leave it open."

Like the prophets and prophetesses in Ezekiel 13, those who call themselves into ministry often bring their own message with them. We should be cautious of those, in particular, who tell us what we want to hear rather than what we need to hear. What could be more dangerous than telling those people not to worry who in reality have much to fear? "We must speak clearly of the tragic and dangerous state of men and women without Christ. They are sinners under the wrath of God, at risk of eternal lostness" (Duguid, *Ezekiel,* 165).

Second, *there are times when preaching against other preachers is necessary.* Prophesying against the prophets will probably not lead to Ezekiel's winning a popularity contest. But then again, "popularity is not a test of truth" (Wiersbe, *Be Reverent,* 73). Generalities will not suffice when specificity is needed. We may not just be able to say, "Here are some general characteristics of false teachers," but may at times need to name names. When this occurs, Thomas offers some wisdom: "Preaching against preachers must never be done out of envy or spite, but always and only out of regard for the truth of God's Word" (Thomas, *God Strengthens,* 96).

Third, *we should avoid being jackals in the ruins or those who whitewash walls* and give people false confidences. We are like jackals when all we care about is ourselves. If we intentionally withhold truth from those who are perishing because we want them to like us, then our real concern is only for ourselves. We whitewash walls when we allow people to feel safe even though they hold convictions contrary to God's Word. We're like those who say, "Peace," when there is no peace. Let us run to the gaps and restore the walls by not being afraid to speak God's Word to those around us.

Fourth, *if we are going to be put to death for proclaiming a message, it better be the right one.* The false prophets and prophetesses paid a real price for a false message. We who carry the gospel, however, know we have already died to self, and any cost that is necessary to proclaim Christ's good news will be worth it.

Will We Deliver God's Word and Desire to Obey Him No Matter the Cost?
EZEKIEL 12:7

I'm not sure any preacher has been asked to proclaim God's Word in more peculiar ways than Ezekiel. From all we saw in Ezekiel 4, digging through walls, carrying baggage at night, and eating and drinking while trembling has now been added. Do you ever wonder what Ezekiel's wife thought about all of this? We know his thoughts: **I did just as I was commanded**.

The prophet's obedience is a challenge to my soul. Whatever he needed to do to proclaim the word of the Lord, he was willing to do. What about us? Are we willing to deliver His message in whatever way He asks us? Like Ezekiel, we've been asked to deliver God's Word to those who are hostile and doing evil (Col 1:21). We are Christ's witnesses (Acts 1:9) and living letters (2 Cor 3:3). He will strengthen us just as He did Ezekiel.

The need to deliver God's Word is just as great in our day as it was in Ezekiel's. While creation and conscience will leave everyone without excuse before the Lord, it takes a lot to get from a pinecone to propitiation without someone filling in the details. We have been given a message. We do not have to be cute or creative with it but faithful. How many will perish today because no one has delivered the message of Christ yet to their people group?

Will We Delight in the Greatest Word God Has Spoken to Us—Christ?
HEBREWS 1:2

As we consider God's word, the prophets who deliver it, and our responses to it, we would be remiss if we did not consider Christ. The author of Hebrews informs us, "Long ago God spoke to the fathers by the prophets at different times and in different ways. In these last days, He has spoken to us by His Son" (Heb 1:1-2). Despite all of Ezekiel's faithfulness, no one has ever done more to deliver the word of God than Christ, who is the Word made flesh (John 1:14). No one has ever given up more or paid a higher price to communicate God's message than the One who left heaven ultimately to be nailed to a cross.

Jesus is God's perfect prophet because He revealed God to us and spoke His word like no one else could ever do. He did not just deliver a message given to Him but was also the message's source and fulfillment. Unlike the false prophets who were jackals in the ruins, Christ came to recover what had been ruined at the cost of His own body and blood.

As His ambassadors (2 Cor 5:20), we act in a prophetic way whenever we proclaim His gospel to a dying world. When we teach and admonish one another in all wisdom, it should be because the message of the Messiah dwells richly in us (Col 3:16). Like Paul, "We proclaim Him, warning and teaching everyone with all wisdom, so that we may present everyone mature in Christ" (Col 1:28). But even on our best days, we are imperfect. Fortunately, a day is coming when we will speak perfectly of God because we will know Him and He will dwell with us like never before. Until that day arrives, let us be diligent to present ourselves approved to God, workers who do not need to be ashamed but who correctly teach the word of truth (2 Tim 2:15).

Reflect and Discuss

1. Has the Lord's "delay" ever caused you to struggle with disbelief? How did you get past it?
2. Why are we tempted at times not to believe God's plans are best?
3. What, if any, consequences have you or others around you experienced because they did not believe some portion of God's Word?
4. Why do we at times delay our obedience to the Lord? Why is this presumptuous?
5. In what ways are you currently delaying obedience, and how do you think this is impacting others?
6. If you were asked to prophesy against false prophets, what, if any, hesitations would you have?
7. How can we know if someone is truly speaking for the Lord today?
8. Is there anywhere or with anyone you would be hesitant to deliver God's Word? Why? How can you overcome this hesitation?
9. In what ways have you been challenged by Ezekiel's obedience to deliver the message he was given?
10. What makes Jesus the greatest One to fill the office of prophet? In what ways can we fulfill a prophetic role today?

Idolatry Leads to Uselessness

EZEKIEL 14:1–15:8

Main Idea: Our sin can never be concealed from God, and it costs us more than it's worth, but it can be covered by Christ.

I. Our Idolatry Cannot Be Concealed (14:1-11).
II. Our Idolatry Always Costs Us (15:1-8).
III. Our Idolatry Must Be Covered by Another (14:12-23).

Have you ever done something wrong but felt like you could keep it concealed? When I was young, I learned, "Our sins will find us out." When I was around four, I went with my mother to visit one of her friends. While there I asked for a glass of water. I then put the water in my mouth, ran to the next room, and released it from my mouth into a vase on a coffee table. Perhaps "around" the vase would be a more accurate description. Needless to say, I made a mess. I chose not to tell Mom what I did. By the time we got home, however, our phone was ringing off the hook. My mother's friend wanted to be sure Mom knew what I had done with the water she gave me. Mom hung up the phone and called me by my full name. I prayed, "Dear God, make me a bird so I can fly far, far away!" I was busted in more ways than one that day.

Spitting water into a vase is indeed child's play compared to some of the sins you and I try to conceal. For whatever reason we think God will ignore our rebellion and go on with business as usual. God never ignores our sin. Rooting out sin in our lives *is* business as usual for God. If He does not do this, then we will not be useful for His kingdom. In Ezekiel 14–15 God is going to expose the idolatry of the exilic elders. Because of their sin Israel has become like a worthless vine. In the end no one will be righteous enough to stop God's judgment on His people.

Our Idolatry Cannot Be Concealed

EZEKIEL 14:1-11

As bad as Jerusalem's leadership was (8:1-18; 11:1-13), God's people in Babylon were not exactly blessed with godly leaders themselves.

Apparently Babylon's taking of Israel's best leaders was not equivalent with taking her holiest ones. In Ezekiel 8 we may have been shocked to see all the idolatry committed by the leaders of God's people who were still living in Jerusalem. As you may recall, some of the exilic leaders were sitting with Ezekiel when he received the vision that comprises chapters 8–11. What we learn in Ezekiel 14, though, is that the elders in Babylon were not any godlier than those in Jerusalem, and some may have even been worse. The elders in Jerusalem brought idols into the temple, but those in Babylon had **set up idols in their hearts** and **put sinful stumbling blocks before their faces** (14:3).

I can imagine the exilic elders shaking their heads when they heard the news of their counterparts' leadership in Jerusalem. They might have even asked, "Can you believe those guys?" But to scoff at those who brought idols into the Lord's temple is foolish when those who've brought idols into their hearts are doing the scoffing.

We may camouflage our hypocrisy with external religious orthodoxy, but nothing can conceal the pagan secrets of our heart from God. How much time and energy do we spend worrying about what others will think about us rather than what God thinks? What does it matter if our peers think we have it all together, when God knows we do not? The beauty of the cross is that Christ has already covered any idolatry we confess. As leaders in our home, let us not conceal sin in our hearts and lead our families away from God, but let us confess sin and lead our families to the only One who can do anything about it.

These elders were not political leaders but were heads of households. They were fathers and grandfathers. They were the shepherds of their homes, and their leadership would not be without effect. Sadly, what was true of them was also true of the entire **house of Israel** who had taken idols into their hearts and become **estranged** from the Lord (14:5). If the fathers and grandfathers were active in idolatry, it should not be completely surprising the practice spread to everyone else.

In bringing the idols into their hearts, the elders brought rivals to where love for God alone was to reside (Deut 6:5). The elders were supposed to teach their offspring what exclusive devotion to Yahweh looked like; instead their affections were divided among many gods. God, however, would once again **take hold of Israel by their hearts** (14:5).

We can learn much about God and the elders through their interaction in Ezekiel 14. First, *God will be sought on His terms and not ours* (vv. 2-3). The **elders of Israel** have done the right thing by coming to

God, but they apparently had not done so with the right hearts. Block notes,

> Even if the Lord invites all to come to Him and knock, seek, and ask, He is under no obligation to respond to everyone who approaches Him, especially not those who demonstrate no covenant faithfulness in their daily lives. To receive a favorable answer from the divine king one must come with sincerity and on his terms, among which is included his exclusive right to one's devotion. God tolerates no rivals. Nor does He permit Himself to be reduced to a sorcerer's agent, disclosing future events and solving the problems of all who appeal for His aid. (Block, *Ezekiel 1–24*, 437)

We are foolish when we think our pursuit of sin will not impact our relationship with God. Setting up idols in our heart always separates us from God (v. 7). We cannot walk toward God and toward sin simultaneously. I'm honestly not sure if the elders in Ezekiel 14 thought they could hide their sin from God or if they just did not think He would care. They were wrong, and God refused to be inquired of by those whose heart did not belong fully to Him. It would have been humorous if God told the elders to consult their idols. How long do you think they would have had to wait for an answer? We are so foolish to turn from the living God and serve nonexistent ones.

Second, *God remains gracious and merciful to all who repent of their sin* (v. 6). Just as inquiring of the Lord is a privilege so is repentance. God is not obligated to plead with us to abandon our adulterous relationships with idols. He can extend judgment and be just as holy as He has always been. God, however, takes no pleasure in the death of the wicked. Though the house of Israel had gone away from Him (v. 5), God lovingly called them to abandon the path of death and to live. How do we treat those who wound us?

Third, *all of God's discipline has the dual goal of His glory and our good* as He conforms us to Christ and pries the idols from our hearts (vv. 5,11). Yahweh wanted to **take hold of Israel by their hearts** (v. 5). Block notes,

> The Lord is never capricious in his judgment. His responses to human sin are consistent with his immutable character and have as their goal the transformation of sinful human beings into a covenant people, pure and exclusive in their devotion to him. (Ibid.)

God disciplined His people **in order that the house of Israel may no longer stray from following** Him (v. 11). In saving us from our sins, God is saving us from ourselves. He graciously steps in and does what we in our fallen state are too weak to do on our own. He helps us release the lifeless idols we are clutching with our hands and storing in our hearts, so that we do not lay our lives down beside them. To die for the living God is one thing, but to die for gods we've created is a tragedy. Our prayer should always be, God help me love You with all my heart and root out any other competitor that I foolishly invite in.

Fourth, *God will give ungodly leaders exactly what they deserve* (vv. 8,23). Those who continue to reject Yahweh will find themselves rejected. If they refused to repent, "God himself would answer their empty inquiry with action, not words" (Alexander, *Ezekiel*, 805). God never judges without cause (v. 23). The nonrepentant elders would set an example for God's people, just not in the way they might have thought. When God enacts the covenant curses on them, they will become a **sign and a proverb** (v. 8) to the rest of the people. Idolatry is foolish, but failing to repent of idolatry is even worse. Thinking on your leadership for a moment, is God teaching others more through your obedience or disobedience? Do those you disciple see you repent of sin quickly or struggle to release it?

Fifth, *if we seek something other than God and His truth, we should not be surprised when we end up deceived* (v. 9). If the elders refused to be honest with God and deal with their idolatry, then God would withhold right counsel from them. God would not put lies in the minds of the false prophets; He would merely let them share the lies they already possessed. The result would be that both the false prophet and those who refused to forsake their idolatry would be destroyed.

Our Idolatry Always Costs Us
EZEKIEL 15:1-8

Nothing will keep the gospel from advancing in us and through us more than our pursuit of sin. Are you ready for an agricultural pop quiz? What is an apple tree supposed to produce? Apples. What is an orange tree supposed to produce? Oranges. What is a pear tree supposed to produce? Pears. I'm sure you get it by now, but let me ask you, What if each of these three trees does not produce their intended fruit? What else are they good for? Perhaps shade or firewood, but neither of these benefits is the primary purpose for which these trees were created.

In Ezekiel 15 we are informed the grapevine exists for one purpose. It is not useful for making furniture (vv. 2-3). It is not useful as a wall peg (v. 3). If the grapevine is not producing fruit, then its only use is for the fire (v. 4). Once burned, the vine is even less useful (v. 5). Like the vine in the illustration, Jerusalem and God's people had become fruitless and worthless.

What led to Israel's uselessness? They acted **unfaithfully** toward God (v. 8). They cheated on God with gods that did not exist and with idols they brought into their hearts. They engaged in disobedience and disbelief. Peter did not want those he loved becoming unfruitful, so he told them how to avoid it:

> *Make every effort to supplement your faith with goodness, goodness with knowledge, knowledge with self-control, self-control with endurance, endurance with godliness, godliness with brotherly affection, and brotherly affection with love. For if these qualities are yours and are increasing, they will keep you from being useless or unfruitful in the knowledge of our Lord Jesus Christ.* (2 Pet 1:5-8)

Even in exile God did not want His people to be useless or unfruitful. Through the pen of Jeremiah, God sent a letter to the exiles. He told them to "seek the welfare of the city I have deported you to. Pray to the LORD on its behalf, for when it has prosperity, you will prosper" (Jer 29:7). For seeking the welfare of their city to even be a possibility "suggests that many Jews managed fairly well in captivity" (Smith, *Prophets*, 253). God always has a purpose for when He places us somewhere. Even exile is a stewardship for God's people.

The exiles are not to be passive, but they are intentionally to seek the good of the Babylonians. Paul told the Galatians, "As we have opportunity, we must work for the good of all, especially for those who belong to the household of faith" (Gal 6:10). We cannot simultaneously seek the good of our cities and join them in sin. Even if the Israelites considered the Babylonians to be their enemies, they were still to intercede for them. This admonition is the same one we have received from Jesus (Matt 5:44).

The greatest good God's people can do for the cities in which they live is to proclaim the gospel. Of course, the gospel will not advance through us if it is not advancing in us. Furthermore, we cannot seek the good of the city if we continually seek ways out of the city. Likewise, we cannot seek the good of the city if we make the walls of the faith community a fortress we stay behind. Uselessness was never a path God chose for His people but one they chose for themselves every time they pursued sin.

How about your faith family? Is your congregation seeking the good of its city, or is it seeking sin just like everyone else? In what ways is your city a better place to live because your church exists? How often does your faith family pray for the good of your city?

I am not sure how much time I have spent pursuing sin in my life, but I do know two things about it. First, I've spent a lot of time in rebellious pursuits. Second, all of that time has been wasted. Sin never provides a single benefit. Instead of seeking sin and becoming useless like those in Jerusalem, let us seek the good of our cities and pray for them. Our exile will one day come to an end as well. Let us always be mindful of Peter's exhortation:

> *Dear friends, I urge you as strangers and temporary residents to abstain from fleshly desires that war against you. Conduct yourselves honorably among the Gentiles, so that in a case where they speak against you as those who do what is evil, they will, by observing your good works, glorify God on the day of visitation.* (1 Pet 2:11-12)

Our Idolatry Must Be Covered by Another
EZEKIEL 14:12-23

Paul once said,

> *I speak the truth in Christ—I am not lying; my conscience is testifying to me with the Holy Spirit—that I have intense sorrow and continual anguish in my heart. For I could almost wish to be cursed and cut off from the Messiah for the benefit of my brothers, my own flesh and blood. They are Israelites.* (Rom 9:1-4)

Could you imagine trading your eternity for the benefit of others? Paul said he almost desired to perish and be forsaken if it meant his people, the Israelites, would not be. I find it most interesting these were the people who tended to bring Paul the most harm, but he was resilient in his love for them and concern for their souls.

Paul's "almost-wish," however, is not a possibility. He is not able to save others because he is not able to save himself. All of Paul's righteousness has been given to him rather than earned by him, and it does not transfer to another designee of his choosing.

As Ezekiel 14 draws to a close, God tells Jerusalem He is going to send **sword, famine, dangerous animals, and plague in order to wipe out both man and animal from it** (v. 21). What's more, no one can stop it. When you think of righteous men mentioned in the Bible, who in particular comes to your mind besides Christ? If you are struggling to generate a roster, the Lord has three suggestions for you. His list includes Noah, Daniel, and Job (v. 14). God includes this trio merely to point out that even if they were in Jerusalem **they would deliver only themselves by their righteousness** (v. 14), but they could do nothing to save the city from God's judgment. In fact, they are powerless even to **deliver their sons and daughters** (v. 16). God's people have chosen idolatry, their idolatry has made them useless, and now God is going to wipe them out for their pursuit of sin and lack of repentance.

In light of the conclusion of Ezekiel 14, we are reminded there is only one whose righteousness can save Jerusalem and every other city. Christ's righteousness alone can be imputed to others. Unlike Noah, Daniel, and Job, Christ can save us from the wrath that is coming because He took it upon Himself (1 Thess 1:10). Since we cannot transfer any personal righteousness to others, the greatest thing we can do is to share the gospel with them and beg them to flee to Christ. If God did not withhold His judgment from His holy city or from His Son when our sin was laid on Him, then He will not withhold His judgment from anyone else.

Conclusion

Secret sin is only a secret to other people. It's no secret to us or to God. As much as we want God to turn a blind eye to our rebellion, He refuses. We were created for His glory (Isa 43:7) and not for our cravings. If God leaves us to ourselves, we will become worthless and will eventually be destroyed. Christ, however, can deliver us from these bodies of death and provide the only means of escaping God's coming judgment (Rom 7:24-25). On our best day our blood could never do the work Christ's has done. We should depend on Christ alone, and we should seek the good of our cities by calling them to turn from their sin and live.

Reflect and Discuss

1. Why do we seem to care more about what others think of our sin than what God thinks?
2. Have you ever concealed sin? How did that turn out for you and others around you?
3. How does sin affect our relationship with God?
4. How can we minimize bringing idols into our heart?
5. How can we maximize loving God with all of our heart?
6. What is our purpose in life, and how does sin work against this?
7. Who would you like to see respond to the gospel more than anyone else? In what ways is God using you in their life?
8. How is your faith family intentionally working for the good of your city?
9. How often do you pray for your city? What do you pray for your city?
10. When you see how powerful the blood of Christ is in atoning for our sin, what words would you use to express your gratitude to Him?

The Gospel According to Ezekiel

EZEKIEL 16:1-63; 23:1-46

Main Idea: At our absolute lowest point of depravity, God still chooses to atone for His people rather than abandoning us.

I. Without God We Are Helpless, Hopeless, and Left for Dead (16:1-5).
II. God's Love for His People Is Not Only Extravagant and Undeserved but Also Transforming (16:6-14).
III. Ingratitude Toward God and Pride in Self Inevitably Lead to Spiritual Harlotry (16:15-34).
IV. God Is as Passionate in His Judgment as He Is in His Love (16:35-43).
V. Our Sin Is More Wretched Than We Care to Acknowledge (16:44-52).
VI. Rather Than Abandon His People God Chooses to Atone for Them (16:53-63).

If Ezekiel 16 and 23 were summarized as one sentence from God to His people, it would be, Though you've been an adulterous nymphomaniac, I love you and will atone for all your whoredom (Stuart, *Preacher's Commentary*, 211). To the church in Rome, Paul wrote, "The law came along to multiply the trespass. But where sin multiplied, grace multiplied even more" (Rom 5:20). If there were ever two chapters in the Bible that demonstrate God's grace is multiplied more than sin, it is Ezekiel 16 and 23. These chapters contain some of the most graphic language in Scripture. If they were sold in the music department of a store, they would come with a warning label for explicit content. When one considers they are words from the Lord, there is even more shock that He would utter such phrases. Why does He use such graphic terminology? Yahweh wants His people to know the depravity of their sin and the steadfastness of His love. He uses the most intimate of phrases to convey how He views their actions. In discussing Ezekiel 16, Piper contends, "God created us with sexual passion so that there would be language to describe what it means to cleave to him in love and what it means to turn away from him to others" (Piper and Taylor, *Supremacy*, 28). Israel's actions have been nothing less than adulterous as she prostituted herself to every nation around her. She turned her back on her true love (23:35; cf. Rev 2:4) and embraced those who only wanted to use and abuse her. In the end we should be more shocked by Israel's sin than by God's semantics.

As we begin our journey in these texts, I want to remind you of a few questions I asked at the beginning of this commentary:

- Have you ever felt like your ability to sin is greater than God's ability to save?
- Have you ever felt like you've overextended your sin limit and God's daily mercies have run out?
- Have you ever felt like you've "done it now" and your sin is going to cause God to finally say, "I'm done with you! I quit"?
- Have you ever felt like God abandoned you in your sin and left you alone to experience the full consequences?

If you answered yes to any of the questions above, then Ezekiel 16 and 23 are exactly what you need to hear from the Lord. Just as it seems Israel's sin has reached a depth of no return, God promises restoration and atonement for His people. As shocking as the actions of His people are in these chapters, it's His love that steals our breath. To a world filled with abandonment where marriages end and mothers or fathers walk out on children, God has given Ezekiel 16 and 23. To those who constantly think God is going to give up on them or drop them or forsake them, God has given Ezekiel 16 and 23. To those who easily forget His "grace is greater than all our sin," God has given Ezekiel 16 and 23 (Johnston, "Grace Greater Than Our Sin").

As remarkable as Ezekiel 16 and 23 are, I'm concerned some of its effect can be lost on those of us who have grown up in a John 3:16 world. We know of His love. We have been informed about it since the cradle roll at our church. We may even *expect* His love and see ourselves as worthy recipients of it. My real fear, however, is that we are more surprised by God's discipline than by His grace. I fear we've come to think that we deserve His goodness because we have earned it. The real question we should be asking in light of these chapters is, "Why are You so good to us, even though we are so bad?" God's discipline is always deserved; His grace is not.

If we are going to love God passionately and others rightly, we must meditate on the cross constantly. We need not go past the gospel but deeper into it. The lost world needs to see the gospel advancing in us and through us and to see that it still amazes us. I love that Ezekiel 16 and 23 show the absolute depth of our depravity and the overcoming love of our God. My prayer is that as we walk through these chapters you

> *may be able to comprehend with all the saints what is the length and width, height and depth of God's love, and to know the Messiah's love that surpasses knowledge, so you may be filled with all the fullness of God.* (Eph 3:18-19)

Without God We Are Helpless, Hopeless, and Left for Dead
EZEKIEL 16:1-5

Ezekiel 16 begins and ends in the same way: the people of Israel are helpless to change their situation, and if God does not intervene, they will die.

Four years ago in Florida, an 18-year-old girl walked into an abortion clinic to terminate her pregnancy. Three days later she was prepped for the procedure, but the doctor was delayed, and she went into labor. She delivered the baby alive. One of the owners of the clinic then took the baby, placed it in a biohazard bag, and threw it out with the trash ("Newborn baby"). Last year in New Jersey a couple claimed to have a stillborn baby and threw the baby in the trash. Prior to this the mother had been seeking an abortion. Do you know what punishment the couple received? Each must each pay fines of $125 and perform 25 hours of community service ("Prosecutor"). In both of these stories, the babies were unwanted. Their parents had no desire for them, and they were discarded with the trash.

I've sat in the operating room for all four of my children's deliveries. I go through the same routine with each C-section my wife has. I sit and try to comfort Tara while her body is experiencing major trauma, and all the while I wait breathlessly it seems to hear that first cry. With our youngest, Alastair, I was most anxious because there were so many unknowns about his condition. Yet, with all four deliveries, my reaction has been the same: I cry, I feel relief, I feel intense love, and then all I want to do is comfort and protect the little one and let them know they are safe. Not one single moment has this word ever come into my mind: UNWANTED.

Jerusalem and Israel's history was one of being unwanted by anyone but God. In Philippians 3 Paul informs us his lineage was once a source of great boasting for him, but in light of Christ, he considered all things rubbish. He was born into the right family who did the right things. Jerusalem, however, was not as privileged as Paul. The city was born in the "wrong" location to the "wrong" parents who ultimately did not want it (Block, *Ezekiel 1–24*, 474–75). Sometimes we forget where we came from, and sometimes we choose to forget where we came from; either way, Jerusalem did not have the beginning you would want to brag about. Jerusalem was born in Canaan to pagan parents (16:3).

After birth Jerusalem was thrown out, hated, and left for dead (16:4-5). No care was provided because no one who cared was present. Instead of being loved and tenderly cleaned, Jerusalem was despised and abandoned in a field. For God to paint a bleaker picture of Israel's beginnings would be difficult to imagine. He is intentionally stressing, No one wanted you!

What happens to babies who experience this? What happens to babies thrown out into a field with no clothes, no protection, and no medical attention? They die. Without God there would be no Jerusalem and no people of Israel. God begins Ezekiel 16 by reminding Israel of her beginning. Jerusalem's beginnings were not that great. And neither were ours. Whatever it takes, always remember where we would be without God: helpless, hopeless, and left for dead (Eph 2:1-4; Col 1:21; 1 Cor 1:26-31). Block points out, "The sentence of death hangs over all of us (Rom 3:23)" (*Ezekiel 1–24*, 520).

God's Love for His People Is Not Only Extravagant and Undeserved but Also Transforming
EZEKIEL 16:6-14

Despite being abandoned because she was abhorred, Jerusalem will be saved by adoption. **"I passed by you and saw you lying in your blood, and I said to you as you lay in your blood: Live! Yes, I said to you as you lay in your blood: Live!"** Duguid notes, "All it took to turn the field from a place of death to a place of life was God's word" (*Ezekiel*, 210). While the child wallowed in its blood, God chose to intervene and to claim parental rights. Jerusalem may have not received any affection from those around her at her birth, but she would have all of God's. What's staggering is that God knows full well what saying "Live" to Israel (and to us) is going to cost Him. On the days the Columbine shooters, Eric Harris and Dylan Klebold, were born, their parents had no idea the grief these boys would cause them and many others. God, however, knew full well how Israel (and we) would grieve Him, but His love is resolute.

Why does He do this? Does He look down a time tunnel and see that Israel will choose Him? Clearly not. Does He look forward in time and see that Israel will be really great one day, make it to the NFL, and buy God a house and car? Definitely not. Block contends, "The source and motivation of divine love lies entirely in God Himself" (*Ezekiel,* 521). God did not choose Israel (or us) because of who we would be but because of who He would make us to be. The potential was His, not ours. He knew what He was going to do with Israel and with us, so He said, "Live!"

As when she was born, God once again stepped in to protect her.

"Then I passed by you and saw you, and you were indeed at the age for love. So I spread the edge of My garment over you and covered your nakedness. I pledged Myself to you, entered into a covenant with you, and you became Mine." This is the declaration of the Lord God. (v. 8)

When she was a baby and naked, she needed protection from the elements and wild animals; now that she is at the age of marriage and naked, she also needs to be protected from those who would use and abuse her (Block, *Ezekiel 1–24,* 482).

God made a covenant with Israel and then displayed unrestrained and extravagant love. He does not love on a budget. His love knows no bounds. The covenant shows His seriousness and commitment, which is a security for His people. He **washed** and **anointed** her (16:9). He **clothed** her with the finest clothes, which would have been fitting for a queen (v.10). He **adorned** her **with jewelry** in every way possible (vv. 11-13). He fed her with the finest foods (v. 13).

What was the result? Transformation. Israel **became extremely beautiful and attained royalty.** Her **fame spread among the nations** because of her beauty. And what was the source of this transformation? It was God's **splendor**, which **he had bestowed on** Israel. God's love is not without effect. When we receive His love, we cannot help but be changed

(2 Cor 3:18). And just as He showered love on Jerusalem, He has done the same for us (Eph 1:3-14). Through Christ, we have received every spiritual blessing the Lord can provide (Eph 1:3).

What about you? In what ways are you different today because God's love has transformed your desires, your thoughts, and your behaviors? How often do you consider how truly powerful His love is that overcame all your rebellion and produced fruit where there had only been death and wretchedness? How often do you consider He is not obligated to love in this manner but chooses to do so? Could we ever think on this truth too much? The more we consider His love, the more we will walk in humility, gratitude, and dependence on Him.

Ingratitude Toward God and Pride in Self Inevitably Lead to Spiritual Harlotry
EZEKIEL 16:15-34

How is it even possible that verse 15 starts with the contrasting word "**But**"? How could this story take such a wretched and wounding turn? Somehow Israel became **confident in** her **beauty** instead of in God (v. 15), and she **did not remember the days of** her **youth** (v. 20). Astonishingly, she forgot God (23:35). Why does Israel seem to suffer from amnesia so much in the Bible? They crossed the Red Sea and days later doubted God's ability to provide food and water for them. When they were weighed down with the treasure God caused the Egyptians to give them, did it not occur to anyone besides Moses that God provides for His people? They witnessed God crush Pharaoh and his army, but did they not believe God could give them Canaan? When the children born in the wilderness finally got to enter the promised land, they acted as if they forgot everything Moses told them. Despite all the Ebenezers Israel raised to commemorate great events, they could never seem to remember it was God who gave them the occasion to raise them.

Enamored with what they had become, God's people forgot from where they came. Their confidence was in how they were made rather than in their Maker. At some point their story line shifted from Sovereign made to self-made, and it would result in their downfall. Are we ever prone to put more emphasis in God's gifts than we do in God? At times Israel loved the ark of the covenant and the temple more than they loved the One whose presence was with both. We are always in trouble if our confidence is in who we are rather than whose we are.

When they were not looking at themselves in the mirror, God's people were staring at other countries and lusting after what they saw (23:12). In particular they were drawn to the men of Egypt, Assyria, and Chaldea (16:23-29; 23:12-21). God describes Israel's actions in some of the most graphic language in the Bible (16:25-26; 23:19-21). The essence of Yahweh's grievance with His people is that they have used His resources to initiate relationships with other nations and have sought security in their embrace rather than in His. Those nations were all too willing to comply (23:21).

In Ezekiel 16:15-34 God states His case against Israel and accuses them of both religious and political adultery. Imagine a married woman has another lover waiting for her at a designated location. Now imagine she goes to her husband and asks for money. She then takes the money and uses it to lavish her lover with gifts. This is what Israel did (16:15-19,32-33; 23:41) and what we do (Jas 4:3-4). Jerusalem used the gifts God gave them to chase after nonexistent gods, and what's worse, they even sacrificed their children to them (16:20-21). God has one word for all of it: **prostitution**.

What had God done that justified this treatment? What good thing had He withheld? Or when was a time He ever proved unreliable? Apparently, Jerusalem thought He could not be trusted alone with their well-being since they sought alliances with other countries and their gods (16:23-29). Their actions were so awful that even the Philistine women were embarrassed by Jerusalem's **indecent behavior** (16:27). In all of it, Jerusalem was no ordinary prostitute because instead of getting paid, she was paying everyone else. She initiated the tryst (23:16), let the other nation have their way with her, and then **turned away from them in disgust** (23:17).

The best way not to end up like Jerusalem is for us never to forget where God brought us from and all that His love has made us to be. How many times are we like Israel and look for love and security in all the wrong places? Why don't we really believe that in His presence is abundant joy and at His right hand are eternal pleasures (Ps 16:11)? When we consider our own lack of faithfulness to God, which sin do we think is not wounding to Him? Which sin is not our looking for satisfaction or security somewhere else? Which sin is not our placing something else above Him in our heart? If there is a greater picture of betrayal and ingratitude in the Bible, I do not know it!

God Is as Passionate in His Judgment as He Is in His Love
EZEKIEL 16:35-43

Has God ever given you something you thought you wanted only for you to realize you did not want it after all? If Israel wanted to expose her **nakedness** (16:36), then He was going to make sure her lovers could see her **completely naked** (16:37), which was not a good thing.

As a consequence of her prostitution, God is going to **gather** all her lovers against her (16:37). He will use those lovers to bring about her **bloodshed** (16:38). Her lovers will **tear down** her **elevated places**. They will also **stone** her, **cut** her, and **burn down** her houses (16:39-41). Though the wording is slightly different, the divine Judge gives a similar sentence in Ezekiel 23:47. The nations Israel prostituted herself to will now execute the Lord's judgment (23:24). Those she delighted in pursuing will now pursue her destruction. Israel will be left naked, penniless, and covered in shame (23:29).

Why was God acting in such a wrathful manner toward His people? Well, one answer is because Jerusalem asked for it. She **enraged** (intentionally provoked) God by not remembering the days of her youth (16:43). But God had another purpose for His discipline: **I will stop you from being a prostitute, and you will never again pay fees for lovers** (16:41). In the depth of their depravity and despite their hearts that were **inflamed with lust** (16:30), God would save His people from themselves. He will bring all their lewdness to an end (23:27). He will work in their lives so they will no longer seek security anywhere but in Him. His discipline of His children is never just punitive but purifying. In the movie *Forrest Gump* (1994), Forrest's love for the wayward Jenny was steadfast but not transformative. His love was insufficient to produce any lasting changes in Jenny's desires and behaviors. God's love, however, is not that weak. His love transforms those who receive it. He will not leave His people in the same condition that He finds them. His plan is that all will be conformed to the image of His Son (Rom 8:29).

Our Sin Is More Wretched Than We Care to Acknowledge
EZEKIEL 16:44-52

As if all God said up to this point was not sufficient to give His people an accurate portrait of their sin and sickness, He provided one more comparison. He wanted them to know they had **behaved more**

corruptly than **Sodom** and that **Samaria did not commit half** their sins (16:47,51). It would have been astoundingly offensive for Israel to hear God's indictments because they considered themselves more pious than the rest. But God's assessments did not lack facts. It was as if Israel had seen Samaria's ways and said, "Anything you can do, I can do far worse" (23:11). God's people had so **multiplied** their **detestable practices** they made Sodom and Samaria appear righteous (16:52). How grieving and how gross that God's people loved sin so much.

It should not be surprising when Gentiles act like those who do not know God, since they do not. When God's people, however, act in like manner, something is terribly wrong. Paul encouraged the Thessalonians to "abstain from sexual immorality, so that each of you knows how to control his own body in sanctification and honor, not with lustful desires, like the Gentiles who don't know God" (1 Thess 4:3-5). He clearly implies those who know God act in one way and those who do not know God act in another. Israel's actions in Ezekiel 16 and 23 were the same as those who did not know God. But Israel did know Him, so they were without excuse when called to give an account for their actions. As Christians, we've been called to holiness (1 Thess 4:7) and have been given His Spirit (1 Thess 4:8). If our pursuit of sin is making those who do not know God appear to be more righteous, we are without excuse as well.

Rather Than Abandon His People God Chooses to Atone for Them
EZEKIEL 16:53-63

If this passage was about a contemporary marriage, then most likely the union would dissolve based on marital infidelity and irreconcilable differences, but for God there is no such thing. Instead of abandoning His people, He will **make atonement for all** they **had done** (16:63). Can we read that once more? Instead of forsaking His unfaithful bride, He will atone for her by forsaking His faithful Son. In making atonement, the Father will treat Jesus as if He was the one who engaged in prostitution. He will treat Jesus as if He worshiped other gods. He will treat Jesus as if He had looked for security somewhere besides the Father. He will treat Jesus as if He had looked at porn, or gossiped, or had an abortion. In short, God the Father will treat Jesus as if He was guilty of every single act of rebellion we have ever committed against God.

To all those who would say, "There is no way God can forgive the filthy things I've done," Ezekiel 16 and 23 stand as a lighthouse shining truth against that lie. He knows all that we have done, and instead of running away from us, He runs to us. Whatever we confess, He has covered with the blood of His Son. When we truly grasp the love displayed in Ezekiel 16 and 23,

> our hearts break because of the unexpected beauty of it. God keeps coming to us, even in our bloody tawdriness, and says, "Live!" And in the end, he gives us his very life through the Son to make just that possible. (Hoezee, "Jeremiah 8:18–9:1")

No sinner is beyond the reach of God's grace. Fanny Crosby led us to sing,

> O perfect redemption, the purchase of blood!
> To every believer the promise of God;
> The vilest offender who truly believes,
> that moment from Jesus a pardon receives.
> Praise the Lord! Praise the Lord!
> Let the earth hear His voice!
> Praise the Lord! Praise the Lord!
> Let the people rejoice;
> O come to the Father, through Jesus the Son:
> And give Him the glory! Great things He hath done!
>   (Fanny J. Crosby, "To God Be the Glory")

If you have been made keenly aware of how awful you are in comparison to the Lord's holy standard, then rejoice, because "there is more mercy in Christ than sin in us" (Sibbes, *The Bruised Reed*).

Reflect and Discuss

1. What steps can we take never to forget what we were like before Christ rescued us? Why should we do this?
2. Why are we tempted to become confident in what Christ has made us instead of being confident in Christ alone?
3. In what ways has God's love transformed you and others around you?
4. Why are we prone to use God's good gifts on our own cravings and pursuits? How can we avoid this?

5. Have you ever considered your sin to be prostitution or adultery in relation to God? Why or why not?
6. Though we may not be like Israel and seek security in other countries, what are some places or things in which we seek security besides God?
7. When was a time in your life that you found God's discipline to be not just punitive but purifying?
8. Why do we often fail to grasp the wretchedness of our sin?
9. Why is it so amazing that instead of abandoning us in our own filth, God has chosen to atone for us?
10. Why do we sometimes feel as if we are too dirty for God? Is that ever truly the case?

Riddle Me This

Main Idea: God is telling the same story of both His judgment and His mercy but in a new way.

I. God's Parable and Its Purpose (17:1-15)
II. God's Punishment of the Puppet King (17:16-21)
III. God's Promise of a Planting (17:22-25)

Ezekiel 17 is not a new message but a new way to reveal the same truths the prophet has been declaring all along. The familiar truths presented in an unfamiliar way are that God is sovereign, He judges those who refuse to do His will, and He has a steadfast plan to preserve a people for His name. Similar to Genesis 37–41, the events noted in Ezekiel 17 reveal a divine hand orchestrating a plan beyond what is just perceived with human eyes. The actions of Nebuchadnezzar are not random but appointed, since judgment has come for Zedekiah. In fact, the king of Babylon is not the King with whom Zedekiah should be most concerned. In the final portion of the parable, a sprig of hope will be planted in the people's hearts as God tells of the planting He will do on Israel's high mountain (17:22-23).

God's Parable and Its Purpose
EZEKIEL 17:1-15

When we see the word "riddle" (v. 2), my generation is more inclined to think of the grumpy old troll who lives under the bridge in one of our children's cartoons than we are to think of God. Mercifully my children have moved beyond this multilingual preadolescent explorer, but I still find myself wondering on occasion where her parents were during all her adventures. At first glance we may wonder ourselves why God is employing a riddle to communicate with His people. In the language of the Old Testament, the word "riddle" means "difficult speech requiring interpretation" (Wilson, *NIDOTTE*, 2:107). God's people were already hardheaded and hardhearted (3:7), so using difficult speech that needs additional information to provide clarity might not sound like the wisest strategy to us, but God always knows the best way to convey His message. Like most riddles there is a question that needs an answer: God wants to know if a specific vine is going to flourish (vv. 9-10). Unlike most riddles however, God is going to supply the answer Himself (vv. 16-21). He desires to be clear with His people and not leave the interpretation of what's unfolding to their best collective wisdom.

God uses various techniques to communicate with His people, but vain repetition is not one of them. His aim in the riddle or parable is not just repeating previous proclamations but giving further revelation of current events for Ezekiel's audience. Entertainment is also not the primary reason for God's shift in communication style but education. He is not merely telling a fairy tale but one grounded in the facts of Zedekiah's rebellion and consequent judgment. With these aims in mind, Ezekiel is told to tell the story of two eagles, a cedar, and a vine.

The summary of the story is simple enough. A beautiful and powerful eagle plucks the top off a cedar tree and then drops it into a city full of commerce. The eagle then takes an interest in farming and plants seed in a place with great potential for growth. The seed becomes a vine that outwardly honors the eagle but beneath the surface remains most loyal to self. The vine reaches out to another eagle for help and rejects what the first eagle has done for it. The question of the riddle is then asked: What's going to happen to the vine after it rejects the first eagle in favor of the second eagle? Specifically the Riddler wants to know if anyone thinks the vine will be in a better position after betraying the first eagle. The answer provided is no. The first eagle will destroy the vine, and it will shrivel and die. The Lord then has Ezekiel ask the people, **"Don't you know what these things mean?"** (v. 12).

If I were in Ezekiel's audience, I would have to answer the Lord, "Nope. Not a clue." In my defense, when David was first told a parable about himself, he did not get it either (2 Sam 12:1-7). As stated previously, the summary of the riddle in Ezekiel 17 is simple enough, but its meaning is another matter. Knowing He was dealing with obtuse people (like us), the Lord provides the interpretation for His parable (vv. 12-15). The first eagle is Nebuchadnezzar and the second eagle is the pharaoh in Egypt. The top shoot of the cedar is Jehoiachin, and the vine is Zedekiah. Though he swore an oath to the king of Babylon, Zedekiah broke his agreement and sought resources and rescue from Egypt. After explaining the parable, the Lord's question remains the same: Is Zedekiah going to flourish by doing evil? Will he get away with failing to keep his word?

A possible answer for Ezekiel's audience to offer could be, "Lord GOD, only You know" (37:3). The question they were given, however, should have been a "softball" for those who had been paying attention to the Lord's messages through His prophet. God already gave the answer to the question concerning Zedekiah's fate (12:1-16). Whether or not Ezekiel's audience was really listening and taking to heart each word from the Lord is not revealed in Ezekiel 17.

A question we might ask at this point is, Why does the Lord use the parable? Why doesn't He just start with the explanation? One reason for the use of the riddle is so the Lord can present the facts of the case without any biases interfering with the message's receipt. For example, Nathan's use of a parable allowed David to hear the injustice that occurred and to determine what action should be taken against the offending party (2 Sam 12:1-7). David's response was exactly as it should be when assessing the facts of the situation. It was not until the interpretation was given that David understood the parable was about his own sinful actions. Likewise, the parable presented in Ezekiel 17:1-10 allows the prophet's audience to formulate their own ideas of guilty and innocent parties based on the facts presented. From the story they could determine the most treacherous character is the vine. He rejected the first eagle's provision and sought care from a lesser eagle. While neither eagle may be fully innocent, the guilt of the vine would be without question.

Perhaps, then, God withheld the names of the people represented by the eagles and vine because some of the exiles were sympathetic toward Zedekiah. We do not know fully what communication was like between the exiles and Jerusalem. We do know a fugitive will be able to relay the news of Jerusalem's downfall (33:21) and that Jeremiah was able to send those in exile a letter (Jer 29:1-29). Block proposes Ezekiel's use of the riddle is because possible "reports of Zedekiah's overtures with the Egyptians were being greeted as an opportunity to throw off the Babylonian yoke, which in turn would enable them to return home" (Block, *Ezekiel 1–24*, 539). The use of the eagles and vine allows Ezekiel's audience to determine that the actions of the vine are wrong, before understanding that the vine represents the current prince in Jerusalem. Block contends Ezekiel's aim "is to expose Zedekiah's treacherous policies and his compatriots' support of them as rebellion against Yahweh"(ibid.). From the use of this parable, we can see once again that God always knows the best ways to engage our hearts and minds. He wants the people to understand His discipline of Zedekiah is not without cause. He also wants them to know if they side with the prince in Jerusalem, they are siding against Yahweh.

God's Punishment of the Puppet King
EZEKIEL 17:16-21

In answer to the questions of the riddle, Zedekiah will not flourish, nor will he escape judgment. Pharaoh will be of no help to Jerusalem's prince in the time he will need it most. Because of his treacherous actions, Zedekiah will die in Babylon. Believe it or not, neither Nebuchadnezzar nor physical death are Zedekiah's biggest problem. By utilizing the word "therefore," Ezekiel informs us God has a point He wants to drive home beyond just telling the parable and its interpretation.

Zedekiah is not just guilty of possessing a poor strategy in foreign policy, but more importantly he has broken the covenant with God. In response Yahweh will use Nebuchadnezzar as His means of judgment in the prince of Jerusalem's life. The events foretold in 12:1-16 happen just as the Lord said they would (2 Kgs 25:1-7). Zedekiah is caught not just in Nebuchadnezzar's snare but in Yahweh's. The prince and his posse will pay the price for acting rebelliously toward God.

In light of Ezekiel 17:16-21, here are a few observations.

Anyone who rejects God's plans will never flourish. Provision was made in Nebuchadnezzar's plan for Zedekiah and the people in Jerusalem to endure (v. 14). Zedekiah, however, refused to believe this was the best plan for his life and felt he could make better arrangements. He paid the price for his foolishness and so did those who followed him.

Seeking refuge in anyone or anything besides God can be a fatal mistake. In the text Pharaoh was not the initiator; rather, it was Zedekiah who first sent ambassadors to Egypt (19:15). As it turns out, Pharaoh did not help Jerusalem's prince, but it would not have mattered if he had. His resources were no match for Nebuchadnezzar's army, especially since the king of Babylon was appointed as God's instrument of justice against Zedekiah. We are always in trouble if we look to our peers for help more than we look to God.

Zedekiah did not "escape" Divine judgment, and neither will we without Christ's aid. There is no place we can run from God. Ask Jonah. Like

Zedekiah we have all gone astray from God and turned to our own way (Isa 53:6). For some reason we feel we make better rulers of our lives than God. Our strongest inclinations, however, do not change the fact there is only one King of the universe. He deserves our absolute loyalty. What Zedekiah did in breaking his oath to Nebuchadnezzar, we have all done to God on a grand scale. God did not ignore the prince of Jerusalem's sin, and He will not ignore ours. Zedekiah is actually a great example of what will be seen next in Ezekiel 18—we will be held personally responsible for our sin. Our only hope for escaping the wrath our treason against God deserves is to flee to Christ who has borne our sins for us. Yes, we turned away, but "the LORD has punished Him for the iniquity of us all" (Isa 53:6).

What is seen has more to do with what is unseen than we may be aware. For many the capture and punishment of Zedekiah was primarily because he broke his oath with Nebuchadnezzar. Yahweh informs us, however, something deeper is occurring (vv. 19-21). The events carried out in the siege of Jerusalem are primarily God's judgments against His own people for all of their idolatry and insubordination. We should be mindful, then, no matter what we see on the news, God is writing a bigger story that will be revealed when time is done.

The worst thing man can do to you when you break a covenant is put you to death; God, however, can put you to second death. Jesus said, "Don't fear those who kill the body but are not able to kill the soul; rather, fear Him who is able to destroy both soul and body in hell" (Matt 10:28). The worst Nebuchadnezzar can do is kill Zedekiah's sons, blind Zedekiah, and then put Zedekiah to death. Admittedly this sounds pretty bad until one understands the punishment from Nebuchadnezzar is now complete. He can do nothing more to harm Zedekiah. For those who reject God's ways, being put to death by men pales in comparison to experiencing eternal death and the wrath of God.

God's Promise of a Planting
EZEKIEL 17:22-25

Every promise of God is a grace not a right. God does not owe a single word of hope to sinners. The fact He gives one should always amaze us. Ezekiel 17 could stop at verse 21 and be similar to the lament in Ezekiel 19. God, however, wants His people to know that He is not finished with them or with David's line. He will plant a sprig from the cedar on top of Israel's high mountain once again (17:22). He will also cause it to flourish (v. 23).

A counsel often provided in a hermeneutics class is to be careful in searching for Christ under every rock and tree in the Old Testament. Greidanus contends, however,

> since the literary context of the Old Testament in the Christian canon is the New Testament, this means that the Old Testament must be understood in the context of the New Testament. And since the heart of the New Testament is Jesus Christ, this means that every message from the Old Testament must be seen in the light of Jesus Christ. (Greidanus, *Preaching Christ*, 51)

In the case of Ezekiel 17, you don't have to look under every rock and tree when Jesus is the tree that is referenced. The ultimate fulfillment of the cedar sprig is Christ. What God says vaguely in Ezekiel 17 about the planting, He says clearly in Ezekiel 34. God will provide the greatest ruler for His people. Jesus is who Helm calls "God's forever King" in the book we repeatedly read to all of our children (Helm, *Big Picture Story Bible*, 411). Though we do not deserve such a wonderful leader, God graciously gives Him to us for our good and His glory.

As Ezekiel 17 closes, Israel's greatest hope for enduring does not lie in Nebuchadnezzar's kindness but in the Lord's. While Nebuchadnezzar had a provision that would allow those in Jerusalem to endure (v. 14), God has a plan that will cause His people to flourish forever (v. 23). He alone is capable of making the "low tree tall" and making the "withered tree thrive" (v. 24). He will do it. He has spoken (v. 24).

Reflect and Discuss

1. When you hear the word *riddle*, what comes to your mind? Why does God have to use various means of communication to help us understand what He is doing?
2. Why do we struggle to believe that God's plans for our lives are best?
3. Have you ever known what God wanted you to do but refused to submit to His will? How did that work out for you?
4. How can we learn not to base our understanding of what's happening in our lives solely on what we see with our eyes?
5. How can we know that God is working His plan not in regard to just some things in our lives but all things?

6. How can we minimize reaching out to those around us for help and security more than we reach out to God?
7. Have you ever felt like you might "get away" with a sin? What can we learn from Zedekiah's life in this regard?
8. How grateful are you that we know who the sprig of cedar is? What difference is this knowledge making in our lives?
9. Why do you think we tend to *expect* hope from God rather than being amazed by it?
10. When you consider Zedekiah's actions and the consequences both he and those he led experienced, how will you be different as a leader in your home, faith family, vocation, or community?

Turn and Live: God's Justice and Our Responsibility

EZEKIEL 18:1-32

Main Idea: The only sin God holds against us is our own, but in His graciousness, He calls us to turn from sin and live.

I. Good News: God Will Not Hold the Sins of Anyone Else Against Us (18:1-20).

II. Bad News: God Will Hold Us Accountable for Our Sins, and Just One of Them Is Worthy of the Full Measure of His Wrath (18:21-29).

III. Greatest News: God Has Laid All of Our Sin on Christ that We Might Turn and Live (18:30-32).

Sometimes we find ourselves in situations because of the choices of others. When I was in fifth grade, there was a teacher who did not want me in her classroom solely because of my father's reputation. My closest friends were in her class, but I was not. She did not want to deal with my father's craziness. Speaking of his craziness, when I was in sixth grade, my father showed poor sportsmanship and was asked to no longer coach our basketball team. As a result, he forced me to quit and miss the second half of the season. I'm certain this is where my future NBA career was derailed.

My situations are mild in comparison to some who suffer greatly because of the decisions of others. There are babies who are born with birth defects because their mother could not stop drinking or using drugs while pregnant. There are Christians whose bodies are mutilated or scarred because this is how their audience responded to their witness of Christ. There are children who will cry themselves to sleep tonight because a parent has walked out on their family. Certainly there are times we suffer because of the decisions of others, but I find most of the consequences I deal with are because of my own decisions.

In Ezekiel 18 the prophet's generation believes they are suffering because of the sins of their fathers and grandfathers. They do not believe they deserve the situation they are in, and they do not think it will change. Above all, they accuse God of injustice. He, however, will confront their fatalistic worldview by calling them to acknowledge their own sin and to turn from it. In turning they will find life.

Both presently and eternally, sin is a matter of life and death. The words "live/life" or "death/die" are used more than 28 times in this text. The repetition reveals the emphasis. Despite all His people had done, God's desire was still for them (and us) to own their sin, turn from it, and find life in Christ. As much as we want to blame others, no one has ever made us choose sin. The world, the flesh, and the Devil may load the gun of temptation, but we pull the trigger. The first person we should blame for the consequences we often find ourselves in is often the last person we hold responsible. Ezekiel 18 is a call to acknowledge our sin and accept God's call to repent and live.

Good News: God Will Not Hold the Sins of Anyone Else Against Us
EZEKIEL 18:1-20

On his desk in the Oval Office, President Truman had a sign with these words written on it: The buck stops here. Sometimes I wonder if anyone in Washington, DC, knows where that sign went. But I digress. From our first journey into sin, humankind has been an expert at blaming everyone else for our sin. Adam blamed Eve, Eve blamed the serpent, and all who have come behind them have been gifted in shifting responsibility. God's people in the time of Ezekiel were no different.

Based on their circumstances, the people of God adopted a fatalistic worldview. They shared this **proverb** with one another: "**The fathers eat sour grapes, and the children's teeth are set on edge.**" Though He knows the answer, God wants Ezekiel to ask His people **what** they **mean** by the **proverb**. Ezekiel's contemporary, Jeremiah, recorded exactly what they meant: "Our fathers sinned; they no longer exist, but we bear their punishment" (Lam 5:7). Ezekiel's peers were blaming their ancestors (and God) for the discipline they were receiving. In essence, their accounts were being debited because of checks written by their fathers.

Beneath their proverb was a conviction of fatalism. Block contends their mind-set was, "This is the way the universe operates. There is an inevitable and uncontrollable determinism. This is how things are; one can do nothing to change it" (*Ezekiel 1–24*, 560). If they were indeed thinking along these lines, it means they believed God did not care about them, or if He did, He was too weak to change anything. Perhaps they felt things were this way because God's ways lack fairness (18:25). Instead of punishing those who committed treason against God, He punishes their children, or so they thought.

You cannot accuse God of wrongdoing and think He will not notice. The Lord has a response for their **proverb**. He tells them, **"You will no longer use this proverb in Israel."** He will silence their popular saying and worldview because it is wrong. He declares, **"Look, every life belongs to Me. The life of the father is like the life of the son—both belong to Me. The person who sins is the one who will die."** In essence God informs them He owns every life and holds each accountable for that person's own actions. No random laws of the cosmos are in operation but only His laws, and He is just.

To further explain how wrong their thinking is, the Lord provides them with three case studies about a father, his son, and his grandson (18:5-17). In the first example God describes a man who **"follows my statutes and keeps My ordinances, acting faithfully. Such a person is righteous; he will certainly live."** In the second example the man's son is described as **violent** and **who sheds blood**, though **the father** did none of these things. According to the Lord, the man's son **will not live** because unlike the father he chose to commit **detestable acts. His blood will be on him.** In the third example the righteous man's grandson sees **all the sins his father committed** and chooses not to **do likewise.** Like his grandfather the grandson **practices** the Lord's **ordinances and follows** His **statutes. He will not die for his father's iniquity. He will certainly live.**

In coming to the conclusion of the three case studies, God wants to drive the point home clearly. In contrast to their popular proverb, God informs Ezekiel's generation each person is held accountable for that person's own sin. Of course, they should have known this already because God has been saying the same thing all along. Because He does not change, neither does His message. In Deuteronomy 24:16 He informed His people, "Fathers are not to be put to death for their children or children for their fathers; each person will be put to death for his own sin." God was also repeating the same message in the exile's generation through Jeremiah: "In those days, it will never again be said: The fathers have eaten sour grapes, and the children's teeth are set on edge. Rather, each will die for his own wrongdoing. Anyone who eats sour grapes—his own teeth will be set on edge" (Jer 31:29-30).

Since none of Ezekiel's audience quoted Deuteronomy 24:16, it's doubtful the word of the Lord was at the forefront of their minds, but had it been, one might have asked, "What about Exodus 34:7?" In proclaiming Himself to Moses, the Lord revealed, "He will not leave the guilty unpunished, bringing the consequences of the fathers' wrongdoing on the children and grandchildren to the third and fourth generation" (Exod 34:7). At first glance this verse appears to justify the claims Israel was bringing against the Lord. Exodus 20:5, however, provides some clarification. In this verse the Lord addresses the idolatry of His people and says, "You must not bow down to them or worship them; for I, the LORD your God, am a jealous God, punishing the children for the fathers' sin, to the third and fourth generations *of those who hate Me*" (Exod 20:5, emphasis added). The key to interpretation and reconciliation with the other Scripture passages is the last phrase. What Ezekiel portrays is a son who sees his father's sins and avoids them, while Exodus has in view sons and grandsons who embrace the sins they have seen and who follow the same pattern.

Both passages in Exodus and Ezekiel affirm the same truth. The only innocent son God has ever punished is His own Son when He laid our guilt on Christ. In all other cases any children that turn from the sinful practices of their parents and obey God will not be punished for what their moms and dads do. Likewise, any children that continue in the rebellious footsteps of their fathers should expect the same punishment.

The case studies the Lord provides in Ezekiel 18 can also teach us additional truths. First, a wicked son cannot be rescued by the righteousness of his father. In the examples the Lord gave, none of the father's obedience and righteousness was credited to the account of the son. For all of us, the only One who can pass righteousness to us is Christ. In all other cases the righteous deeds of a parent will not be credited to the account of the child.

Second, just because a father chooses wickedness and rebellion toward God does not mean his children have to walk in the same path. For those of us who have had an ungodly parent, the example given in the third case study should give us hope. The grandson sees what his father did and chooses to walk in the path of his grandfather instead. Josiah is one of the greatest examples of breaking the cycle of sin that is handed down from parents (2 Kgs 22:1-2). His father and grandfather were evil kings, but Josiah chose another example to follow—David. Just because our parents may have rejected the ways of the Lord does not mean we are doomed to the same path.

Third, righteousness is more evidenced by practice than profession. With both the man and the grandson, righteousness was not talk but deed. They did things such as give their bread to the hungry and cover the naked with clothing (18:7,16). They refused to oppress others and treated their neighbor's wife with purity (vv. 6-7,15-16). None of these acts earned righteousness but evidenced it. They followed the Lord's statutes and ordinances, and righteousness was revealed.

Fourth, when the Lord disciplines us, we should not look for anyone else to blame but ourselves. Ezekiel's generation wanted to know why they were suffering. They know now their exile is not because God is unjust or because He laid on them the sins of their parents. It was time for Israel to stop blaming others and accept responsibility for their own actions. We should too. As a pastor I frequently meet people who cannot get over some aspect of their past. Though we may blame certain circumstances on our fathers, we cannot blame our sins on them. We alone make our choices, and we alone will be held accountable for them.

Bad News: God Will Hold Us Accountable for Our Sins, and Just One of Them Is Worthy of the Full Measure of His Wrath
EZEKIEL 18:21-29

The Lord's kindness leads us to repentance (Rom 2:4). To be led by the Lord to acknowledge our sins and to turn from them is a grace to us. In the initial moments of conviction, we may not view our experience as a period of grace, but anytime the Lord does not leave us in our sin, it is nothing but grace. The very reason Israel is thinking and processing sin is because they have been disciplined. Their problem was they were thinking on the sins of their fathers and not their own. God, however, is about to change this practice.

The people of Judah did not just need to be rescued from Babylon; they needed to be rescued from their sin. Block notes, "One's appreciation for grace is directly proportional to one's consciousness of sin. A prophet does no one a favor by promoting a sense of well being when one is governed by the law of sin and death" (Block, *Ezekiel 1–24*, 590). If what they heard from the Lord in Ezekiel 18:5-20 was true, then what they claimed in Ezekiel 18:2 was false. If God deals justly with each generation, then they too must be guilty. And they were (20:30-32). Their parents had certainly committed sin (20:4-29), but their generation continued to defile themselves by practicing idolatry (20:31). Something bad was not happening to a people who were good. No, God was using something bad to discipline people who were bad, ultimately to produce a good result. God disciplines His people for the purpose of repentance and restoration and not for ruin.

To help Israel understand their accountability for their actions, the Lord provides Ezekiel with two more examples. In the first example a wicked person turns from his sins, follows the Lord's way, and lives (18:21-23). In the second example a righteous person turns from the Lord's ways, practices iniquity, and faces death (v. 24). In one example there is a person who has turned from sin and in the other example, a person who has turned to it.

What can we learn from the examples? First, we do not have to stay the way we are. What a great word of hope! Those who have walked in wickedness can be counted among the righteous. Just because Israel walked in idolatry up to that point did not mean they had to continue in it. Ezekiel's generation could recognize their sin and repent of it. In the New Testament there are real-life examples of what Ezekiel was telling them. For instance, there were the tax collectors, Matthew and Zacchaeus, who turned from their practices and followed Christ. There was also Paul, who went from persecuting the people of God to pastoring them. The Lord's grace can bring true and lasting change in our lives.

Second, past righteousness never covers present sin. The second example is one the church crowd might want to give special attention. We cannot live in obedience to God the first portion of our life and then use that as a righteous slush fund to spend our credits on disobedience. Faith is demonstrated in a consistently godly life. With regard to righteousness, there is no time like the present. Is there current evidence of the fruit of the Spirit? Are we growing today as a disciple in Christ? As much as Ezekiel was to exhort the wicked to turn from their ways, he was also to encourage the righteous to continue in theirs.

I fear in my denomination eternal security has been emphasized far more than the call to persevere in Christ. The concept of New Testament conversion is not "I'm saved, so now I can do what I want," but "I'm saved, and for the first time I can do what He wants." Some seem to think that as long as one confesses the "sinner's prayer," then it does not matter what happens with the rest of their lives. The second example provided to Ezekiel should serve as a reminder to us that righteousness is not merely to be professed once in our lives but practiced daily.

However much we may glean from the two examples God provided, Ezekiel's audience did not like them. They said, **"The Lord's way isn't fair."** They struggled to process what they were hearing from the Lord. How could one who was wicked not be punished, and how could one who walked in righteousness face punishment? God cut to the heart of Israel by saying the issue was not His own fairness but theirs (vv. 25,29). God is not being arbitrary or unpredictable. He is punishing the one who turns to sin and forgiving the one who turns away from it, and He will do the same for the exiles (v. 30). For Israel to want Him to do otherwise reveals they are in no position to declare what is fair and what is not.

Greatest News: God Has Laid All of Our Sin on Christ that We Might Turn and Live
EZEKIEL 18:30-32

As Ezekiel 18 comes to a close, one might expect the Lord to grow weary with His obstinate and ignorant people. If His fairness was what they questioned, then perhaps He should give them a full taste. He, however, has a better plan.

We are sinners born from sinners; therefore we should not be surprised by the Lord's judgment but by His mercy. Judgment is deserved, but mercy is not. The fact the One we have rebelled from is the One who begs us to repent should not be lost on us. We should never cease to be amazed Ezekiel 18:30-32 is recorded in the Bible. After enduring their rebellion and their accusations, God offers His people (and us) grace and life instead of judgment.

God, the offended party, pleads with us, the offenders, to **repent and turn from all** our **transgressions, so they will not be a stumbling block that causes** our **punishment.** His desire is for us to **throw off all the transgressions** we **have committed and get** ourselves **a new heart and a new spirit.** He takes **no pleasure in anyone's death.** As obstinate as His people have been in their sin, He is as steadfast in His love. To punish sin, God is being nothing but fair, but to forgive it, He is being nothing but gracious.

What Israel needed was a proper vision of God. Theirs was clearly flawed with thoughts of His weakness and injustice. What they learn is that He does punish the wicked, but He takes no pleasure in it. What they also learn is that their lives are precious to Him. He has stepped in and disciplined His people because if they continue on the path of sin it will lead to only one thing—death. He is pleading with them to turn from their rebellion and live.

In order for God to forgive, His people must **repent** and **throw off all** of their **transgressions**. What does it mean to repent? It means we turn from sin and from ourselves and turn to God. Repentance is not the same as remorse, which means we feel bad for a little while but then keep walking the same path. No, repentance involves not merely a momentary change but a fundamental one. We walk differently because we have been made different.

True repentance requires a new spirit and a new heart. From where will these come? God. He does for His people what we are incapable of doing for ourselves. He says,

> *I will give you a new heart and put a new spirit within you; I will remove your heart of stone and give you a heart of flesh. I will place My Spirit within you and cause you to follow My statutes and carefully observe My ordinances.* (36:26-27)

All that God expects from His people, He provides for them. The only way to "get" a new spirit and a new heart is to go to God.

Where exactly should one throw all of their transgressions? There is no other place but Christ. He alone has taken our sins upon Himself and paid the price for them. For those who repent, the only place God remembers our sin is at the cross of Christ. God's offer of life to His people comes only through the death of His Son.

At the close of Ezekiel 18, I cannot help but wonder if we are as passionate with our pleading with sinners as God is. The last words in the chapter are, "**Repent and live!**" He is calling sinners to abandon the path of death and choose His path of life. Is this how we treat people who wound us? Do we seek their best though they have sought our harm? One of the clearest ways we can image God is to initiate reconciliation with those who have sinned against us. Instead of waiting for them to come to us, like God we should go to them.

God still appeals to sinners today to turn and live. His appeals are offered through us. Paul contends, "We are ambassadors for Christ, certain that God is appealing through us. We plead on Christ's behalf, 'Be reconciled to God'" (2 Cor 5:20). The pleading of Paul was the pleading of God, and it is the same through us. If any of our loved ones, coworkers, neighbors, or friends perish, may they do so only with our pleading ringing in their ears.

Reflect and Discuss

1. Why are we tempted at times to blame anyone but ourselves for our sin?
2. Has there ever been a time when you felt God was punishing you because of someone else's sin?
3. Has there ever been a time others have had to deal with the consequences of your sin?
4. Have you ever considered God to be unfair? With regard to our sin, why should we desire grace rather than fairness from God?
5. When is a time God stepped in to "save you from yourself"? In what ways are you thankful He did?
6. Why do we not immediately embrace God's discipline as a grace to us? How can we grow in this area?
7. When you see God, who is the offended party, initiating reconciliation and calling for the offenders to repent, in what ways do you want to praise Him?
8. How can we look like God when we initiate reconciliation with others?
9. Is there anyone who has wounded you that you do not want to initiate reconciliation with or to forgive? How can the Lord help you be like Him in this area?
10. Is God's passionate call to sinners to repent being heard clearly through you? Why or why not?

Weeping for Those Who Lead Us

EZEKIEL 19:1-14

Main Idea: When our leaders refuse to walk in God's ways, we should weep for their failure and seek deliverance in another King.

I. We Should Weep for Our Leaders When They Intentionally Reject God's Ways (19:2-4).
II. We Should Weep for Our Leaders When They Are Full of Pride (19:5-9).
III. We Should Weep for Our Leaders When They Refuse to Listen to God (19:10-14).

In a letter to his protégé, Paul urges Timothy that as a first priority, "petitions, prayers, intercessions, and thanksgivings be made for everyone" and, in particular, "for kings and all those who are in authority" (1 Tim 2:1-2). The reason prayer should be offered for the leaders is "so that we may lead a tranquil and quiet life in all godliness and dignity" (1 Tim 2:2). Because of these instructions I regularly pray for our political leaders when our faith family gathers in worship, when our elders meet, and during my personal conversations with the Lord. In my prayers I ask God to give our leaders an awareness of the stewardship He has entrusted to them, to silence all voices of influence in their lives but His own, and to provide all that our leaders need to guide and serve us well. So let me ask you, is prayer a priority in your life? If so, is praying for the leaders of your nation, state, and city a matter of first importance?

What Paul does not tell Timothy, however, is when he should weep for those same leaders. We know Paul wept over the lost (Phil 3:18) and over his teaching (Acts 20:31), but we do not have any incident recorded of Paul shedding tears for those in authority over him. The same cannot be said for Ezekiel. In fact, God commanded the prophet to lament for the princes of Israel (19:1). The question is, Why did God want Ezekiel to cry for these leaders, and when should we cry for ours?

A lament is a form of song used to help individuals or groups of people "to express struggles, suffering, or disappointment to the Lord" (Fee and Stuart, *How to Read the Bible*, 194). Laments were often used at funerals in praise of the one who died and to express grief over their death. What happens in Ezekiel 19, however, is not just a pure funeral dirge. In one sense Ezekiel is told to lament (v. 1) and that what he sings should be used as a lament (v. 14), but the content of the song itself lacks the usual trappings of this genre. For instance, the song does not contain a call for its hearers to join in the lamenting. Block contends, "Contrary to the original hearers' and many modern readers' expectation, like ch. 17, this is a riddle, not a funeral song; it deals enigmatically with a living reality—the fate of the Davidic dynasty"(*Ezekiel 1–24*, 595). Unlike Ezekiel 17, God does not provide a specific interpretation for Ezekiel's song but leaves the content of Ezekiel 19 to stand on its own.

While the customary phrases of a lament may not be present, the Lord informs His prophet that what he sings is to be used as a lament (v. 14). In contrast to Tom Sawyer, most of us do not get to attend our funeral while we are alive. The Davidic rulers of Judah may not be present for their funeral either, but based on this song, they can know it is coming. The essence of the song is to convey the failure of Judah's leaders and the certainty of their doom. In this lament there will be no praising of the good done by the departed, only a shameful heralding of failed leadership. These princes (Ezekiel's preferred word for rulers) are being lamented not because they have been so great but because they have been so evil. If Zedekiah is indeed one of the rulers described in Ezekiel 19, then we can know he will not heed the Lord's admonition in Ezekiel 18 to turn and live. Following Ezekiel 18, we can also know the men mentioned in this lament are being held responsible for their actions and not those of other leaders. For those in exile with Ezekiel, the lament indicates any hope of being delivered by a king from home should be abandoned. If God's people are to be delivered, it will not be from those who have ruled them. Were it not for Ezekiel 17:22-24, they might even wonder if the scepter has been removed permanently from the house of David. A time for weeping has arisen indeed.

We Should Weep for Our Leaders When They Intentionally Reject God's Ways
EZEKIEL 19:2-4

In Genesis 49:9-11 Jacob blesses the tribe of Judah in this way:

> *Judah is a young lion—my son, you return from the kill. He crouches;*
> *he lies down like a lion or a lioness—who dares to rouse him? The*

scepter will not depart from Judah or the staff from between his feet
until He whose right it is comes and the obedience of the peoples
belongs to Him. He ties his donkey to a vine, and the colt of his donkey
to the choice vine. He washes his clothes in wine and his robes in the
blood of grapes.

Ezekiel's use of the "lion" and the "vine" clue us in that Ezekiel 19 is about Judah's rulers, but what he describes is far different from what Jacob ever considered.

Though he is not mentioned specifically, the details provided in 19:2-4 refer to Jehoahaz. His father was Josiah, who was one of Judah's greatest kings. Unfortunately, Jehoahaz chose to emulate his grandfather and great-grandfather and do what was evil in Yahweh's sight (2 Kgs 23:32). His reign in Jerusalem lasted three months before the one who killed his father, Pharaoh Neco, imprisoned him in Egypt where he would eventually die (2 Kgs 23:34). The summary of Jehoahaz's reign from Ezekiel's perspective was one of devouring people (19:3). Though his leadership of God's people was brief, it was clearly more of a burden than a blessing.

How could Josiah's son rule in such a way? Unlike the kings before him, Josiah "turned to the LORD with all his mind and with all his heart and with all his strength according to all the law of Moses" (2 Kgs 23:25). Josiah cleaned out the temple of pagan artifacts, tore down the altars and high places used to worship false gods, and put to death those who led God's people astray (2 Kgs 23:4-20). Unfortunately for Israel, no one like Josiah "arose after him" (2 Kgs 23:25).

Jehoahaz had what many lack: a godly father in his home. He also had God's Word, which had been recovered in the temple (2 Kgs 23:24). His decision to lead God's people away from Him is even more despicable because he not only rejected the Lord's ways but also his father's example. His decisions were not fueled by ignorance but by insolence. He intentionally rejected what he knew to be right. As a result, God's people suffered as they always do when ungodly leaders rule. People who are continually led to go against God's ways should not expect blessings to be poured out from heaven. Much of Ezekiel 17–22 is God's revealing of His discipline of Israel's disobedient leaders.

What should we do when those who are ungodly lead us? We should weep, pray, and even fast for them. We should ask God to reveal their sin to them and empower their repentance. In all things that are not sinful, we should do our best to comply with their leadership. But once they try to lead us away from God, we should pray to be as bold as the Hebrew young men who told Nebuchadnezzar, "Even if He does not rescue us, we want you as king to know that we will not serve your gods or worship the gold statue you set up" (Dan 3:18). The lament in Ezekiel 19 and the warnings in the surrounding chapters reveal that God holds Israel's leaders most responsible for the nation's sin, but in reality the people always had a choice. They just chose to follow their earthly king rather than their heavenly One.

We Should Weep for Our Leaders When They Are Full of Pride
EZEKIEL 19:5-9

Applied to the current lament, the phrase "same song second verse" could not be truer. In 19:5-9 a different lion is chosen, but his actions and consequences are similar to those of the first. The ruler identified with this lion is debatable. The possibilities include Jehoiakim, Jehoiachin, and Zedekiah (2 Kgs 23:34–24:20). Of those three candidates Jehoiakim is the only one who was not exiled from Jerusalem. If the lioness image is pressed, then Jehoahaz and Zedekiah shared the same mother whose name was Hamutal (2 Kgs 23:31; 24:18). If the lioness image refers to Judah itself, then Jehoiachin could be considered one of her cubs. Regardless, the second lion devoured people, devastated their strongholds, and destroyed their cities (Ezek 19:6-7). What is unclear is whether these acts were carried out on his enemies or enacted on his own people because of his evil leadership.

The consequences of the second lion's behavior will be the same discipline as for the first lion but in a different destination. Instead of being carried to Egypt, the second lion will be yoked or put in a cage and led away to Babylon (v. 9). The roar of this lion will never be heard in Israel again, which simply means his time as the leader of God's people is done.

What drove the second lion to his actions? Pride. Ezekiel says the second lion prowled or strutted among the lions (v. 6). Jehoiachin and Zedekiah were 18 and 21, respectively, when each became king. As leaders, both men did what was evil in the Lord's sight (2 Kgs 24:9,19). Nothing drives these actions more than pride. To not regard what God says is holy is not only foolish but the height of arrogance. Both of these kings made decisions as if they were not accountable to Another for the stewardship of their reign. Unfortunately, their pride not only led to their own downfall but also to the destruction of many others (Ezek 19:7).

What should we do if someone leads us who is full of pride? We should pray for God to humble them, perhaps not in the same manner as Nebuchadnezzar (Dan 4:28-33) but certainly with the same result: "Now I, Nebuchadnezzar, praise, exalt, and glorify the King of heaven, because all His works are true and His ways are just. He is able to humble those who walk in pride" (Dan 4:37). We should pray for them to be led to give God glory rather than seek their own (Acts 12:23). We should pray for the fear of the Lord and true knowledge to be produced in their lives (Prov 1:7). We should pray for them to understand that all authority has been given to Christ (Matt 28:18). Ezekiel 19 is a strong testimony that "pride comes before destruction, and an arrogant spirit before a fall" (Prov 16:18). Above all, if our leaders are going to take pride in something, let us pray it is "in the name of Yahweh our God" (Ps 20:7).

As ministers we need to pay careful attention to everything in Ezekiel 19 but the issue of pride in particular. There is no place for arrogance in the pastorate. If your congregation is growing, it is due to the Master Builder's doing His work more than your being especially skilled or wise (Matt 16:18). Every fruit of Christ produced in the congregation you lead is due to the Spirit of Christ using the Word of Christ. When our time of leadership is complete, I hope we can all point to our humble service (Acts 20:19) and our singular boast in the "cross of our Lord Jesus Christ" (Gal 6:14).

We Should Weep for Our Leaders When They Refuse to Listen to God
EZEKIEL 19:10-14

The image in the lament shifts from a lioness to a vine. The vine grows strong due to its proximity to plentiful waters and produces many strong branches that are fit for the scepters of rulers (vv. 10-11). Pride consumes the branches, so the vine is uprooted and replanted in a dry and thirsty land (vv. 11-13). Fire from the main branch has consumed the fruit of this vine with the result that there is no longer a branch strong enough for a scepter (v. 14).

The vine in these verses is Judah, and the branches for ruling represent the Davidic line. God placed Judah in a prime location for prosperity and growth. From David to Zedekiah, 22 kings came from Judah. But as we saw in Ezekiel 15, vines that fail to produce fruit have little other use (15:1-8). The evil leadership of Judah's kings has stored up God's wrath, and now He will uproot the vine "in fury" (19:12).

The sentence of doom falls heaviest in verse 14. Stuart notes, "Verses 2-9 spoke of the end of the reigns of two kings; verses 10-14 speak of the end of the reigns of all the kings. If this is the case, it is almost certain that the 'fire' of verse 14 is Zedekiah himself" (Stuart, *Ezekiel,* 162–63). Zedekiah could have submitted to the Lord's plan (27:12-15), but he refused to listen. His legacy in the lineage of David will be as the guy who brought the family down in a blaze of glory. I use the phrase "will be" because at the time of Ezekiel 19, the events of verses 10-14 were still in the future. Ezekiel is told to sing the funeral song, though, because Zedekiah's doom is certain. He will refuse the Lord's calls to repent and to submit to Nebuchadnezzar's leadership, and as a result he will bring many people to ruin.

What can we do if our leaders refuse to listen to God? We can first of all pray that God will silence all false counsel in his or her ears. Zedekiah's counselors were advising him in direct contrast to the Lord's revelation (2 Kgs 27:14). Zedekiah decided to accept their worldview over God's. For our leaders we should pray they will give most attention to the Ancient of Days rather than men whose lives are but a vapor. If our leaders are refusing to heed the Lord's wisdom, then we should pray and ask God to do for our leader what they cannot do for themselves. We should ask God to turn their hearts toward His instruction and incline their wills toward His (Prov 21:1). Zedekiah was not the only Davidic king who refused to listen to God, but he would be the last one for his generation. We should pray for our leaders who refuse to listen to God to repent before the opportunity to do so is removed.

Conclusion

Unlike Ezekiel 17, Ezekiel 19 ends without any promise of a planting of a sprig or any mention of a forthcoming shepherd-prince (34:23). If this were the only chapter in Ezekiel addressing the Davidic line, then we would be inclined to think the reign of this family is finished. I believe the Lord wants the heaviness of the situation to weigh on those who are listening to Ezekiel. The majority of their leaders have been evil, and now the time of their reign is over.

Ezekiel's audience most likely has questions. Is David's line done forever? Will we have a deliverer? First, God does not have to repeat His promises for them to hold true. What God said in Ezekiel 17 has not changed based on His declarations in Ezekiel 19. He does not need to be reminded to plant a sprig of hope (17:22). The cedar shoot originated in His heart and not theirs. I believe God does not add anything to this lament because His focus is just that—lamenting. He wants His people to weep for the wretched leadership they have endured. Hope has been provided in other places in Ezekiel and that hope is certain. In Ezekiel 19 the time has come for grief. Our appreciation for deliverance is in proportion to our understanding from what we have been delivered. Knowing that Christ is our substitute does not mean we should think less of the gravity of sin's cost. Perhaps if we paused and considered the wretchedness of sin more, we would not so easily run to it.

Second, God's people should not be looking for deliverance to come from an earthly ruler but from their heavenly One. God alone rescues His people. The announcing of the burned branches means deliverance from man is impossible but not deliverance from God. He brings beauty from ashes every day. Ultimately, God will deliver His people and give them the greatest King possible from David's line (34:23).

Lastly, we must ask, What kind of leaders are we in our homes and our jobs? Are we leaders who know God's Word but are rejecting it? Are we leaders who are full of pride and attribute our accomplishments to our own greatness? Are we leaders who think we can devise a better plan than God? How would our children describe our leadership? What phrases would our coworkers use to describe the way we lead in our jobs? We should not read Ezekiel 19 and merely grieve for Israel's lack of godly leaders, but we should also seek God's empowerment so that what was true of them will never be said of us. Wragg exhorts,

> It is the godly character of a leader that determines the level of beneficial and long-term influence in spiritual matters. If others are to be effectively launched in a God-ward direction a leader must ignite the fuel of his own intimate walk with Jesus Christ. (Wragg, *Spiritual Leadership*, 21)

Reflect and Discuss

1. Are you more prone to speak negatively about ungodly leaders or to pray for them?
2. What is your intentional plan of intercession for the leaders of our nation, state, and city? How often does your faith family corporately intercede for our leaders?
3. How familiar are you with laments in Scripture? What are ways laments can be used in both our personal and our corporate prayers?
4. Why do we refuse to learn from God's discipline of others? Why do we see so many examples of God's punishment for disobedience in the Bible and think He will hold us less accountable than them?
5. As political or business leaders, why is pride a constant temptation? What measures have you taken to minimize this sin in your life and to maximize your boasting in Christ?
6. As spiritual ministers, how can we minimize succumbing to the temptation of pride and maximize boasting in Christ alone?
7. If you have someone in your congregation who follows the ways of the Lord, but his or her children have rejected the same path, how would you counsel your church member?
8. If someone you know has a boss who repeatedly wants them to engage in an occupational practice that is both unethical and sinful, how would you counsel them?
9. As a leader, what are you doing to help equip godly leaders in the homes closest to you?
10. What words would our spouses and children use to describe our leadership? Would those outside our home speak differently about how we lead? Which is more important?

Like Fathers, like Sons . . . but Not Forever

EZEKIEL 20:1-44

Main Idea: Despite our lineage of sin and continued propensity toward it, God will set our hearts and hands free from the idols we treasure.

I. **God Will Be Sought on His Terms, Not Ours (20:1-3,30-31).**
II. **God's Kindness, Mercy, and Love Toward His Rebellious People Is Without Equal (20:4-31).**
III. **God Does Not Lower His Standards but Raises His People (20:32-44).**

Is there a specific sin you cannot seem to stop? How long has it been part of your life? A week? A year? Decades? How many times have you "given it to Jesus" only to find you pick it back up some time later? With Christ we have the power to put away besetting sin (Rom 6:1-23). In the power of the Spirit, we should be intentional to put to death anything in our flesh that would lead us away from God (Rom 8:13). Memorizing His Word can help us in our battle against sin as well (Ps 119:11). Confessing our sins to one another and praying for one another are ways a faith family can pursue holiness together (Jas 5:16). Despite all of these extraordinary resources, perfection will not come until our glorification.

While we await glorification, our sanctification is a process. Sometimes it can even be a slow and painful process. In our hearts a daily war rages between the flesh and the Spirit (1 Pet 2:11; Rom 7:23). These powers are not equal, for the One who is in us is greater (1 John 4:4), but the draw of the flesh has not been completely removed from our lives. In considering these matters, Paul cries, "What a wretched man I am! Who will rescue me from this dying body?" (Rom 7:24). There is only one answer: "I thank God through Jesus Christ our Lord" (Rom 7:25).

What about those, however, who are not crying to be set free from their sin? What about those who show no sign of struggle but only pure embracing of their rebellion? In Ezekiel 20 Israel's history and current pursuit of idolatry are revealed. Every generation of God's people since

Egypt has engaged in the worship of other gods besides Yahweh. The real wonder is that Israel still exists. At various times God has considered wiping His people out, but for the sake of His name, He has withheld His wrath. Instead of lowering His standards, He will one day raise His people and set them free from their cycle of sin.

I believe the true depth of the gospel can only be appreciated by studying chapters like Ezekiel 16; 20; and 23. In these chapters facing the facts of our depravity shatters our notions of "we are not that bad." In reality we are far worse than we know, and God is far more merciful than we realize. Ezekiel 20 reveals that no matter how bent we are on pursuing sin, God is even more determined to save us from ourselves (v. 32). In the battle of wills, God's grace will ultimately overcome all our rebellion and rip our hands and hearts free from the idols we would have clutched until they killed us. In Christ, God forgives every treacherous act of our turning our back on Him and turning our hearts to gods we create. In Christ, He forgives our lack of trust in Him and His ways. All who see how His grace transforms us will marvel because there is no other who could produce such change. For all eternity, we will be portraits of His grace (Eph 2:7) testifying that God is able to save His people through Christ (Heb 7:25). All will know He is Yahweh (Ezek 20:38). In the current text He wants Israel's elders to know they cannot seek His counsel and simultaneously ignore their sin. Let's turn to this now.

God Will Be Sought on His Terms, Not Ours
EZEKIEL 20:1-3,30-31

God is not a genie in a lamp who is bound to grant our wishes. We cannot prance into His presence and make our petitions known without any regard for His perspective on our lives. For some reason the elders of Israel were slow to learn this lesson. Whether the group in Ezekiel 20:1-3 is the same group of elders who came to consult God in Ezekiel 14:1-3 is not known. In both cases, however, God let these men know that halfhearted seeking never warrants His wholehearted response (Jer 29:13).

Why were they consulting God anyway? We know whatever He told them they would not obey (33:31-32). We also know they did not believe what He said, or if they did, they at least considered His words to be for those coming behind them (12:22,27). Their specific motive for approaching God is not revealed in the text, but God's seizing of the opportunity to say what they needed to hear most is.

God refuses to be consulted by those who continue to ignore sin in their lives. Our pursuit of sin reveals that His will is not our priority. His counsel is not to be an add-on to our life, but His words are to be our very life (Deut 32:47). Until Israel turned from their idolatry, everything else was secondary. To enter into God's presence is a privilege. His refusal to leave us in our sin is a grace. Israel's elders are about to receive a history lesson in the idolatry of their ancestors and a confrontation of their own idolatry. God's purpose, however, is not just to inform these elders of what they most likely knew well but also to call them to repentance. When we come to God, we may not receive what we asked for, but we will always receive what is for our best.

Here's one final thought for those of us who readily take advantage of the privilege we have to draw near to God through Christ (Heb 10:19-22). Had these elders felt they could consult God on their own, they would have done so. Prior to Pentecost, Stuart asserts "believers in general often did not think of themselves as having direct access to God's guidance, approaching instead prophets through whom God could provide guidance to them" (*Ezekiel,* 168). What a blessing we have in our opportunity through Christ to ask, seek, and knock with the promise that "everyone who asks receives, and the one who searches finds, and to the one who knocks, the door will be opened" (Matt 7:8). Because of our Mediator, we can seek the Lord's wisdom at any time and any place (1 Tim 2:5). But let us not make the same mistake as the elders of Israel, who tried to seek His wisdom without sincerity in their heart.

God's Kindness, Mercy, and Love Toward His Rebellious People Is Without Equal
EZEKIEL 20:4-31

In his opening paragraph of *Let the Nations Be Glad,* John Piper writes,

> Missions is not the ultimate goal of the church. Worship is.
> Missions exists because worship doesn't. Worship is ultimate,
> not missions, because God is ultimate not man. When this
> age is over, and the countless millions of the redeemed fall on
> their faces before the throne of God, missions will be no more.
> It is a temporary necessity. But worship abides forever. (Piper,
> *Let the Nations,* 17)

Worship is and has always been a purpose of God's having a people for the sake of His name. Worship is God's aim in delivering His people not only from Egypt but also from sin. Duguid contends, "The goal of exodus, indeed of all salvation, is a purified people worshipping the one true God" (*Ezekiel*, 270).

Historically, Israel does not have a problem with worship. Their problem is the object—or better, objects—of their worship. If Israel were on a modern television show, it would be *Intervention*. On this show families confront loved ones whose addictions are destroying their lives. Israel was addicted to idolatry and had been since its creation (v. 8). Their treacherous actions were driven by their heart's desire to be like the nations and worship wood and stone (v. 32). Why would they want to be like everyone else when they had been chosen to be unique (v. 5; cf. Ps 135:4)? More importantly, why would they want to embrace false gods and reject the one true living God?

Stuart provides some insights on why Israel and other nations frequently worshiped idols they created. He asserts,

> Ancient people believed that if they made an image (idol) of a god no matter how crudely it may have been fashioned and no matter how partially it may have represented the god, it nevertheless captured its essence. Therefore, with idols they could guarantee that the gods would be with them, right in their presence, taking note of their offerings and automatically hearing their prayers. (Stuart, *Ezekiel*, 166)

Despite the customs of the day, however, God clearly instructed His people not to have other gods besides Him and not to make an idol for themselves (Exod 20:3-4).

The history of God's people is not a pretty one. It may not have been so bad in the memories of the people, but God's memory is the only one that counts. When stories were passed from generation to generation, I'm uncertain how many examples of Grandpappy's idolatry were heralded, but there were plenty of possibilities. The summary of God's brief history lesson to the elders of Israel is that God's people have been idolatrous in Egypt (vv. 4-9), idolatrous in the wilderness (vv. 10-17), idolatrous in the wilderness again (vv. 18-26), idolatrous in Canaan (vv. 27-29), and idolatrous even in exile (vv. 30-32). All along they have worshiped; they have just not worshiped Yahweh alone. Each new generation and each new location brought the same old situation as God's people pursued idols.

With each act of idolatry, God was tempted to exhaust His anger by pouring out His wrath on His people (vv. 8,13,21). But with each generation, He resisted for the sake of His name (vv. 9,14,17,22). In covenanting with His people, God tied His reputation and renown to them, and His treatment of them always accorded with what brought Him the most glory. His withholding of His wrath did not mean its removal, only its delay. It also did not mean there were no consequences for His people's rebellion. There were. Their idolatry cost one generation the opportunity to enter Canaan (v. 15) and another generation the opportunity to stay there (v. 23).

In Ezekiel 20 the goodness of God and the wretchedness of man are on full display. God initiates a relationship by choosing them and then covenants Himself to them (v. 5). Of His own accord, He promises to deliver Moses' generation from Egypt and bring them to "the most beautiful of all lands," which He searched out (and made) Himself (v. 6). During their 430-year stay in Egypt, they picked up some detestable practices and idols of the "host" country. For their own good God tells them to throw away their idols because He is Yahweh their God (v. 7). How was God's kindness rewarded? They rebelled against Him and refused to listen to Him, and none of them—did you get that? *zero* of them—threw away their detestable things or let go of their idols. God considered bringing them to an end in Egypt, but He resisted for the sake of His name (vv. 8-9) and brought them out of Egypt instead.

If given the opportunity to talk with Moses' generation, one question I would ask is, Why would you bring gods out of Egypt that could not bring you out of Egypt? I would follow with another question: When you carried your carved images out of Egypt, did it occur to you that these gods could not carry you anywhere? God's people may have been liberated from their oppressors, but they were still in bondage to their sin.

Perhaps all Israel needed in order to release their idols fully was a fresh walk through the wilderness. After drowning Pharaoh and his army, God continued to initiate kindness to His people. He gave them His statutes and explained His ordinances to them. He also gave them Sabbaths (vv. 11-12). His rules and His rest were for setting His people apart as holy (v. 12). They were not intended to be burdens but blessings. The law was not a means of earning righteousness, but it was good, and the one who walked in it would not be put to death for rebellion (v. 13). The walk in the wilderness, however, did not change Israel's hearts, nor did they release the idols from their hands. They rebelled against God and rejected His ordinances, statutes, and Sabbaths. It's as if they collectively shook their fist at God and said, "We do not care what You want!" God considered killing them all but refrained for the sake of His name (vv. 14,17). Instead, He would not allow their generation to enter Canaan because their hearts went after their idols (vv. 15-16).

Once the exodus generation walked around in the wilderness until they all died, God was ready to move forward with their children. Because He was Yahweh their God, He charged them not to follow the statutes of their fathers or pursue their idols (v. 18). The apple, however, did not fall far from the tree. They did all the evil their fathers had done and raised the ante by sacrificing their firstborn children to pagan gods (v. 26). God considered wiping them out as well but once again withheld His wrath for the sake of His name (v. 22). Because their eyes were fixed on their father's idols, God promised to disperse them and allowed them to follow statutes and ordinances that were no good (vv. 23,25). Every child sacrifice brought them nothing but defilement (v. 26).

Perhaps if God could just lead His people into Canaan, then the next generation would be fully obedient. Wrong. They quickly adopted the practices of the Canaanites and offered sacrifices on any high hill or under any leafy tree (v. 28). Instead of following the command to participate in the yearly festivals in Jerusalem, God's people desired convenience over obedience. Any ol' hill will do if you do not want to put too much effort into worship. They were a far cry from David's desire not to offer the Lord anything that cost him nothing (2 Sam 24:24). Like their fathers and grandfathers they received good from God and returned to Him nothing but bad.

At this point in Ezekiel's relaying of God's history lesson to the elders of Israel, they might have been saying to one another, "I told you we were being punished for the sins of previous generations." God, however, had already cleared this up in Ezekiel 18 and would soon reveal that Ezekiel's generation was no innocent bystander. In fact, they were doing the same evil their ancestors had done, including sacrificing their children (20:31).

Why? Of all the pagan practices, why did Israel add this to their repertoire of disobedience? Stuart believes,

Thinking themselves likely to gain the lifetime favor of the
gods in this way, the Israelites borrowed child sacrifice, too,
from their neighbors and began killing their firstborn infants
and burning them on altars as a means of sending them to
the false gods they were worshipping. It is evident that such
people really wanted the gods to love them and were willing to
"give their all" to gain such love. (Stuart, *Ezekiel*, 175)

How foolish! They were trying to gain the love of gods that did not exist,
all the while shunning the love of the God who does. They were seeking
to earn the love of their idols, while Yahweh's love had been given freely.

As God comes to the end of His recounting of Israel's idolatry, He
reveals to the elders who were there with Ezekiel that they may not
consult Him (v. 31). If they want His wisdom, then they must do something about their sin. He has been nothing but faithful while they and
their ancestors have been nothing but unfaithful. He has initiated love
to each of their generations only to be met with rejection. He is done
being consulted by people who have their own agendas. The question
remains, though, is He finally done with His people? Will He finally
destroy them in His wrath? By now, however, we know the answer. He
will not destroy them, but He will discipline them. Best of all, the punishment will also be a means of purification. God is not done with His
people, but He is done with their idolatry.

When you read through Ezekiel 20:4-31, what are your thoughts?
Are you disgusted with Israel's consistent rebellion and rejection? Are
you overwhelmed by God's steadfast love? Are you amazed by God's
restraint and withholding of wrath? Are you surprised that after all of
God's goodness, His people still refused to put away what pulled them
away from Him? When encountering a passage like this, we want to
make sure we are not wearing our rose-colored classes when we consider our own past. We were no better than Israel. All of us turned away
from God, and none of us sought Him on our own (Rom 3:11-12). His
love for us is just as staggering since while we were still sinners, Christ
died for us (Rom 5:8). The wrath God withheld with each disobedient
generation would ultimately be atoned not through exile but through
the cross of His Son. What He withheld from Israel (and us), He poured
out on Jesus. I wonder then if His forgiveness of and patience with sinners is evident in our lives? Are our Father's traits of long-suffering and
mercy being displayed in us and through us? Are there any idols we are

foolishly carrying around that we need to "throw away" (Ezek 20:7)? Are there any ways we are trying to earn His love rather than resting in what Christ has earned already? How can the cycle of sin be stopped for Israel and for us? The answer to this question is in the next part of the passage.

God Does Not Lower His Standards but Raises His People
EZEKIEL 20:32-44

That Israel has a history beyond verse 8 should amaze all of us, but the fact they are given the promises of verses 32-44 should leave us in absolute wonder of God's mercy. For Israel (and us), what has always been will not always be. Despite all their running away, God never does anything but run to His people. He knows changing generations and changing locations in themselves will not produce lasting change in His people. Up to this point, they have produced no change. God, however, will set His people free from their greatest bondage, which is sin.

The cycle of idolatry will be broken because God will demonstrate His holiness *through* His people and not just *to* them (v. 41). He will not let their desire to "be like the nations, like the people of other countries, worshiping wood and stone" be their final lot (v. 32). God graciously rescues us from ourselves. He will rule over His people, He will bring them from the peoples and gather them from the nations, He will lead them into a new wilderness and judge them, He will make them pass under the rod for the purpose of bringing them back into the bond of the covenant, and He will purge from their presence all who rebel and transgress against Him (vv. 33-38). These are not just possibilities but certainties. He *will* do what He is declaring.

God's purifying work in His people will be so effective they will one day no longer defile His holy name with their gifts and idols (v. 39). In fact, they will hate the evil things they used to do (v. 43). Not just some of the people He preserves will serve on Israel's high mountain, but all of them, the entire house of Israel, will be accepted and bless Him with holy offerings (v. 40). His people will be a pleasing aroma to the Lord (v. 41). Despite generations of idolatry, God will deal with His people for the sake of His name rather than according to their evil ways and corrupt acts (v. 44). He will not treat them as they deserve but will bless them for their good and His glory. When all this occurs, both His people and the nations will know He is Yahweh (vv. 42,44).

In considering Ezekiel 20:1-44, Block confesses,

> The experience of divine mercy drives true covenant people
> to their knees. . . . God did not express his love in Jesus Christ
> in response to our worthiness, but to redeem us from our
> unworthiness. The fundamental problem with most of us is
> not deficient self-esteem but an inadequate divine-esteem. As
> we submit ourselves to God, recognizing that ultimately he
> operates for his own name's sake, and that his investment in us
> relates to agendas far greater than ourselves, we will treasure
> the grace with which he reaches out to us. (Block, *Ezekiel*,
> 658–59)

Block's point is that we should never look at the love God demonstrates
for us in the cross of Christ and think to ourselves, "Of course He wants
to save me. I'm great." Instead, with Watts we should ask,

> While all our hearts and all our songs
> Join to admire the feast,
> Each of us cry, with thankful tongues,
> "Lord, why was I a guest?
> "Why was I made to hear Thy voice,
> And enter while there's room,
> When thousands make a wretched choice,
> And rather starve than come?"
> 'Twas the same love that spread the feast
> That sweetly drew us in;
> Else we had still refused to taste,
> And perished in our sin.
> (Isaac Watts, "How Sweet and Aweful Is the Place," 1707)

As I said in the beginning, God's grace will ultimately overcome
all our rebellion and rip our hands and hearts free from the idols we
would have clutched until they killed us. Despite all our unfaithfulness
He chooses to forsake His Son so that He does not have to forsake us. It
was the offering of His Son that atoned for our sins and not the burning
of any of ours. He did not give up on Israel in Egypt or in the wilderness or in Canaan because He brings to completion the work He starts
(Phil 1:6). Ezekiel 20 gives us a better picture of just how much work was
required in Israel and in us. God does not treat us according to our sins

because He treated Christ according to them and treats us according to Christ's righteousness. May our mouths never cease to offer Him praise and to announce to a lost world the good news of Jesus Christ. There is no sinner His grace cannot deliver!

Reflect and Discuss

1. Why did Israel exhibit so little gratitude for God's kindness and love? In what ways are you different?
2. Why was letting go of idols so difficult for Israel? How has God pried your hands free of a besetting sin?
3. What are your thoughts as you examine Israel's depravity and God's steadfast love? How have you experienced these in your life?
4. In what ways did the idols of the fathers influence the sons? In what ways are our children being influenced by what we treasure?
5. Why would Israel ever seek to earn another god's favor? In what ways have you ever tried to earn God's?
6. Why is changing locations or even habits not enough to ultimately free us from sin?
7. In what ways does God demonstrate His holiness *through* us and not just *to* us?
8. How can we balance loathing our previous sin and moving forward in God's grace?
9. How often do you consider that God does not deal with us according to our evil ways and corrupt acts because He laid these on Christ?
10. In what ways is God's patience with and forgiveness of sinners evident through you?

God's Fire and God's Sword

EZEKIEL 20:45–22:12

Main Idea: The time of God's judgment approaches, and unless there is an intercessor, all will be consumed.

I. How Should We Proclaim God's Judgment (21:6,12)?
II. What Can We Learn About God's Judgment?
    A. God's judgment is complete (20:45–21:7).
    B. God's judgment is controlled (21:8-23).
    C. God's judgment is with cause (21:24-27; 22:1-12).
    D. God's judgment is consuming (21:28-32).
III. How Can We Avoid God's Judgment?

In Ezekiel 19–20 God reveals the sin of Israel's leaders and its people. In Ezekiel 18 God reveals that each will be held responsible for his or her sin. In Ezekiel 20:45–22:12 God reveals what it will be like when the day of reckoning arrives. God's judgment will be like a fire and a sword. His judgment will be complete, controlled, with cause, and consuming. He will judge His people as well as other nations. Let's consider His judgment now.

How Should We Proclaim God's Judgment?

EZEKIEL 21:6,12

Ezekiel 21 is a heavy chapter about God's judgment, not only of His people but also of those who have harmed Israel. Fee and Stuart exhort us to

> bear in mind that the prophets did not invent the blessings or curses they announced. They may have worded these blessings and curses in novel, captivating ways, as they were inspired to do so. But they reproduced God's word, not their own. Through them God announced his intention to enforce the covenant, for benefit or for harm depending on the faithfulness of Israel, but always on the basis of and in accordance with the categories of blessing and curse already

contained in Leviticus 26, Deuteronomy 4, and Deuteronomy 28–32. (*How to Read the Bible,* 168)

In the case of Ezekiel 21, Yahweh's prophet is asked to announce a message of "harm" for those who have broken His covenant.

In preaching, the tone of the text should always be the tone of the sermon. Piper laments what he considers to be

> a preaching atmosphere and a preaching style plagued by triviality, levity, carelessness, flippancy, and a general spirit that nothing of eternal and infinite proportions is being done or said on Sunday morning. (Piper, *Supremacy of God,* 52)

He adds, "It is a sign of the age that we preachers are far more adept at humor than tears" (ibid., 58). If we decide to introduce our sermon on Ezekiel 21 with a joke, we will have completely missed the tone of this text. Much like the prophets our goal in preaching is not to get our audience to like us but to respond to the word we have been given to declare. This does not mean there is never a place for humor in the pulpit. It just means humor should not be used to "break the heaviness" of God's message when its original intent was to overwhelm the audience with God's seriousness about His holiness.

Ezekiel will not deliver the words of judgment in this chapter in a happy or trite manner. God commands Ezekiel to groan bitterly with a broken heart (v. 6) and to wail and strike his thigh in grief (v. 12). God's people are being severely disciplined, and His mouthpiece is told to communicate the message with all the emotion appropriate for such judgment. Some might say Ezekiel is just acting, but considering he probably knows some of those who are going to be destroyed, I imagine not all of his tears are a theatrical production. The prophet is meant to feel the gravity of the events God describes and he declares. Interestingly, Ezekiel will be allowed to grieve more in communicating Jerusalem's judgment than when mourning the death of his wife (24:17).

What about us? Does the tone of the text drive the tone of our sermons? Are our sermons marked by "intensity of feeling, the weight of argument, a deep and pervading solemnity of mind, a savor of the power of godliness, fervency of spirit, (and) zeal for God" (Piper, *Supremacy of God,* 50)? Can people grasp the seriousness of heaven's and hell's reality by the way we preach (ibid., 55)? The judgment Ezekiel was asked to proclaim was nothing but serious. God's people may have treated His holiness as if it were a joke, but God's fire and His sword of judgment are no laughing matter. For Ezekiel's audience the matter was settled, and there would be no escape, but for our audiences a time for repentance remains open. They just need a messenger who grasps the eternal significance of the proclamation event and calls them to turn and live (18:32). Another communication matter needs to be addressed before going further. Someone has said that a picture is worth a thousand words. In Ezekiel 20:45-48 God provides a picture of a blazing flame that consumes everything in its path. In Ezekiel 21:1-32 God provides a picture of a sharpened and polished sword that in the hand of the slayer flashes like lightning and slashes right and left. In our rush to provide applicable teaching points from the text, we do not want to miss the form in which they were originally preached. Like a batter pulling a ball where it would not naturally go, we do not want to forsake the original form of a text just to force it into our favorite style of sermon presentation. Duguid has some helpful thoughts on this matter:

> The Bible is a book filled with images and imagery. God delivers his message not in the cold tones of propositional statements (although we may certainly deduce from the Bible propositions about who God is and what he is like) but in a welter of pictures. Supremely, his self-communication takes the form of the visible enactments of the prophets and most particularly of the final prophet, Jesus Christ, the Word become flesh.
>
> Ironically, however, much expository preaching, which seeks to faithfully deliver the message of the Bible, begins by abstracting the proposition (the so-called "big idea of the passage") from its surrounding imagery. That imagery is then tossed away like so much used wrapping paper, while the "big idea" is repackaged in an entirely new format for its delivery to the contemporary congregation. Could that be one reason why people find so much of our preaching boring? We have lost the vivid directness of the fire-filled Word of God, replacing it by the cool logical flow of classical rhetoric. If we wish to regain the power of the original proclamation, we would do well to consider more fully how we can deliver messages about fires that burn and words about the sword that cut to the heart. (Duguid, *Ezekiel*, 280)

What Can We Learn About God's Judgment?

God's Judgment Is Complete (20:45–21:7)

Nothing can prevent the fire God is about to bring to the forestland in the Negev. Of course, had God's people turned from their sins, this judgment could have been avoided, but they did not, and the time for repentance has passed.

God tells Ezekiel to face the south and prophesy against the forest in the Negev. He is about to ignite a fire that will not be extinguished (20:47-48). The fire will rage until it consumes every green tree and every dry tree, regardless of the potential for flammability. The fire will consume all in like manner. The flame will rage with such heat "every face from the south to the north will be scorched by it" (v. 47). There will be no doubt who caused and fueled the fire. Everyone will be able to identify Yahweh's work.

As faithful as Ezekiel was in delivering the message, the hardheaded and hardhearted people in his audience responded with "Huh?" As with Ezekiel 17 and 19, they felt God's prophet was once again spinning riddles. Whatever Yahweh was intending to tell them, they did not comprehend it. To provide clarity but not necessarily comfort, Yahweh changes the image from a fire to a sword. Foregoing coded language, God tells Ezekiel to prophesy against Jerusalem, against the sanctuaries where God's people have practiced idolatrous worship, and against the land of Israel itself. How's that for clarity?

Instead of trees being consumed by fire, God's people will be cut down with the sword. None will escape (cf. 9:5-6). They are informed the sword will strike "both the righteous and the wicked," and "everyone from the south to the north" (21:4). Like the fire that will not be extinguished, the sword will not be sheathed (v. 5). What effect Ezekiel's sermons are having on his audience is debatable (33:32), but when this judgment occurs, "every heart will melt, and every hand will become weak. Every spirit will be discouraged, and every knee will turn to water" (21:7). God is bringing judgment on His people, and nothing will stop His fire or sword.

The idea of Yahweh wielding a sword of judgment was not new to Israel (Deut 32:41; Isa 34:5-8; Jer 50:35; Zeph 2:12). They, however, were accustomed to His enemies being the targets. Yahweh says in Deuteronomy 32:40-41,

I raise My hand to heaven and declare: As surely as I live forever,
when I sharpen My flashing sword, and My hand takes hold of
judgment, I will take vengeance on My adversaries and repay those
who hate Me.

A great illustration of this is found in Joshua 5:13-15 where the
Lord's sword is drawn in judgment against the inhabitants of Jericho.

When they learned God would be bringing the sword against His
own people, at least two places in Scripture should have entered the
minds of Ezekiel's audience. The first would have been in the first book
of the Law and with the first humans ever created. When Adam and Eve
sinned and God sent them away from Eden, He "stationed the cherubim
and the flaming, whirling sword east of the garden of Eden to guard
the way to the tree of life" (Gen 3:24). The second place in Scripture
Ezekiel's peers should have remembered was the covenant between God
and His people. In Leviticus 26:25 God informs Israel that if they break
the covenant and reject His discipline, He "will bring a sword against
[them] to execute the vengeance of the covenant." Based on the history
lesson in Ezekiel 20, Israel never demonstrated much desire to keep their
end of the agreement, but God was completely determined to keep His.

How is it that both the green tree and the dry tree are consumed, or
more explicitly, both the righteous and the wicked (20:47; 21:4)? Is God
going back on His word from Ezekiel 18 and punishing the righteous
for the sins of others? No. God never speaks out of both sides of His
mouth. The picture of the all-consuming fire and sword in Ezekiel 21
represents God's complete judgment. His wrath is kindled and what is
poured out on Jerusalem's inhabitants will not be partial judgment. All
will be either killed or scattered. The righteous will not bear the penalty
of the actions of the wicked, but they may suffer the consequences. For
example, when the Lord gave Jericho to His people,

Achan son of Carmi, son of Zabdi, son of Zerah, of the tribe of Judah,
took some of what was set apart, and the Lord's anger burned against
the Israelites. (Josh 7:1)

Achan's sin brought consequences on all of Israel (Josh 7:5,11-12).
In Ezekiel 21 all will be caught up in the Lord's judgment as a consequence of the pervasive wickedness in Judah and Jerusalem.

A consideration of the Lord's judgment with a fire and a sword
would be incomplete if the ministry of Jesus were not considered. When

Matthew and Luke were each reporting the same teaching of Christ, they described the two images of judgment found in Ezekiel 21. In Matthew's Gospel, Jesus cautioned His disciples, "Don't assume that I came to bring peace on the earth. I did not come to bring peace, but a sword" (Matt 10:34). In Luke's account Jesus says, "I came to bring fire on the earth, and how I wish it were already set ablaze" (Luke 12:49). Paul tells us that Jesus will one day bring fire again. He told the church at Thessalonica,

> *This will take place at the revelation of the Lord Jesus from heaven*
> *with His powerful angels, taking vengeance with flaming fire on those*
> *who don't . . . obey the gospel of our Lord Jesus.* (2 Thess 1:7-8)

After their physical death, those who do not obey God will experience eternal destruction in a fire that will never be extinguished (Rev 20:15). For all eternity, the Lord will be against His enemies, and His sword of judgment will never be sheathed (Ezek 21:3,5) God's sword and fire have come and are coming again. Are we ready? Are those we love ready? What are we doing to sound the alarm?

God's Judgment Is Controlled (21:8-23)

Neither the fire nor the sword operates with its own agenda. Both have purposes ordained for them, and both belong to God. Yahweh not only sharpens and polishes the sword but also appoints it for slaughter at all the gates to which the people may try to flee Jerusalem (v. 15). God's sword has been unsheathed for a massacre (v. 14) of His own people (v. 12). The sword will be placed into the slayer's hands, and he will slash to the right and turn to the left (vv. 11,16). All the while the Lord will be applauding (v. 17). Anyone want to tell Jerusalem, "Don't worry, because God has a wonderful plan for your life?" How can these images not move us? How can we not tremble before such a holy God?

Make no mistake, the Lord is not clapping because He takes pleasure in the death of His people (18:32). The applause is for the satisfaction of His wrath and the demonstration of His holiness. Sin will be punished.

In placing His sword in Nebuchadnezzar's hand, the Lord still retains control. To demonstrate His sovereignty, God tells Ezekiel to mark out a road from Babylon that leads to a fork. One way will lead to Rabbah and the other path will lead to Jerusalem. Ezekiel is to enact Nebuchadnezzar's divination practices that he uses to discern which path to take. The answer given will be Jerusalem, which some will think is a mistake because they swore an oath. But as we learned in Ezekiel 17, Zedekiah broke that oath. God will expose the guilt of His people.

I want us to consider two thoughts. First, even when he functions as God's instrument of justice, Nebuchadnezzar does not choose His own path. God certainly does not approve of the king of Babylon's divination practices, but He does reign over them. Just like the fire and the sword are controlled by God, so is the pagan king. God does not do violence to Nebuchadnezzar's will; He just lets it carry him to the places ordained. Second, no matter what fortifications are in place, no city can withstand God's sword of judgment. The word "fortified" is provided to show us there is no man-made refuge that is safe from God's wrath. Jerusalem could not build a bulwark high enough or thick enough to stop God's discipline.

God does not start a fire and let it blaze its own trail. Neither does He release a sword and let it cut down lives at will. Both His fire and His sword are evidences of controlled judgment. His discipline is never arbitrary but specific. His judgment is also never without reason.

God's Judgment Is with Cause (21:24-27; 22:1-12)

Neither the people of Jerusalem nor their prince were innocent in the Lord's eyes. In Ezekiel 22 God provides a laundry list of their sins that include bloodshed, idolatry, treating parents with contempt, exploiting the sojourner among them, oppressing widows and orphans, despising God's holy things, profaning His Sabbaths, sexual immorality, incest, and usury (22:1-12). And these were God's people? They were a light to the nations? No wonder God's revelatory purpose of demonstrating He is Yahweh is so important to Him. His people certainly are not doing Him any favors with regard to the nations who are watching.

Pertaining to His judgment, Israel cannot plead ignorance or innocence. The sins of God's people have finally led to their capture (21:24). The sins of the prince will also lead to the Davidic line having to yield the scepter for the time being (v. 26). The result for Jerusalem, for God's people, and for Zedekiah will be ruin, ruin, ruin (v. 27). The day of punishment has arrived. Payment is required for their pervasive rebellion.

A question remains about how to interpret 21:27. According to a footnote in the HCSB, another possible translation is, "Yet this will not happen until He comes to whom it rightfully belongs, and I will give it to Him." A traditional understanding utilizing the variant reading is that the scepter of Judah would be taken from Zedekiah, but it would not be permanently removed from the linage of David but given to the Messiah. In blessing Judah, Jacob said, "The scepter will not depart from Judah or the staff from between his feet until He whose right it is comes and the obedience of the peoples belongs to Him" (Gen 49:10). There is One to whom the right of kingship over God's people genuinely belongs (Taylor, *Ezekiel*, 163). There is no question that Genesis 49:10 is ultimately fulfilled by Christ, but is Ezekiel thinking of the Messiah when he utters verse 27?

The majority of the translation team who worked on the HCSB believes the best rendering of 21:27 includes, "Yet this will not happen until He comes; I have given judgment to Him." Block affirms, "'Judgment' in the sense of punishment suits the context perfectly" (*Ezekiel 1–24*, 692). He goes on to say the prophet's pointing to the Messiah would not be out of the question but "such a ray of hope would be quite unexpected from Ezekiel at this point" (ibid.). Block does think Ezekiel is thinking of Genesis 49:10, but he uses a "sinister reinterpretation of the ancient promise" not to laud Judah but to speak of its judgment (ibid., 692–93). Regardless of whether Ezekiel is referring to Nebuchadnezzar or to the Messiah, God is the One who gives the **judgment to Him**. This truth is further evidence of God's judgment being controlled even when He has cause. Neither Nebuchadnezzar nor the Messiah will appoint themselves as instruments of judgment. Lastly, if Nebuchadnezzar is the fulfillment of Ezekiel 21:27; Christ alone is the One to whom Genesis 49:10 points. Nebuchadnezzar's holding of Israel's scepter would be for just a moment, but Christ will hold it for all eternity.

God's Judgment Is Consuming (21:28-32)

Though it is doubtful any Ammonites were listening to Ezekiel's message, this did not stop the Lord from announcing their fate. When God judges the nations in Ezekiel 25–32, He starts with the Ammonites (25:1). If, for some reason, some from this people group were present in Babylon, then they no doubt were relieved when Nebuchadnezzar was led to take the road to Jerusalem instead of to Rabbah (21:22). God's delayed judgment, however, should never be confused with an acquittal. The Ammonites have acted with evil intent toward God's people (25:3,6), so He has appointed a sword for their slaughter (21:28).

There is some question whether 21:30-32 is about the Ammonites or about Nebuchadnezzar and Babylon. Because Ammon receives the same pronouncement of judgment in 25:10 as is recorded in 21:32, I am inclined to believe 21:30-32 is a continuation of God's address to the Ammonites. They will be totally consumed by God's judgment. Their punishment of not being remembered means their people group will be "annihilated, permanently deleted" (Block, *Ezekiel*, 698). "To the Semitic mind nothing could be more terrible: no prospect of restoration, no continuance in succeeding generations, no memorial, not even a memory. Oblivion" (Taylor, *Ezekiel*, 163). As bad as Judah's punishment sounded, Ammon's was worse. Jerusalem would be ruined, but it would also be remembered. The same could not be said for Ammon. First Peter 4:17 is a good summary of Ezekiel 21: "For the time has come for judgment to begin with God's household, and if it begins with us, what will the outcome be for those who disobey the gospel of God?" Just consider Ammon and you will have your answer.

How Can We Avoid God's Judgment?

In Ezekiel 21 God's judgment cannot be avoided. He will satisfy His wrath on Jerusalem, on the sanctuaries, on the land, on the people, on Zedekiah, and on the Ammonites. There will be no intercessor between the sinful parties and the Holy God. There will also be no substitute, but each one mentioned will bear the punishment for their rebellion. Which leads us to an important question: Is there any way we can avoid God's judgment? The simple answer from Ezekiel 18:32 of turning and living is echoed in Christ's call to repent and believe (Mark 1:15). But how will we escape God's sword and His fire?

God gave Zechariah the answer long before Christ's incarnation. The Lord said, "Sword, awake against My shepherd, against the man who is My associate—this is the declaration of the LORD of Hosts" (Zech 13:7). Christ did not come just to wield God's sword of judgment but also to receive it. The reason we will not be slashed is because Christ was. This also means God's fires of judgment will refine us rather than ruin us (Zech 13:9). Christ absorbed the blazing flame of God's wrath so that our faces might not be scorched. Hallelujah, what a Savior!

Reflect and Discuss

1. In communicating God's judgment, why are we at times prone to levity instead of gravity?
2. What steps do you take to make sure the tone of the biblical text is the tone of your sermon?

3. How can the pursuit of "principles" when developing sermons sometimes dull the effect of the images provided in the biblical text? How can we grow in our communication of the images God employs in His word?

4. When you consider God's judgment through the lens of a flame and a sword, what effect is produced in your heart/mind? What effect is produced in your actions?

5. How can we know God's judgment is controlled?

6. Why is it comforting to know that God's judgment is never meted out on innocent people? Why is this also discomforting?

7. Why do we sometimes perceive God's delayed judgment as an acquittal? How do we know it's not?

8. What gives God the right to judge not only Israel but also Ammon?

9. How often do you consider what it means for us that Christ was slashed with God's sword and burned with God's flame when our sin was laid on Him?

10. What are you doing to help others flee to Christ so that they will not have to face the judgment of God?

Judgment, Sacrifice, and a Glimmer of Hope

EZEKIEL 24:1-27

Main Idea: In light of the approaching day of judgment, we should warn all others at all costs.

I. **God's Judgment Is Never Without Cause (24:1-14).**
    A. God's judgment is certain.
    B. God's judgment is irrevocable.
    C. God's judgment is intense.
    D. God's judgment is deserved.
    E. God's judgment can be avoided.
II. **God's Message Is Never Without Cost (24:15-24).**
III. **God's Hope Is Never Without Comfort (24:25-27).**

I often think of Psalm 96:13. In this verse David informs us the Lord is coming and "He is coming to judge the earth. He will judge the world with righteousness and the peoples with His faithfulness." Beside this verse in my Bible, I've written the question, "Do they know?" When I see the Lord is coming to judge the earth, the world, and the peoples, I cannot help but be broken over those who have no idea He came the first time. David speaks of a judgment that is not just a possibility but also a certainty. One day the Lord *will* return, and He *will* judge all peoples.

Adoniram Judson was often overwhelmed that people were being swept away into eternity with a lack of truth. He was broken to think they would face judgment without having an opportunity to hear the gospel. As convicted as he was, Judson was no fool. He knew taking the good news of Christ to difficult places would not come without cost. Whatever was required, however, he was willing to give it. His awareness is revealed in a letter he wrote to his fiancé about the suffering they might face for the sake of the gospel:

> January 1, 1811. Tuesday Morning.
> It is with the utmost sincerity, and with my whole heart, that I wish you, my love, a happy new year. May it be a year in which your walk will be close with God; your frame calm and serene; and the road that leads you to the Lamb marked

with purer light. May it be a year in which you will have more
largely the spirit of Christ, be raised above sublunary things,
and be willing to be disposed of in this world just as God shall
please. As every moment of the year will bring you nearer the
end of your pilgrimage, may it bring you nearer to God, and
find you more prepared to hail the messenger of death as a
deliverer and a friend. And now, since I have begun to wish, I
will go on. May this be the year in which you will change your
name; in which you will take a final leave of your relatives
and native land; in which you will cross the wide ocean, and
dwell on the other side of the world, among a heathen people.
What a great change will this year probably effect in our lives!
How very different will be our situation and employment! If
our lives are preserved and our attempt prospered, we shall
next new year's day be in India, and perhaps wish each other
a happy new year in the uncouth dialect of Hindostan or
Burmah. We shall no more see our kind friends around us, or
enjoy the conveniences of civilized life, or go to the house of
God with those that keep holy day; but swarthy countenances
will everywhere meet our eye, the jargon of an unknown
tongue will assail our ears, and we shall witness the assembling
of the heathen to celebrate the worship of idol gods. We shall
be weary of the world, and wish for wings like a dove, that
we may fly away and be at rest. We shall probably experience
seasons when we shall be "exceeding sorrowful, even unto
death." We shall see many dreary, disconsolate hours, and feel
a sinking of spirits, anguish of mind, of which now we can
form little conception. O, we shall wish to lie down and die.
And that time may soon come. One of us may be unable to
sustain the heat of the climate and the change of habits; and
the other may say, with literal truth, over the grave—
    "By foreign hands thy dying eyes were closed;
    By foreign hands thy decent limbs composed;
    By foreign hands thy humble grave adorned;"
    but whether we shall be honored and mourned by
strangers, God only knows. At least, either of us will be
certain of *one* mourner. In view of such scenes shall we not
pray with earnestness "O for an overcoming faith," etc.?
(Judson, "Letter")

After 21 chapters of prophesied judgment, the possibility exists of our having become numb to the message Ezekiel is proclaiming. I pray not. In Ezekiel 24 the judgment on God's people will no longer be delayed. In this chapter Ezekiel will be asked to deliver his costliest sermon, all of which causes me to wonder: How does the certainty of God's judgment and the beauty of His gospel impact our lives each week? Are we weeping in prayer over those we know walk as enemies of Christ? Are we setting up meetings to share the gospel with those we know are still under His wrath? Are we willing to proclaim God's message at all costs? Ezekiel did, and so should we.

God's Judgment Is Never Without Cause
EZEKIEL 24:1-14

Nine years, ten months, and ten days after Ezekiel and his peers were taken into exile, **the king of Babylon laid siege to Jerusalem**. Through this king and his army, God is going to let His temple be desecrated, His city be destroyed, and His people be disciplined. Though His judgment could have been avoided, the time for repentance is past, and the time for reaping the cost of their rebellion has arrived.

The first half of Ezekiel 24 is a parable about a boiling pot. God gives Ezekiel this word not because He is hungry but because He is holy. He has tried to purify His people, but they have **frustrated every effort** (v. 12) and **would not be purified from** their **uncleanness** (v. 13). The time has come to **pile on the logs and kindle the fire** of His judgment (v. 10). The parable, however, is not for those in Jerusalem but for the exiles in Babylon. As they see and hear what God is doing, they can learn important truths about God's judgment—and so can we.

God's Judgment Is Certain

At one point the exiles were skeptical the Lord was going to bring the judgment on Jerusalem that Ezekiel kept telling them about. They were saying, "The days keep passing by, and every vision fails" (12:22). God's response was "whatever message I will speak, . . . it will be done. It will no longer be delayed. For in your days, rebellious house, I will speak a message and bring it to pass" (12:25). He told them they would live to see His judgment, and they did.

In the ninth year, in the tenth month, on the tenth day, the Lord told Ezekiel, **"Write down today's date, this very day."** The day of reckoning had arrived, and the days of delay were done. In the years to come this day would be marked as a fast day so that His people would always remember their rebellion and the Lord's retribution.

The certainty of God's judgment should have led to contrition in the hearts of his people; instead, delay led to doubt. No matter how many times He told them, **"It is coming, and I will do it,"** they went about their lives as if there were nothing to be worried about. Fueled by their delusion (11:3,15), they ignored every **declaration of the Lord God.** Now it was too late; the opportunity to repent was gone.

Like Ezekiel's audience we've been warned of a day of judgment. We know God "has set a day when He is going to judge the world in righteousness by the Man He has appointed. He has provided proof of this to everyone by raising Him from the dead" (Acts 17:31). We also know that "we must all appear before the tribunal of Christ, so that each may be repaid for what he has done in the body, whether good or worthless" (2 Cor 5:10). Because we know this, Paul says, "We seek to persuade people" (2 Cor 5:11), knowing that "anyone not found written in the book of life" will be "thrown into the lake of fire" (Rev 20:15).

Because we are certain of God's judgment, we should "rescue those being taken off to death, and save those stumbling toward slaughter" (Prov 24:11). We will not be able to plead ignorance before the Lord. "If you say, 'But we didn't know about this,' won't He who weighs hearts consider it? Won't He who protects your life know? Won't He repay a person according to his work?" (Prov 24:12).

The certainty of God's judgment cannot be seen any clearer than at the cross of Christ. God does not leave sin unpunished forever. If He did not spare His own Son when sin was laid on Him, why would anyone think He would spare him or her? Those who will not flee to Christ now will face Christ then, and on that day they will say "to the mountains and to the rocks, 'Fall on us and hide us from the face of the One seated on the throne and from the wrath of the Lamb, because the great day of Their wrath has come! And who is able to stand?'" (Rev 6:16-17). Not even death, however, will be a means of escaping God's wrath.

I hope we will learn from those in Jerusalem during Ezekiel's day. I also hope we will not go about business as usual. The Lord is not going to change His mind. We need to heed Paul's exhortation:

> *The time is limited, so from now on those who have wives should*
> *be as though they had none, those who weep as though they did not*
> *weep, those who rejoice as though they did not rejoice, those who buy*

as though they did not possess, and those who use the world as though they did not make full use of it. For this world in its current form is passing away. (1 Cor 7:29-31)

God's Judgment Is Irrevocable

Perhaps Ezekiel's peers thought God would change His mind and not bring judgment on His people. If they did, then they were foolish, because He told them, **"I will not refrain, I will not show pity, and I will not relent"** (24:14). He was not going to hold back or turn back until He satisfied His wrath on them (v. 13).

One of the differences between God's wrath being poured out on the cross of Christ and God's wrath that will be poured out in hell is that on the cross Jesus was able to cry, "It is finished" (John 19:30). In hell this phrase will never be uttered. God will pour His wrath without pitying or relenting. He will hold nothing back, nor will He ever turn back from His eternal judgment of those who perish.

God is not going to change His mind. He is the One who declares

the end from the beginning, and from long ago what is not yet done, saying: My plan will take place, and I will do all My will. . . . Yes, I have spoken; so I will also bring it about. I have planned it; I will also do it. (Isa 46:10-11)

Everything will turn out just as He has said it will. What we need to do is heed what He said next through Isaiah: "Listen to me, you hard-hearted" (Isa 46:12).

God's Judgment Is Intense

God's judgment is awful. For those in Jerusalem, He was going to **"make the pile of kindling large"** (24:9). In essence they would feel the full heat of His wrath. He instructed, **"Pile on the logs and kindle the fire! Cook the meat well and mix in the spices! Let the bones be burned! Set the empty pot on its coals so that it becomes hot and its copper glows"** (vv. 10-11).

Jesus taught us a lot about the intensity of God's judgment. He used phrases such as "weeping and gnashing of teeth" (Matt 13:42) to describe what those who experienced it would be doing. He said those who are judged would be thrown into "outer darkness" (Matt 8:12; 22:13; 25:30), and it will be like they are blind forever.

Jesus taught us the most about God's intense judgment, however, around three o'clock on the afternoon He was crucified. It was then

He "cried out with a loud voice, 'Elí, Elí, lemá sabachtháni?' that is, 'My God, My God, why have You forsaken Me?'" (Matt 27:46). The most intense part of God's wrath will not be the fire but the forsakenness. The soul God judges will be cut off from His mercy, grace, and love forever. The day is coming when God's wrath will be released in its full capacity, and it will never be diminished. His fire will not be extinguished, and His sword will not be sheathed.

God's Judgment Is Deserved

God never punishes the innocent. His judgment is always deserved. For those in Jerusalem, God was going to **judge** them **according to** their **ways and deeds** (v. 14). Those who questioned His fairness (18:25) will find His judgment is unquestionably right. God's people were guilty of **bloodshed** (24:6,7,9), **indecency**, and **uncleanness** (v. 13). They were like a pot whose **thick rust will not come off** (vv. 6,12). They were not even concerned with covering their sin (v. 7).

Innocent people have nothing to fear from God. The problem is, there are no innocent people. All have sinned and fall short of His glory (Rom 3:23); therefore, all should fear His judgment. But there is hope because "He made the One who did not know sin to be sin for us, so that we might become the righteousness of God in Him" (2 Cor 5:21). Many phrases will be cried from hell, but "innocent" is not one of them.

God's Judgment Can Be Avoided

At one point God's judgment in Jerusalem was avoidable. He reminded them, **"I tried to purify you, but you would not be purified from your uncleanness"** (v. 13). For generations He sent prophets to warn His people, but His people killed His prophets (1 Kgs 19:14). The opportunity to repent and live had been given, but now it was gone. All that was left for Jerusalem was judgment without pity.

Though we know the Lord's judgment is certain, it can be avoided. Our problem is we often look for security in all the wrong places. Edwards warned, "Men's hands cannot be strong when God rises up. . . . There is no fortress that is any defense from the power of God" (Edwards, *Sinners*, 18). There is only one place we can flee from the wrath of God, and that is to the One who has already faced it. John said, "The one who believes in the Son has eternal life, but the one who refuses to believe in the Son will not see life; instead, the wrath of God remains on him" (John 3:36). Let us then "seek the LORD while He may be found" and "call to Him while He is near" (Isa 55:6).

God's Message Is Never Without Cost
EZEKIEL 24:15-24

Up to this point Ezekiel has preached difficult sermons through difficult means. In Ezekiel 24, however, God asks His prophet to preach his costliest sermon. Ezekiel's wife is going to die, and he will not be allowed to display the customary signs of grief and mourning.

In these verses we see a side of Ezekiel that has not been revealed previously. Taylor notes, "While not wishing to romanticize Ezekiel in any way, it is worth commenting that often a man is seen for what he really is only when he is seen in conjunction with his wife" (Taylor, *Ezekiel*, 177). For Ezekiel his wife was **the delight of** his **eyes**. She was precious to him. He loved her.

What right does God have to ask Ezekiel to preach this sermon? What right does God have to take Ezekiel's beloved wife? God has every right. He is the sovereign and holy King. Without question this is a painful providence, but God's holiness ensures that His ways are always right and good. God is free to use His people in the way He knows is best. For Jeremiah this meant not marrying. For Hosea this meant marrying an unfaithful wife. For Ezekiel this meant the sudden loss of the one he deeply loved.

Speaking honestly, this would be a brutal price to pay for ministry. The disobedience of the Israelites now will cost Ezekiel his wife because God wants to use this drastic measure to get through to them. How does Ezekiel not resent them or, worse, God? How does he still deliver messages to them, knowing that had they and their families repented earlier, his wife would not have been taken?

There is a great teaching point here: not all suffering is punishment. Sometimes our "best life now" actually involves suffering—not because suffering is good but because God is good and He uses our pain to produce a good result. Ezekiel's wife is being taken not because of his or her disobedience. Up to this point Ezekiel has done everything the Lord has asked Him to do in the way He asked the prophet to do it. God is not disciplining Ezekiel. He will use Ezekiel's suffering to preach a sermon like no other.

Several years ago a couple in the first church we served suffered numerous miscarriages. Others, outside our faith family, told them the death of these babies was due to disobedience in their lives. In October of 2006 my wife and I lost a baby in the second trimester of pregnancy. Through tears I preached Proverbs 3:5-6 the following Sunday.

> *Trust in the* Lord *with all your heart,*
>   *and do not rely on your own understanding;*
> *think about Him in all your ways,*
>   *and He will guide you on the right paths.*

My wife and I felt God allowed us to experience this pain for many reasons, but discipline or consequences were never one of them. We believed He was sanctifying us to minister to the previously mentioned couple like never before.

For Ezekiel and his wife, there would be no long good-byes. As a matter of fact, he could not say anything to her and had not been able to for a while (3:26-27). That his wife is still with him after all the "crazy" sign acts he was asked to perform says a lot about her. We know she did not sign up to be a prophet's wife when they were first married, since Ezekiel was a priest, but she had stuck with him through this new ministry in exile. All of this makes it more amazing that Ezekiel says, **"I spoke to the people in the morning, and my wife died in the evening. The next morning I did just as I was commanded"** (v. 18). May the Lord strengthen us as He did Ezekiel, that we might be as obedient and sacrificial for the sake of the gospel.

The good news is that Ezekiel's actions were not lost on his audience. They responded to his peculiar behavior by asking, **"Won't you tell us what these things you are doing mean for us?"** At least by now they know that when Ezekiel does something strange it's not because he is crazy. No, the Lord has something He wants to say to them, and they now know enough to ask, "What are you trying to say to us?"

Ezekiel would provide the reason behind his actions. He told them,

> *The word of the* Lord *came to me: "Say to the house of Israel: This is what the Lord* God *says: I am about to desecrate My sanctuary, the pride of your power, the delight of your eyes, and the desire of your heart. Also, the sons and daughters you left behind will fall by the sword."* (v. 21)

The Lord's people would respond to their loss just as Ezekiel did to the loss of his wife: **"You will not lament or weep"** (v. 23).

Ezekiel knows now that his suffering has spoken to God's people in a way that no other sermon could communicate and that it will achieve its purpose. The people will come to know that God is Yahweh. God's plan is never arbitrary or "just for kicks." He always knows what He is doing, why He is doing it, and the best way to do it. He also knows the measures He has to take to speak into the depths of our depravity.

Sadly, God's people had replaced love for God with love for God's temple (Jer 7:4). The place of God was more precious to them than the person of God. Perhaps they felt secure as long as the building was standing, but the temple itself could do nothing to protect them. They cared more about the building's destruction than the Lord's departure.

Ezekiel is not the only one paying a price in Ezekiel 24. God is going to allow His sanctuary to be desecrated. He does so because "nothing, not even the temple, is more sacred to God than a sanctified people" (Block, *Ezekiel 1–24*, 797). For some reason God's people often have the "propensity to transform legitimate religious symbols into idolatrous images" (ibid.). Our generation is no different. Sometimes we worship musical worship instead of the One to whom the song is sung. There are times we can be enamored with a great sermon rather than a great Savior. We can even make our church building or church family an idol. Thankfully, God often steps in and reminds us we are missing the main point—Him!

Seeing what Ezekiel sacrificed and the purpose for which it was intended should lead us to assess whether we are "all in" for the sake of the gospel. Ezekiel is not the only messenger of God to sacrifice a spouse during the course of ministry. John Paton, Adoniram Judson, and William Carey all buried their wives while sharing the gospel in difficult places. Paton even dug his wife's grave with his bare hands.

As we consider these sacrifices, we should bear in mind that no one will be asked to give more than God has given for the cause of the gospel. God willingly offered His Son in whom He delighted (Matt 3:17). In addition, we have been "bought at a price," and we are no longer our own (1 Cor 6:20). All we have belongs to Him, and He is free to use everything as He sees best. Sacrifice and suffering provide an opportunity for us to entrust ourselves to a faithful Creator (1 Pet 4:19).

God's Hope Is Never Without Comfort
EZEKIEL 24:25-27

With the death of Ezekiel's wife and the destruction of the temple, Ezekiel 24 is indeed full of doom, but there is a glimmer of hope. The Lord told Ezekiel,

> *"Son of man, know that on the day I take their stronghold from them, their pride and joy, the delight of their eyes and the longing of their hearts, as well as their sons and daughters, on that day a fugitive will come to you and report the news. On that day your mouth will be opened to talk with him; you will speak and no longer be mute. So you will be a sign for them, and they will know that I am Yahweh."*
> (vv. 25-27)

Almost three years to the day after Ezekiel was given this word, everything happened just as the Lord said it would (33:21-22). Though the fall of Jerusalem and the temple would be devastating to God's people, it would also mark a turning point in their exile. Instead of discipline, the message would now be one of hope and deliverance. Ezekiel's mouth would no longer be bound just to communicate God's judgment, but now he would be able to speak of God's blessings. God's wrath will be satisfied (24:13), and the people will know He is Yahweh.

Just as the destruction of the temple seemed like the darkest moment for God's people, so did the death of God's Son. God would lay our sin on His Son and pour out the full measure of His wrath. The darkness of the crucifixion, though, would soon give way to the light of the resurrection. What seemed like defeat would ultimately be victory.

Unlike Ezekiel we do not have to wait three years to see how everything is going to turn out. We know that in the cross of Christ the wrath of God was satisfied. Our tongues have been set free to proclaim a message of deliverance. The discipline has passed. Hope has come.

Reflect and Discuss

1. How often do you think about the certainty of God's coming judgment? How could being more intentional to consider this truth make a difference in our daily lives?

2. Why do you think people delay repentance in their lives? What would make them feel this is acceptable?

3. Has there ever been a time when God "tried to purify you, but you would not be purified"? Why did you cling to your sin rather than run to repentance?

4. Is there any area now where God is trying to get you to let go of sin? How will you heed His loving call?

5. In what ways are you challenged by Ezekiel's faithfulness and sacrifice?

6. Would you obey the Lord if you knew it would cost the lives of your family? Why are we hesitant to obey even when the costs are far less?

7. How can the gospel empower us to proclaim God's message in difficult places and without regard for the cost?

8. In what ways have you been challenged by those who've given so much for the sake of the gospel?

9. Though it may not be the temple for us, we are often tempted to replace worship of God with worship of something God has given us. How have you seen this in your own life? How can we minimize these times?

10. How can we have hope and expectation as we await the fulfillment of all God has promised us? What should we do while we wait?

The Nations Will Know That I Am Yahweh

EZEKIEL 25:1–32:32

Main Idea: God is going to judge the nations who hurt or hoped to take advantage of His people, in order to show them that He is Yahweh and to pave the way for Israel's restoration.

I.   **God Is Sovereign over Every Nation (25:1–32:32).**
   A. Ammon (25:1-7)
   B. Moab (25:8-11)
   C. Edom (25:12-14)
   D. Philistia (25:15-17)
   E. Tyre (26:1–28:19)
   F. Sidon (28:20-23)
   G. Egypt (29:1–32:32)
II. **What Can We Learn About God?**
   A. God has no equal.
   B. God has authority over everyone and everything everywhere.
   C. God's standards do not change based on one's location.
   D. God keeps His promises.
   E. God often uses human kingdoms or governments as His means of divine justice.
   F. God receives glory both in extending mercy and in withholding it.
   G. God's discipline of the nations is for the good of His people (28:24-26; 29:21).
III. **What Can We Learn About Us?**
   A. The world will often rejoice when God's people struggle.
   B. Everything we look to for security besides God will ultimately fail us.
   C. Not everything that seems important now, really is.
   D. If God rewarded the pagan Nebuchadnezzar for his work, how much more will He reward those who love Him and walk in His ways?
   E. We have work to do.

Leaving vengeance to God is not always easy. When I was a senior in college my father died from a massive heart attack. His death occurred in a dorm room my stepmother used when she took courses at a nearby university. The back of his hands had what I felt was unusual bruising. For a while I struggled whether something more had happened to my father. Then the Lord brought me to what Paul shared with the church at Rome: "Friends, do not avenge yourselves; instead, leave room for His wrath. For it is written: Vengeance belongs to Me; I will repay, says the Lord" (Rom 12:19). The Spirit used this verse to free me from my concern and to know that one day God will take care of all wrongs.

As we come to this portion of Scripture in Ezekiel, let me ask you, when is the last time you preached or heard a sermon preached from Ezekiel 25:1–32:32? Thought so. In these chapters we enter into what I believe are some of the least proclaimed passages in the entire book. This dearth is to our detriment because there is much to learn in these passages about God's sovereignty, justice, mercy, and glory.

Perhaps now would be a good time to remind us where we are in the book. Ezekiel 1–3 consists of Ezekiel's call and commissioning. God's judgment on His people comprises Ezekiel 4–24. Our focus text, Ezekiel 25–32, is God's judgment of seven nations that are around His people. Restoration and hope can be found in Ezekiel 33–39. And God's new temple and future blessings are in Ezekiel 40–48.

Before jumping into our text, it would be helpful to remember that God reigns over every parliament, every congress, every president, every king, and every dictator. In Isaiah 40:22-24 we are told,

> God is enthroned above the circle of the earth; its inhabitants are like grasshoppers. He stretches out the heavens like thin cloth and spreads them out like a tent to live in. He reduces princes to nothing and makes judges of the earth irrational. They are barely planted, barely sown, their stem hardly takes root in the ground when He blows on them and they wither, and a whirlwind carries them away like stubble.

There is no one to compare God to because He has no equal (Isa 40:25). Misplaced trust in leadership has been the ruin of many people. The psalmist tells us, "It is better to take refuge in the LORD than to trust in nobles" (Ps 118:9). We are warned again, "Do not trust in nobles, in man, who cannot save" (Ps 146:3). We are also told, "A king's heart is like streams of water in the LORD's hand: He directs it wherever He chooses" (Prov 21:1). Above every earthly ruler is the one King of all.

He reigns over every country and requires not their permission, passport, or political vote. He does, however, call for their repentance (Acts 17:30).

What occurs in Ezekiel 25–32 is the Lord's keeping His promise to Abraham. He told Abraham, "I will bless those who bless you, I will curse those who treat you with contempt, and all the peoples on earth will be blessed through you" (Gen 12:3). God will hold all others accountable for how they treat His people. In these chapters we are reminded once again that the Lord of all the earth will judge every nation. Speaking of those nations, Peter once asked, "For the time has come for judgment to begin with God's household, and if it begins with us, what will the outcome be for those who disobey the gospel of God?" (1 Pet 4:17). These chapters in Ezekiel will show that the outcome will be eternally awful.

God Is Sovereign over Every Nation
EZEKIEL 25:1–32:32

In the movie *Braveheart* (1995) William Wallace is charged with treason against the king of England. In his defense he admits he never swore allegiance to the king. The response from the judge was, "It matters not. He is your king." In Ezekiel 25–32 we see that God is King over all nations and not just over those who acknowledge or swear allegiance to Him. Their not having anything to do with Him does not mean He has nothing to do with them.

After 21 chapters of hearing all the Lord was disciplining them for, I'm sure Ezekiel's audience was somewhat relieved to see His judgment move on to others. In these chapters God informs seven countries they will face His judgment. The countries are Ammon (25:1-7), Moab (25:8-11), Edom (25:12-14), Philistia (25:15-17), Tyre (26:1–28:19), Sidon (28:20-23), and Egypt (29:1–32:32). Of the seven Tyre and Egypt receive the longest prophecies and have specific words for their rulers.

Each prophecy contains similar elements for all seven countries. First, the country is named. Second, we are told what they did or what they failed to with regard to God's people. Third, we are informed what is going to happen to them as judgment. Finally, we are told why God is bringing about these judgments. For six countries the purpose is the same: that people **"will know that I am Yahweh"** (25:5,7,11,17; 26:6; 28:23; 32:15). Edom, however, would experience God's judgment so that they would know His vengeance (25:14).

Ammon (25:1-7)

The first people, besides Israel, to receive God's judgment in the book of Ezekiel were the **Ammonites**. In case you have forgotten who they were, these were the descendants of Lot's son who was birthed by his younger daughter (Gen 19:38). Yes, you read that correctly. Talk about a jacked-up family tree. God, however, is not holding them accountable for their ancestry but for their actions. They delighted in Israel's discipline.

God was judging the Ammonites, **"Because you said, 'Good!' about My sanctuary when it was desecrated, about the land of Israel when it was laid waste, and about the house of Judah when they went into exile"** (v. 3). He was also judging them because they **clapped** their **hands, stamped** their **feet, and rejoiced over the land of Israel with wholehearted contempt** (v. 6). As punishment the Ammonites would be handed over to Nebuchadnezzar as well. The **people of the east** would **set up their encampments and pitch their tents** among the Ammonites. They would also **eat** Ammon's fruit and **drink** Ammon's **milk** (v. 4). The land of Ammon would be turned into a **pasture** and a **sheepfold** (v. 5). The Ammonites would be cut off, eliminated, and destroyed (v. 7). They will also be forgotten (v. 10). When all this occurs, the Ammonites will know that God is Yahweh (vv. 5,7). How tragic it is for those who only come to know God is Yahweh through His judgment rather than His mercy.

Moab (25:8-11)

The second group to receive a prophetic judgment from the Lord was the Moabites. These people were descendants of Lot's son by his older daughter (Gen 19:37). Yes, you read that correctly as well. Seriously, can you imagine these family reunions? Their sin was to say, **"Look, the house of Judah is like all the other nations."** In essence, the Moabites were saying there is nothing special about Judah or their God. Their punishment will be the same as their cousins. The **cities** they took such pride in will be given as a **possession** to the **people of the east**. As a result the Moabites will know God is Yahweh and that they misspoke about Him and His people. The God they once viewed as weak will reveal His strength, and they will know they were wrong.

Edom (25:12-14)

Edom is next in the Lord's prophecy against the nations. The Edomites are the descendants of Esau, who was Jacob's brother (Gen 36:1).

According to the Lord, the Edomites **acted vengefully against the house of Judah and incurred grievous guilt by taking revenge on them**. We also know through Obadiah that Edom "stood aloof" and did not help God's people, they gloated over Judah and boastfully mocked them, they looted Jerusalem after it fell, they stood at the crossroads and cut off those fleeing from Jerusalem, and those of God's people that Edom did not kill they handed over to Nebuchadnezzar (Obad 10-14).

Because of their actions against His people, God was going to destroy the Edomites. He told them, "**I will stretch out My hand against Edom and cut off both man and animal from it. I will make it a wasteland; they will fall by the sword from Teman to Dedan**" (25:13). Paul's exhortation about God's vengeance in Romans 12:19 is clearly illustrated in Ezekiel 25:14. The Lord said, "**I will take My vengeance on Edom through My people Israel, and they will deal with Edom according to My anger and wrath. So they will know My vengeance.**" If you think God failed to do this, then just look for Edom's flag at the next Olympics.

Philistia (25:15-17)

The fourth country to be judged by God was Philistia. The Philistines occupied a sliver of land between Judah and the Mediterranean Sea and had been a constant thorn in Israel's side. Just ask Samson and David. The current generation of Philistines, however, **acted in vengeance and took revenge with deep contempt, destroying because of their ancient hatred**. As they harmed God's people, maybe they shouted, "This one's for Goliath!" We do not know their battle cry, but we do know that what they were consumed with ultimately consumed them. The hatred passed to each Philistine descendant would ultimately lead to their destruction. The **furious rebukes** of God's **vengeance** would lead to Philistia knowing God is **Yahweh**.

Tyre (26:1–28:19)

After four summary judgments for the previous nations, the Lord wants to say more to the people of Tyre. What He said in a paragraph with the others, He will spread over two and a half chapters to Tyre. These people dwelled northwest of Israel and along the Mediterranean Sea. They were the commercial capital of their day and full of wisdom and wealth. Of all the nations described, they most remind me of the United States.

So what did the people of Tyre do against God and His people? First of all, they saw Israel's discipline as an opportunity for their own economic gain (26:2). Second, Tyre was full of pride, to the point of declaring, **"I am perfect in beauty"** (27:3; cf. 28:17). Third, their leader thought he was a god (28:2,6), which is always foolish unless you are God. Fourth, they were proud of their wealth (28:5) and felt secure in it. Lastly, they were **filled with violence, sinned, profaned** their **sanctuaries**, and had a **magnitude of iniquities** (28:16,18).

In judgment God was going to make the "beautiful" Tyre **an object of horror** (26:21; 27:36; 28:19). He would cause Tyre to cease to exist so they would never be found again by anyone who sought them (26:21). Those they traded with will **mock** them (27:36). Those who knew them will be **appalled** at Tyre (28:19).

God had a special judgment for Tyre's ruler. The Lord said,

> *Because you regard your heart as that of a god, I am about to bring strangers against you, ruthless men from the nations. They will draw their swords against your magnificent wisdom and will defile your splendor. They will bring you down to the Pit, and you will die a violent death in the heart of the sea. Will you still say, "I am a god," in the presence of those who kill you? Yet you will be only a man, not a god, in the hands of those who kill you. You will die the death of the uncircumcised at the hands of strangers. For I have spoken. This is the declaration of the Lord God.* (28:6-10)

Because of the judgment both the people of Tyre and their ruler would know God is Yahweh (26:6). About Tyre's fall Duguid notes,

> The rapidity with which her demise can be described contrasts starkly with the lengthy description of her beauty. Her beauty and security count for nothing when the storm strikes. (Duguid, *Ezekiel*, 336)

There is only one safe refuge, and that is the Lord.

Sidon (28:20-23)

Squeezed between the lengthier treatises to Tyre and Egypt is a word for **Sidon**. Like Tyre the people of Sidon dwelled northwest of Israel and along the Mediterranean Sea. At a minimum we know they, like Israel's other adversarial neighbors, treated God's people with **contempt** (v. 24). What else **Sidon** was guilty of was not revealed to Ezekiel. In judgment God will **display** His **glory within** them and **demonstrate** His **holiness through** them. They will receive a **plague,** and **bloodshed** will be in their streets. The **slain** will **fall** in Sidon, and the **sword** be against her on **every side**. When the punishment is executed, they will know God is **Yahweh**.

Egypt (29:1–32:32)

The last country to receive a judgment prophecy from the Lord was one of the first who should have expected it. **Egypt** and Israel had an interesting relationship. At one point Egypt held God's people in slavery making "their lives bitter with difficult labor in brick and mortar and in all kinds of fieldwork" (Exod 1:14). The Pharaoh even commanded all his people to "throw every son born to the Hebrews into the Nile" (Exod 1:22). The Lord would deliver His people from their slavery and destroy Pharaoh in the process (Exod 1:28). The one who was responsible for the drowning of so many Israelite children would himself be drowned.

Despite the brutal history, one of the first places Israel would flee for help in times of trouble was Egypt. Why we keep such short memories or repeatedly return to those who want nothing but our harm I'll never know. In Ezekiel's day Egypt had power and resources, and God's people sought their help rather than His. God considered Israel's solicitation of Egypt to be adultery and used the most graphic of terms to describe the relationship between the two nations (16:26).

God knew that Egypt was **a staff made of reed to the house of Israel** (29:6). They were not the crutch on which Israel should have leaned for help in the journey because they were a false support. God told Egypt, **"When Israel grasped you by the hand, you splintered, tearing all their shoulders; when they leaned on you, you shattered and made all their hips unsteady"** (29:7). Egypt's lack of support wounded Israel, and God will hold them accountable.

Besides their lack of trustworthiness, God had other issues against Egypt. He could not stand their pride (31:10) or their pharaoh. Like Tyre, Egypt had a ruler who thought he was a god. He would say, **"My Nile is my own; I made it for myself"** (29:3). If "the fool says in his heart, 'God does not exist'" (Ps 14:1), then what term should be used to describe the one who thinks he *is* a god?

God's judgment of Egypt will be exhaustive (32:15). They and their leader will be given **to the beasts of the earth and the birds of the sky as food** (29:4-5). Egypt's wealth and land will be given to Nebuchadnezzar as compensation (29:19-20). Their allies will be destroyed (30:5-6). There will be nowhere for the Egyptians to run for help when God enacts His judgment. Egypt will be a total wasteland (29:8-16; 30:13-19). They will be destroyed (32:12) and sent to Sheol (32:17-32). When all this occurs, they will know God is Yahweh (32:15) and Pharaoh was no god at all.

What Can We Learn About God?

When studying the Bible, we do not ask, "What does this passage mean to me?" but, "What does this passage mean?" We also do not first ask what a passage can teach us about ourselves but what it can teach us about God. After walking through eight chapters of God's judgment on pagan nations, what can we learn about Him?

God Has No Equal

There is none like Him. He is neither impressed with nor afraid of man's kingdoms. There is not currently, has never been, and will never be a real threat to His authority. He has been, is, and will forever be in control. He needs no counsel. He does not even need sleep (Ps 121:4). The rulers of Tyre and Egypt "thought" they were gods, but Yahweh knows He is and that He is alone.

God Has Authority over Everyone and Everything Everywhere

We have seen this truth previously in this book, but in Ezekiel 25–32 it is especially clear. He does not reign over just His people. He is not standing at the border of countries and waiting for them to validate His passport. His reign is not determined at the ballot box or in accordance with a congressional bill. Whatever He desired in these eight chapters is what would be done. In the discipline of these nations, He would even use other pagan countries. If that's not sovereignty, then I do not know what is!

God's Standards Do Not Change Based on One's Location

He does not excuse sin based on geographical markers or the borders of countries. He is holy, and He expects all people to walk according to His ways. This is true even for peoples who do not have Scripture in their language. He will judge all peoples for both their attitudes and their actions. In these chapters God did not look past the sins of certain people just because they were not in Jerusalem or had never acknowledged His existence. He also did not punish them for general reasons but for specific causes. Somehow, without the FBI, CIA, KGB, or any other information gatherers, God had detailed knowledge of every nation and what they had done or not done in accordance to His will. He will judge all people based on His holiness. In one sense all religions do lead to God but just not in the way most people think.

God Keeps His Promises

As was already noted, what occurs in Ezekiel 25–32 is God keeping His promise to Abraham in Genesis 12:3. God has little tolerance for those who harm His people or lead them away from Him. Furthermore, no one had to remind God to keep His word. Neither Ezekiel nor his peers suggested that God offer retribution for what the other countries did to them. Without setting an alarm as a reminder, God knows when and how is the best way to honor His promises. He will bless all those who bless His people, and He will curse all those who curse them. We should be careful then in how we treat His other children in our faith families and our biological families.

God Often Uses Human Kingdoms or Governments as His Means of Divine Justice

The pagan nations may not even realize they are being used to accomplish His will. In these eight chapters God was going to use Nebuchadnezzar to be His agent of justice (26:7; 29:19-20; 30:24; 31:11). Scripture nowhere records God asking Nebuchadnezzar to partner with Him or asking his permission to use him. With Nebuchadnezzar and every ruler, God can exercise His sovereignty and "accomplish His will without destroying either their freedom or their accountability to Him" (Wiersbe, *Be Reverent*, 160). How does God do this without violating a person's will? He guides them, He strengthens them, and He uses what is already in their heart. When Joseph's brothers sold him into slavery, God did not put the evil in their heart. It was already there. He just had a plan that would turn to good what they intended as harm. Likewise, God did not have to put the desire to conquer other nations into Nebuchadnezzar's heart. He just used what was already there.

The book of Habakkuk is a great illustration of God's using pagan nations while simultaneously holding them accountable. Habakkuk is grieved because of the injustice and violence among God's people (Hab 1:1-4). God tells him to sit tight because He has a plan. He's going to raise a pagan nation to discipline His people (1:5-11). Any guess which nation God is talking about? You guessed it. Good ol' Chaldea, or in other words, the home of the Babylonians. Habakkuk has a lot of questions about that plan but asks them humbly (1:12-17). God tells him not to worry because He will hold the pagan nation accountable for its actions as well (2:2-20). Habakkuk determines to trust God no matter what he sees around him (3:1-19).

God Receives Glory Both in Extending Mercy and in Withholding It

God is not obligated to extend mercy at all. God is not obligated to extend mercy to all. He told Moses, "I will be gracious to whom I will be gracious, and I will have compassion on whom I will have compassion" (Exod 33:19). In Ezekiel 25–32 Israel receives mercy. In these same chapters Ammon, Moab, Edom, Philistia, Tyre, Sidon, and Egypt receive judgment. In both cases God receives glory.

While some aspects of how God does things may be difficult for us to grasp, it does not make them less true. What we do not want to miss in these eight chapters is that every single nation including Israel deserved judgment and every single nation except one received it. The choice belongs to God, and He always does what He knows will bring Him the most glory. Israel's discipline would be for restoration, but all the other nations experienced God's judgment for ruin.

God's Discipline of the Nations Is for the Good of His People (28:24-26; 29:21)

His children "**will no longer be hurt by prickly briers or painful thorns from all their neighbors who treat them with contempt**" (28:24). After God gathers **the house of Israel** and brings them to **their own land**, He wants them to **live there securely, build houses, and plant vineyards** (v. 26). His people will dwell **securely** after He **executes judgments on all their neighbors who treat them with contempt** (v. 26). All He does, He does for His glory and our good.

What Can We Learn About Us?

Ezekiel 25–32 contains points of application that we can take with us.

The World Will Often Rejoice When God's People Struggle

Several of the countries in these chapters rejoiced and gloated over what happened to Israel. They even mocked them. In this world we will have trouble too (John 16:33). We should not be naïve and think everyone is going to love us just because we love Jesus. We should also do all we can to minimize bringing shame on God or causing people to doubt His power or goodness when they look at our lives.

Everything We Look To for Security besides God Will Ultimately Fail Us

Tyre had pride in all it had accumulated (28:5). Egypt took pride in what it had achieved (31:10). Philistia at one time had confidence in its giant. All refuges besides God will be found wanting. Our greatest need for security is from the wrath of God, and this refuge is found only in the cross of Christ. What are you placing your confidence in? Your seminary degree? Your mission trips? Your hours of service to the kingdom? Whatever else we look to for security besides Christ cannot even protect itself from God's wrath, much less protect us.

Not Everything That Seems Important Now, Really Is

How many coins from Tyre do you think lie on the ocean floor? What lies buried in the sand of Egypt that seemed so precious in Ezekiel's day? We do not even know the names of the rulers of Tyre and Egypt, though they considered themselves extremely important. What matters above all is knowing God's will and doing it. We are a mist and a vapor in the timeline of earth's history. How many plans of Egypt were drowned in one afternoon? It's only God's plan that will remain when all other kingdoms have passed away. Are we spending our time on what really matters?

If God Rewarded the Pagan Nebuchadnezzar for His Work, How Much More Will He Reward Those Who Love Him and Walk in His Ways?[3]

God compensated Babylon's king for his work as God's agent of justice (29:17-21). I fear many of us rarely consider kingdom rewards. C. S. Lewis contended,

> If we consider the unblushing promises of reward and the staggering nature of the rewards promised in the Gospels, it would seem that Our Lord finds our desires not too strong,

---

[3] Duguid, *Ezekiel*, 362.

but too weak. We are half-hearted creatures, fooling about
with drink and sex and ambition when infinite joy is offered
us, like an ignorant child who wants to go on making mud
pies in a slum because he cannot imagine what is meant by
the offer of a holiday at the sea. We are far too easily pleased.
(Lewis, *Weight of Glory*, 26)

At the same time, Jesus reminds us, "When you have done all that you
were commanded, you should say, 'We are good-for-nothing slaves;
we've only done our duty'" (Luke 17:10).

We Have Work to Do

Jesus commissioned us to "go, therefore, and make disciples of all
nations" (Matt 28:19). We have seen in these chapters that every nation
and every person will be held accountable to God's holy standards. Paul
also tells us, "No condemnation exists for those in Christ Jesus" (Rom
8:1). After 29 chapters of judgment, let that truth wash over you for just a
moment. Actually, strive to let that truth wash over you every moment of
every day. Then notice the preposition "in." Only those who are *in* Christ
are free from condemnation because He was condemned in our place.

For those who are *not in* Christ, however, there is complete condemnation. How can they know and believe it is "Jesus, who rescues us from
the coming wrath" (1 Thess 1:10)? "Faith comes from what is heard, and
what is heard comes through the message about Christ" (Rom 10:17).
Indeed then, "How beautiful are the feet of those who announce the
gospel of good things" (Rom 10:15).

May we consider these eight chapters and tremble before a holy
God. May we consider His judgment on these nations and know we are
just as deserving of such treatment. May we then look to the cross and
shake our heads in wonder at the substitutionary atonement of Christ.
May we in response not go past the gospel but deeper into it, and may
the good news of Christ advance in us and through us for the glory of
God and the good of others.

Reflect and Discuss

1. If someone were to ask you, "How do you know God reigns over
every nation and not just His people?" what would you tell them?
Why do you think some believe He is just the King over those who
believe in Him?

2. In what ways is God's sovereignty over every nation impacting your prayers?
3. In what ways is God's sovereignty over every person impacting your evangelism?
4. In what ways is God's future judgment of all peoples driving how your faith family seeks the global spread of the gospel? What are you doing specifically in this regard?
5. Are there any ways we are like the people of Tyre and feel secure in what we have rather than in the One who has us? Why do we so easily feel secure in false refuges?
6. Israel would often look to Egypt for help despite knowing Egypt never had Israel's best interest at heart. How are we like this when we repeatedly run to our lovers: the world, the flesh, and the Devil? Why do we go to them so often even though they only want to wound and destroy us?
7. Have you ever leaned on God for support and found him to be a "splintered staff" like Egypt was for Israel? Have you ever thanked Him for His steadfastness?
8. How grateful are you that you have come to know that He is Yahweh through His mercy instead of through His judgment?
9. How often do you consider kingdom rewards? Why can we so easily become distracted with matters that really are not that important from the eternal perspective? How can we stay focused on what matters most with each day the Lord gives us?
10. After 29 chapters of seeing God's judgment on full display, how grateful are you that there is no condemnation for those of us who are in Christ? How is this gratitude revealed in your daily life?

The Watchmen of Our City

EZEKIEL 33:1-33

Main Idea: God provides the means, the message, and the motivation for us to serve as watchmen for the world.

I.   Will We Share the Word (33:1-9)?
II.   Will We Believe the Word (33:10-20)?
III. Will We Listen to the Word (33:23-29)?
IV. Will We Obey the Word (33:30-33)?
V.   Will We Deliver the Word (33:21-22)?

Late one night in fall of my senior year in college, I was studying for an exam. My roommate was asleep in his room upstairs, and I was jealous. While studying, I began to notice a strange aroma but was uncertain of its origin. While investigating the smell, I began to hear some commotion outside our apartment. There was a light tap on our back door. As I opened it, I barely heard someone's voice trailing away in the distance say the word, "Fire!" I stepped out on the sidewalk and saw the apartment with which we shared a common wall was engulfed in flames.

My first thought was of my sleeping roommate. I ran upstairs as quickly as I could only to find him sound asleep. I began to yell for him to wake up. He did not budge. I yelled more. He still did not budge. As a last resort I went to his bed, shook him, and screamed, "Wake up!"

He finally rose from his slumber and said, "I smell smoke."

I said in the most sarcastic of tones, "You think so? It's a fire bro. We've got to get out of here."

I can point to many graces of the Lord on that night. First are the people who helped us get some of our belongings. Second was a friend who gave up his bed for me that night and slept on the floor so I would have a place to stay. A third blessing was that the ceiling did not fall in my roommate's room until we had gotten out. A fourth blessing was that my professor let me postpone my exam . . . for a day. (Sure I am homeless now, but taking your exam is top on my priority list.)

As I have had time to process the events of that night, it has occurred to me of all the sounds we heard one was glaringly absent: our smoke detector in our apartment never made a single sound. Smoke was slapping it in its plastic face but still not a peep. The smoke taunted it and even hit it, but nothing. The smoke alarm failed to do what it was created to do.

Warning can be a matter of life and death. The sailors who slept on the *USS Arizona* and other Navy vessels at Pearl Harbor had no warning on the morning of December 7, 1941, that pilots from Japan were on their way to attack. As a result, 2,335 U.S. servicemen were killed and 1,143 were wounded. People working in the two towers of the World Trade Center in New York had no warning that planes were going to slam into their buildings on the morning of September 11, 2001. As a result, 2,606 people would lose their lives in the collapse of the buildings. More would die in the planes and at the Pentagon. Yes, warning can be a matter of life and death.

More importantly, however, warning can be a matter of eternity. We live in a world where at least two billion people currently lack access to the gospel. The only knowledge they have of God is enough to condemn them to hell for all eternity. How many die each day having never been warned to flee to Christ? How many in our cities will die lacking the same knowledge? There is no plan B for how God will spread His gospel globally. His church is His plan. We are the watchmen who are called to sound the warning in our cities and in the nations.

In Ezekiel 33, themes we encountered in Ezekiel 3 and Ezekiel 18 will be brought back to our attention. Ezekiel will be reminded of his responsibility as **a watchman for the house of Israel** (33:7). Israel will be reminded of God's call to repent and live (v. 11). Ezekiel will finally be set free from the muteness the Lord imposed on Him (v. 22), which means he will have more to share than just judgment. When all is said and done at the close of the chapter, God's people **will know that a prophet has been among them** (v. 33).

Will We Share the Word?
EZEKIEL 33:1-9

My greatest failures in evangelism have not been in saying the wrong things but in saying nothing. Few things are worse than having an opportunity to speak up for the gospel but letting it pass. We should be ready and eager to share the good news of Christ. Peter said, "But honor the Messiah as Lord in your hearts. Always be ready to give a defense to anyone who asks you for a reason for the hope that is in you" (1 Pet 3:15). If we just sit and wait, however, until everyone asks us why we are so hopeful, then few people will hear the gospel. We are called to be proactive in our proclamation (Acts 1:8).

Perhaps one reason many do not share the gospel is fear of rejection. We have to get over this apprehension. Finding our acceptance and approval in the cross of Christ frees us from seeking it in other places and persons. Emboldened by what God has done for us in Jesus, we should share His good news freely. Of course, if the gospel is not in our hearts and on our mind, then it will not come out of our mouths. I often tell the people I shepherd that, if we are going to love God passionately and others rightly, we must meditate on the cross constantly. As we delight in the cross, we are moved to declare its glorious message. Remember, our task is to bring the gospel to our listeners' ears, and the Spirit is tasked with bringing it to their hearts.

What also aids our overcoming a fear of rejection is the knowledge of two truths. First, as God makes His appeal through us (2 Cor 5:20), He is the One who is ultimately rejected and not us. Second, we need not fear rejection because we are not held accountable for how they respond to our message. They are. As a watchman, Ezekiel is informed that he is not responsible for the reactions of the people but for warning them (33:7-9). If God tells Ezekiel to warn a wicked person to turn from his iniquity but the prophet refuses to pass along the message, then the prophet will be held responsible for the blood of the wicked one (v. 8). If, however, Ezekiel warns the wicked one but he ignores or rejects the warning, then the prophet will be released from accountability for the wicked man's decision. What Ezekiel is warned not to be is a **watchman** who **sees the sword coming but doesn't blow the trumpet, so that the people aren't warned, and the sword comes and takes away their lives** (v. 6).

Ezekiel's position as watchman was not based on popular vote. God told the prophet, "**I have made you a watchman for the house of Israel**" (v. 7). The issue then is not whether Ezekiel is a watchman but whether he is a good one. He has been appointed and so have we. We are God's watchmen as well (Acts 1:8; 2 Cor 5:20). There is no other plan. No one will be held more responsible for the cities we live in than us—particularly since God determines both when and where we live (Esth 4:14; Acts 17:26).

How then can we be the watchmen we need to be for our cities, our states, and the nations?

First, we should pray for opportunities to proclaim the gospel. Paul asks the church at Colossae to "pray also for us that God may open a door to us for the message, to speak the mystery of the Messiah, for which I am in prison" (Col 4:3). How many in our faith families are praying this and asking others to pray this for them on a daily basis? How many of our pastors are praying in this way? How would our cities be different if our churches asked God every day for opportunities to share the gospel?

Second, we should pray for opportunities to proclaim the gospel clearly. The next part of Paul's request was, "so that I may reveal it as I am required to speak" (Col 4:4). As he had opportunity to share the message, his prayer was to be able to reveal the mystery of Christ clearly. One thing is certain: if the gospel is not clear to the church, then it will not be clear to the city. I have been amazed as a pastor to see how unclear the gospel is to some people who have spent years in faith families. I have heard longtime members struggle to articulate the good news of Christ.

One of the highest priorities of my ministry as a pastor is making sure our people know the gospel, have received the gospel, are growing in the gospel, and can clearly share the gospel. We use the four words—*God, man, Christ, response*—as key markers in our discussions of the gospel. We even have the gospel posted in every room where we meet as a faith family.

Third, we should trust God's provision of the exact words to say. Paul will go on in Colossians to say, "Your speech should always be gracious, seasoned with salt, so that you may know how you should answer each person" (Col 4:6) Canned evangelism plans are fine, but I do not know any canned people. Every person is unique, and we must meet each in his or her situation. Our speech should be gracious. No one wants to hear about God's grace from someone who demonstrates little of it. In each encounter pray not to remember the presentation you memorized, but trust "you will be given what to say at that hour, because you are not speaking, but the Spirit of your Father is speaking through you" (Matt 10:19-20).

For our role as watchmen, the Lord has provided us with the message, the means, and the motivation for proclamation. God told Ezekiel, **"When you hear a word from My mouth, give them a warning from Me"** (33:7). The warning is not from Ezekiel but from the Lord because the word is not from Ezekiel but from the Lord. Nowhere in the book of Ezekiel is a failure recorded on the prophet's part in delivering the message entrusted to him. No matter how difficult the message, Ezekiel proclaimed it exactly as he received it. In the gospel of Christ, we have been given the greatest word from God. Are we giving His warning from His word? May we be faithful watchmen for our world with the word entrusted to us as Ezekiel was for Israel.

Will We Believe the Word?
EZEKIEL 33:10-20

As we share the word we have been given, not everyone will believe it. Some may even accuse God of wrongdoing. But nothing could be further from the truth. God knew His people were struggling beneath the weight of their sin. He listened to their cries, "**Our transgressions and our sins are heavy on us, and we are wasting away because of them! How then can we survive?**" (v. 10). God had a simple solution for them. He told Ezekiel,

> *Tell them: As I live . . . I take no pleasure in the death of the wicked, but rather that the wicked person should turn from his way and live. Repent, repent of your evil ways! Why will you die, house of Israel?* (v. 11)

All Israel had to do to be relieved of the burden of their sin was to turn away from their wickedness and turn to God.

The fact the prophet is given the same message in chapter 33 as he was in chapter 18 reveals that God's people still did not get it. Despite years to consider the message, they were still having trouble believing God; and, worse, some were still accusing Him of being unfair (33:17,20). They could not seem to comprehend that grace is based on God's mercy and not our merit. The one who turns to sin will die, and the one who turns from sin will live.

Once again Ezekiel is given two scenarios. The first one involves a **righteous person** who turns to **wickedness** and **will die because of the iniquity he has committed** (vv. 12-13). The second example is of a **wicked person** who **repents of his sin and does what is just and right** (v. 14). He **will certainly live** because **none of the sins he committed will be held against him** (v. 16). This does not seem like rocket science, but for God's hardhearted people this message was difficult to accept.

Though they never say it plainly, it seems God's people believe that the one who walked in righteousness but then turned to sin should be cut some slack by God. When you see grace as earned, there will always be a problem. We cannot **trust** in our **righteousness** and then commit **iniquity** (v. 13). Apparently, Ezekiel's crew ignored the word from Isaiah that "all of us have become like something unclean, and all our righteous acts are like a polluted garment" (Isa 64:6). Trusting in our righteousness means we are confident we have done enough good things to impress God. We may even be deluded enough to think He owes us because of the "righteous" acts we have achieved.

If anyone ever had "righteous points" it was Paul. He was from the right family and had done all of the right things—and with more zeal than any of his peers. But when he totaled his accomplishments and compared them with Jesus, he said,

> But everything that was a gain to me, I have considered to be a loss because of Christ. More than that, I . . . consider everything to be a loss in view of the surpassing value of knowing Christ Jesus my Lord. Because of Him I have suffered the loss of all things and consider them filth, so that I may gain Christ. (Phil 3:7-8)

Paul resolved, "But as for me, I will never boast about anything except the cross of our Lord Jesus Christ" (Gal 6:14)—which should lead us to ask, whose righteous acts do you have the most confidence in: yours or Christ's?

The one who turns to sin and forsakes the righteous path should always have fear before the Lord. No matter how many good things were accomplished prior to his bounding down the path of sin, **none of his righteousness will be remembered** (v. 13). God is not adding up our righteous points and then deducting wicked points and hoping we have more good than bad in the end. We do not want to be those who confess to be righteous for a season but those who continue on the path of righteousness with our Savior.

Admittedly, the gospel at times can sound too good to be true. That God would reconcile us to Himself and not count our sins against us should always amaze us (2 Cor 5:19). That "He made the One who did not know sin to be sin for us, so that we might become the righteousness of God in Him" should leave us shaking our heads in wonder (2 Cor 5:21). As unbelievable as it sounds, the exchange of our unrighteousness to Christ and His righteousness to us is completely true. But Ezekiel's peers were struggling to believe what they were hearing.

God told them,

> When I tell the wicked person, "You will surely die," but he repents of his sin and does what is right . . . none of the sins he committed will be

held against him. He has done what is just and right; he will certainly live. (33:14,16)

In reality repentance reveals righteousness. The one who was once wicked now "**returns collateral, makes restitution for what he has stolen, and walks in the statutes of life without practicing iniquity**" (v. 15). This person is evidencing faith, not earning it. Turning and doing are good descriptors of genuine repentance. Righteousness is not just professed but practiced.

Ezekiel's audience just could not fathom the outcome of God's two illustrations. They believed the first person had earned God's good treatment and the second person would never deserve God's favor. The reality is that neither person deserved God's mercy. Also, if their thinking was correct, then one had better be fortunate enough to start on the righteous path; otherwise there was no hope. To all this God asked, "And yet you think I'm the one being unfair?"

God's pro-life stance is affirmed again. He takes **no pleasure in the death of the wicked** but is begging for the wicked person to **turn from his way and live** (v. 11). God asks His people one more time, "**Why will you die, house of Israel?**" If we walk in wickedness, we will perish; but if we turn from it, we will live. There is not a person that is too wicked to be covered by the blood of Christ. Paul declared, "I am not ashamed of the gospel, because it is God's power for salvation to everyone who believes" (Rom 1:16).

What about us? Are we currently walking the righteous path, or are we turning from it and embracing sin? Do we believe we have earned enough points to impress God with our goodness? Are we doing all we can to encourage others to continue on the righteous path? Do we really believe the blood of Christ can cleanse our deepest sin? One thing is certain, God will **judge each** person **according to his** or her **ways** (v. 20). Let us believe what God says and turn from our sin and live.

Will We Listen to the Word?
EZEKIEL 33:23-29

While Ezekiel's peers are struggling to believe what they are hearing from God, we learn things are not any better in Judah. **Those who** were living **in the ruins in the land of Israel** were saying, "**Abraham was only one person, yet he received possession of the land. But we are many; the land has been given to us as a possession**" (v. 24). The difference between them and Abraham, however, was not in number alone but also in faithfulness. He was faithful, they were not. God's promises work through faith and not apart from it (Duguid, *Ezekiel*, 388).

Those who remained in Israel certainly were not repentant, and they who lived in the ruins would soon be ruined themselves. Unfortunately, they were self-deceived and believed that just because they remained in the land, they would receive the land. God informed them they could not be more wrong. He said to them,

> You eat meat with blood in it, raise your eyes to your idols, and shed blood. Should you then receive possession of the land? You have relied on your swords, you have committed detestable acts, and each of you has defiled his neighbor's wife. Should you then receive possession of the land? (33:25-26)

In reality the remnant in Israel should have known better. Jeremiah had already told them that those who refused God's plan of exile but remained in the land were not chosen but condemned. God would send "the sword, famine, and plague against them until they . . . perished from the land [He] gave to them and their ancestors" (Jer 24:10). Those who remained in Judah clearly did not listen to the word of the Lord, and not listening always comes with consequences. Refusing to see things as God sees them is the height of arrogance and insubordination.

Those in the ruins may have escaped the destruction of the temple, but they would not escape the discipline of the Lord. They would not be delivered. They were doomed (33:27,29).

Why are we so often like those who remained in Israel? Why do we ignore the Lord's Word? Why do we refuse to see ourselves as He sees us? Why do we think we know better than the Ancient of Days? Why do we think that because of our position in Christ it does not matter what we practice in life? Why do we seek God's blessings but withhold our obedience? Because they would not listen and receive God's word, they perished, and so will we if we follow their path. If we ignore God's Word, we do so at our own peril.

Will We Obey the Word?
EZEKIEL 33:30-33

After all that has been covered in Ezekiel up to this point and the previous passage in particular, can you believe these four verses are what comes next? How in the world could there be people in Ezekiel's group who were still only listening to the word but not obeying it? After hearing all that was happening to those in Judah who refused to do what God said, how was Ezekiel's audience not lining up to be the first to obey? We are dull and depraved people indeed!

The Lord told Ezekiel His people were drawn to Ezekiel's sermons much like one seeking to be entertained. They would encourage one another to come and hear the message of the Lord (v. 30). They would gather in crowds, sit in front of Ezekiel, and hear his words, but they would not obey them (v. 31). They would talk about how wonderful the sermons were, but in their hearts they pursued dishonest profit (v. 31). God told Ezekiel, "**To them you are like a singer of love songs who has a beautiful voice and plays skillfully on an instrument. They hear your words, but they don't obey them**" (v. 32).

Like Ezekiel's generation our problem is not access to God's Word but acting on it. Unlike the crowd who heard Jesus' Sermon on the Mount, we should not want just to be amazed by His sermon but also to submit to His authority (Matt 7:28-29). Obedience is not optional. Jesus asks, "Why do you call Me 'Lord, Lord' and don't do the things I say?" (Luke 6:46). The ones who refuse to do the will of the Father should not be surprised when they have to depart from the Son (Matt 7:23). It is not the one who just hears Christ's words who is compared to the wise builder but the one who hears His words and does them (Matt 7:24).

As much as I marvel that any of Ezekiel's peers would still lack obedience, we should be even more dismayed in our day. We, after all, are reading what they heard proclaimed and so much more. We have both testaments, and the mystery of Christ has been revealed. Their knowledge was but a matchstick compared to our sun.

How then are we approaching God's Word? Are we treating it as an artistic piece to be placed on the wall but never touched? Are we entertained by it, or are we eating it? Do we receive it with parameters? Are our mouths saying one thing about the Word but our hearts another? In the end, how much of His Word we have heard will not be nearly as important as how much we have lived. When all was said and done, Ezekiel's peers would know he had not been just some performer but a **prophet** who had been among them (33:33).

Will We Deliver the Word?
EZEKIEL 33:21-22

For seven years Ezekiel has been faithfully delivering the Lord's message of discipline to His people. **In the twelfth year** of the **exile, in the**

tenth month, and **on the fifth day of the month**, a message is delivered to Ezekiel (v. 21). **A fugitive from Jerusalem came to** him **and reported, "The city has been taken"** (v. 21). Just as the Lord had told him three years previously (24:26), Ezekiel's **mouth was opened, and** he **was no longer mute** (33:22).

Can you imagine for a moment what it was like for Ezekiel? For seven years he could only share with the people the messages the Lord had given him. He was not allowed to say anything more or anything less. There was no idle chatter. There was not even any small talk with his wife. On top of these burdens, the messages he was allowed to speak all consisted of God's judgment. As fatigued as we may be of walking through these chapters filled with God's wrath and discipline, imagine what it was like to preach that sermon series for seven years.

Of all the responses Ezekiel received from the listeners of his messages, repentance and appreciation are not recorded. How many of them dreaded to see Ezekiel come out of his house knowing he had another message of judgment for them? How many of them after seven years no longer even bothered to listen? One day the full story of Ezekiel's ministry will be told in heaven, but for now it's enough to know he was one of Israel's most faithful watchmen. Our full story will be revealed as well. Will we be found faithful in delivering His Word?

Ezekiel's tongue being set loose means the messages of discipline will now give way to sermons of deliverance. From this point forward in the text, hope and restoration will be proclaimed to those in exile. The midnight of condemnation has passed; the dawn of compassion is breaking.

Reflect and Discuss

1. In what ways are you serving as a watchman for your city?
2. How can we handle negative responses to the warnings we provide of God's coming judgment?
3. Are you trusting in your righteous acts or in Christ's? Are you thinking perseverance does not matter?
4. Do you think you are too dirty to be cleansed by God? Do you think Christ could atone for all sins except yours?
5. Are you refusing to listen to God's truth about you and your situation?
6. Why do we often just hear the Word of God but not do it? How can we not only listen to the Word but also obey it?

7. In what ways are you helping others to have access to God's Word and to act on it?
8. What's your approach and response to God's Word? How much is your heart and mind and body involved in your response?
9. How can we avoid looking just for immediate response and recognition for our faithful service to the Lord?
10. When you consider Ezekiel's seven years of having to preach only judgment, what are your thoughts? How thankful are you to be able to proclaim God's judgment but also His gospel?

Our Great Shepherd-King

EZEKIEL 34:1-31; 22:6-31

Main Idea: Christ is our Shepherd-King, and as His under-shepherds we should lead for His glory and the good of His people.

I. **When Ungodly Leaders Lead God's People, Everyone Suffers (34:1-10,17-22; 22:6-31).**
   A. God cares not only about who leads His people but how they lead them.
   B. God's people lacked godly leaders (34:2-6; 22:6-31).
   C. Where there are bad shepherds there will most likely be bad sheep (34:17-22).
   D. God will not let His people suffer under ungodly leaders forever (34:2,10).

II. **There Is No Greater Leader for God's People Than God Himself (34:11-16,23-31).**
   A. God will give His people protection and provision (34:11-16).
   B. God will give His people a prince (34:23-24).
   C. God will give His people peace (34:25-31).
   D. God will give His people a place (34:27,29).

III. **Godly Leaders Are Still Needed Today in Both Our Families and Our Faith Families, and God Is Still Providing Them.**
   A. God continues to provide leaders for His people.
   B. As they hear us and see us, our families and faith families should know what Jesus is like as a leader.

When you think of the phrase *godly leader*, who comes to mind? Whom you remember or know now? What made them a godly leader, or what stands out to you about them?

As a young man from a divorced home and one who lacked a Christian father, I was blessed in high school to have a godly football coach. Coach Smith served as a deacon in my home church but brought his ministry to the school and field. Though my father was a constant problem for him, Coach Smith's graciousness toward me never wavered. When my father made an ugly scene at our church, my coach came and found me and offered comfort. When my father had a heart attack while I was at football practice, my coach offered prayers and wisdom. To have one godly leader certainly is a grace, but I have been blessed many times by godly leaders who were my youth minister, college ministers, and seminary professors.

As a young minister, I was two weeks into my first pastorate when a member of our congregation died suddenly. He served as a manager for a local Walgreens and had been a godly leader in every way. At his funeral I listened as employee after employee gave testimony to how this man pointed them to Christ, how he would pray with them, how he sacrificed for them, and how he served them. They had been blessed in a secular environment to have a sanctified leader.

The fact I lacked a godly example in my home growing up does not exempt me as a young husband and father, from being one now. One of my passions is equipping the men in our church to lead their families well for Christ. This passion was born out of my own need to know and do what godly leaders do. Unfortunately, I have often failed to image God in my leadership. Instead of learning that God is slow to anger, my children are likely fearful He has a quick temper. Instead of washing my wife with His Word, I have often showered her with just my own thoughts, and they have definitely not been a blessing. What does it profit a pastor to gain his entire congregation but lose his family? With each week, progressing as a godly leader in my home is one of my most earnest prayers.

In Ezekiel 34 we see leadership at its best and at its worst. God will no longer allow His people to be led by those who are self-absorbed. The shepherds of Israel had failed to provide for and protect God's sheep, so He was going to do it Himself. He would also provide a shepherd who would lead His people like no other. As we see God chastise and discipline the awful leaders and as we see Him reveal how He will lead His people, we can glean much from these chapters about leading our families and faith families.

When Ungodly Leaders Lead God's People, Everyone Suffers

EZEKIEL 34:1-10,17-22; 22:6-31

God Cares Not Only About Who Leads His People but How They Lead Them

There will never be a time that we inform God of something He does not already know. We may act like there is, but there is not. When we look at the world and the leaders in it, we may have seasons we think God cannot be aware of all they are doing, but He is. He knows what our president and congressional leaders are doing. The actions of our governor and state legislators do not catch Him off guard. He is not unaware of what our mayors, bosses, and principals are doing either. But perhaps we should be most reminded that He is keenly aware of what the leaders in our homes are doing. He knows all. He sees all. As Ezekiel 34 reveals, He cares both who is leading His people and how they are leading them, and He is fully aware of both.

God's People Lacked Godly Leaders (34:2-6; 22:6-31)

When ungodly leaders lead God's people, everyone suffers. One of Israel's greatest mistakes was rejecting God as their only King (1 Sam 8:1-22). Despite Samuel's warnings of how great the cost would be for them to have earthly kings, Israel refused to listen. Of Israel's 43 kings, only David, Hezekiah, and Josiah were consistently loyal to God. One wonders how many of our presidents have been godly as well.

In Ezekiel 14 a lack of godly elders was revealed, and in Ezekiel 34 we are shown a lack of godly shepherds, but in Ezekiel 22 we see that godliness was missing in every phase of leadership. Jerusalem's princes had used their strength to shed blood (22:6). Her prophets devoured people, seized wealth and valuables, and multiplied the widows within Jerusalem (v. 25). The priests in Jerusalem did violence to the Lord's instruction and profaned His holy things. They were not teaching the people basic truths about holiness (v. 26). With leaders like these, is it any wonder the people practiced extortion and committed robbery, oppressed the poor, and exploited the foreign residents among them (v. 29)? People learn by example.

Jerusalem had an absence of godly leadership in every way. As a result, God lamented, "I searched for a man among them who would repair the wall and stand in the gap before Me on behalf of the land so that I might not destroy it, but I found none" (v. 30). The people needed a leader like a certain youth minister I had who, when he wanted to challenge us to holiness on church trips, would hit repeat on Al Denson's "Be the One." For Jerusalem there was no leader on the political front, the religious front, or the home front to stand in the gap because they had all forgotten God (v. 12).

Instead of having leaders who were consumed with the glory of God and leading well for the good of the people, Israel's shepherds were only concerned with **feeding themselves** (34:2). They saw leadership as an opportunity for their advancement rather than the growth of those they led. They were selfish and lazy (v. 3). The shepherds wanted the benefits of leadership but not the burdens. Full of **violence and cruelty**, Israel's leaders had not **strengthened the weak, healed the sick, bandaged the injured, brought back the strays, or sought the lost** (v. 4). Unlike the shepherd in Christ's parable who leaves the 99 sheep in the open field and goes after the lost one until he finds it (Luke 15:3-7), Israel's leaders have lacked compassion and failed to exercise even basic care over the Lord's people.

As a consequence of lacking **a shepherd**, God's people **were scattered** and **became food for all the wild animals** (34:5). Yahweh's **flock went astray on all the mountains and every high hill. They were scattered over the whole face of the earth, and no one was searching or seeking for them** (v. 6).

Where There Are Bad Shepherds There Will Most Likely Be Bad Sheep (34:17-22)

While in college, I knew of a fraternity that had a history of hazing. At the end of my first semester, all of the actives were kicked out of the fraternity for how they treated their pledges, especially during initiation week. Having endured such brutal exercises, one would think as the newest and only actives now in the fraternity that last pledge class would change the cycle of cruel leadership. They did not. They treated the ones who came behind them in the same ways they had been treated. Bad leadership rarely fails to leave a wretched legacy.

The selfish leadership of Israel's shepherds was not without effect. What started with the leaders spread to the people. They were also greedy and destructive (vv. 17-19). Some of the stronger lay leaders abused the weaker ones (vv. 20-22). Their actions contributed to the Lord's flock being scattered (v. 21).

What effect is our leadership having on those for whom we are accountable? As a boss, elder, parent, coach, troop leader, or mentor, what example are we providing? Are there any negative actions you can identify in the people you lead that can directly be traced back to what you have demonstrated to them? Ungodly leadership on any level is never without consequence.

God Will Not Let His People Suffer Under Ungodly Leaders Forever (34:2,10)

Through Ezekiel, God is communicating to the shepherds of Israel that the time for fancying themselves has come to an end. He will say to them, "**Woe**," and, "**I am against [you]**." He would **demand** His **flock from them** and **prevent them from shepherding** ever again. **The shepherds** would **no longer feed themselves** because God was going to **rescue** His **flock from their mouths so that they will not be food for them.** The time for giving account as leaders to the Chief Shepherd arrived, and Israel's leaders were found wanting. God was going to step in and exercise care for His flock.

There Is No Greater Leader for God's People Than God Himself
EZEKIEL 34:11-16,23-31

God Will Give His People Protection and Provision (34:11-16)

When I was a child, one of my favorite TV shows was *The Dukes of Hazard*. At least once every week Uncle Jesse would grab his CB radio and call to his two nephews, "Shepherd to lost sheep. Shepherd to lost sheep. Y'all got your ears on?" Though God is chastising Israel's shepherds in Ezekiel 34, He will also comfort His people. He has a message for His lost sheep.

God may have given Israel different leaders, but He never gave Israel up. They were always His sheep, and He was always their ultimate Shepherd. Unlike their earthly leaders, God always led for their good. Through His prophet God informed His people that He would search for them (vv. 11-12,16), rescue them (vv. 10,12,22), gather them (v. 13), bandage them (v. 16), feed them (v. 14), strengthen them (v. 16), provide for them (vv. 14-15,29), and protect them (vv. 16-17,20,22,25,28). Can anyone remind me again why Israel wanted a different king than God?

What about us? God has authority over everyone and everything everywhere (Ps 95:3-5), but He uses His authority for our best (Ps 96:6-7). Instead of ruling like a harsh tyrant, God has chosen to relate to His people like a shepherd who leads his sheep. Because He always leads for our good, immediate obedience to Him is always in our best interest, and disobedience is always at our own peril.

What is staggering is that we do not deserve this type of leadership. In case we are viewing ourselves as defenseless, fluffy, innocent sheep who are worthy of a sacrificial leader, we should remember that, like Israel, we have often rejected God's leadership. Perhaps we have even hated it. In fact, every sin we commit is a profession we are really in charge. Each sin is an assertion of our reign and a demotion of His. And we are all guilty of it: "We all went astray like sheep; we all turned to our own way" (Isa 53:6).

Despite all of our rebellion and rejection, God has never wavered. He has rescued us and reconciled us to Himself. No other leader has loved us and led for our good like our God. Also, no other leader has sacrificed as much as God has in giving us His Son.

God Will Give His People a Prince (34:23-24)

On top of all the other blessings, God promised to give His people a true shepherd. He would **appoint over them a single shepherd**, His **servant David, and he** would **shepherd them**. The One Yahweh designated would **tend** God's people **himself and** would **be their shepherd. Yahweh** would **be their God,** and His **servant David** would **be a prince among them**. About this promise, Duguid asserts,

> The change to be wrought in Israel's situation is not so much
> a change in the nature of the office as in the nature of the
> occupant. God's solution to a history of bad shepherds is not
> to replace shepherding with a better system, but to replace the
> bad shepherds with a good shepherd. (Duguid, *Ezekiel*, 396)

What do we know about the shepherd God is describing? First, we know He will be appointed. There will not be an election by the people. God knows best, and He will give His people the best. Second, because He will be the single shepherd, He must be a sufficient one. Yahweh will not give His people many leaders but just one. Third, we know the shepherd will not be David because David is dead at the time Ezekiel is prophesying. That would be a bummer, would it not? Imagine God saying, "Hey, I've got this really great leader I'm going to give you. Only catch is, he's dead." So if David is not going to be resurrected to rule, then why is he referenced? I believe God is talking about David's lineage and also his legacy. David was Israel's greatest king. One will come from his line but will be even greater than David. Lastly, the One Yahweh appoints will not be aloof but will be among His people. He will not just exercise His reign above them but will establish His residence with them.

For the exiles in Babylon, this had to be wonderful news. They and their ancestors had suffered under ungodly leaders for generations. God would give them hope. God's words were not empty rhetoric on a campaign trail. He would provide a prince for His people who would reign with His heart.

What was good news for the exiles is even greater news for us. Unlike Ezekiel we know who the Shepherd-King is that God gave to His people. Luther wrote, "Dost ask who that might be? Christ Jesus it is He!" ("A Mighty Fortress Is Our God"). Jesus Himself has told us, "I am the good shepherd" (John 10:11). As our good shepherd, He is everything God told those in exile He would be. First, He is personal (John 10:1-6). He knows His sheep and helps them. Second, He provides for his flock (John 10:7-20). To His sheep He gives access (John 10:7-9) and abundance (John 10:10). For His sheep He makes atonement (John 10:15-18) for the purpose of their adoption. Finally, He protects His sheep (John 10:25-30). As the good shepherd He will never let His sheep perish, and He will never let them go. He will always be our shepherd (Rev 7:17).

Jesus is also our true Senior Pastor. After

> raising Him from the dead and seating Him at His right hand in the heavens, . . . [God] put everything under His feet and appointed [Christ] as head over everything for the church, which is His body, the fullness of the One who fills all things in every way. (Eph 1:20,22)

God has given His people the greatest leader the world has ever known. The One who has all authority is the One who has been appointed to be our Shepherd. This truth brings us to some important questions: Is it evident Jesus is the senior pastor of your faith family? Can people tell that He is your shepherd or does it look more like you are leading Him? Based on the description we have seen in Ezekiel 34 and John 10, why would we think anyone would be a better leader for us than Jesus?

God Will Give His People Peace (34:25-31)

God not only promised His people a prince but also **peace**. Yahweh would protect them (v. 25) and provide for them (vv. 26-27). They would be secure and feel safe because they would no longer have to fear (v. 28). Though at one time Israel had much reason to be anxious (12:17-20), God would make a **covenant** with them so they could **live securely in the wilderness and sleep in the forest** (34:25).

How would God give His people peace? By giving them His prince. Through Micah, God told Bethlehem,

> *One will come from you to be ruler over Israel for Me. His origin is from antiquity, from eternity. . . . He will stand and shepherd [God's people] in the strength of Yahweh, in the majestic name of Yahweh His God. They will live securely, for then His greatness will extend to the ends of the earth. He will be their peace.* (Mic 5:2,4-5)

Do you see it? He will not just *bring* them peace. He will *be* their peace because He is the Prince of peace (Isa 9:6).

One of the first verses I memorized as a child in Bible drill was Psalm 56:3. David says, "When I am afraid, I will trust in You," which is a bold claim considering he had been seized by the Philistines in Gath. I fear that too many of God's people live in fear today instead of peace. One reason they lack peace is because they lack prayer. They do not take advantage of the Lord's nearness and bring their requests to Him but would rather cling to their anxiety (Phil 4:5-6). I believe a second reason they lack peace is they have not grasped the full implications of the gospel. Maybe they believe there is some sin that is too wretched for the blood of Christ to cleanse. Perhaps they believe Jesus did a great work on the cross, but on top of that they just need to add their giving, and Bible study, and serving, and on and on. Christ, however, said, "It is finished" (John 19:30). For God's people every sin has been atoned, and the only work necessary has been achieved. May each of us rest in this gospel truth: "Therefore, since we have been declared righteous by faith, we have peace with God through our Lord Jesus Christ" (Rom 5:1). Our Prince is our peace.

God Will Give His People a Place (34:27,29)

In addition to protection, provision, a prince, and peace, God promises to give His people a place. God said, "**My flock will be secure in their** land," and "**I will establish for them a place renowned for its agriculture.**" In the land all the promises would accomplish their appointed purpose so God's people "**will know that I, Yahweh their God, am with them, and that they, the house of Israel, are My people**" (v. 30). Goldsworthy asserted that the main point of the Bible is the kingdom of God, and by this He means God's people in God's place under God's rule (*Gospel and Kingdom*, 54). Vaughn Roberts has amended Goldsworthy's definition to include God's blessing, for those under God's rule will certainly be blessed (v. 26) (*God's Big Picture*, 21).

Through Ezekiel, God will give His people in exile hope that Babylon will not be their final dwelling place. God will bring His people back to their land and will **make them and the area around** His **hill a blessing** (v. 26). The greatest blessing, however, will not be the place but His presence. John saw the ultimate fulfillment of this passage in the vision he received while on the isle of Patmos:

> *I saw a new heaven and a new earth, for the first heaven and the first earth passed away, and the sea no longer existed. I also saw the Holy City, new Jerusalem, coming down out of heaven from God, prepared like a bride adorned for her husband. Then I heard a loud voice from the throne: Look! God's dwelling is with humanity, and He will live with them. They will be His people, and God Himself will be with them and be their God.* (Rev 21:1-3)

What John sees is exactly what God described to Ezekiel. What a place!

Godly Leaders Are Still Needed Today in Both Our Families and Our Faith Families, and God Is Still Providing Them

God Continues to Provide Leaders for His People

Though Christ is our ultimate leader, He has continued to provide undershepherds for both our families and our faith families. To our congregations,

> *He personally gave some to be apostles, some prophets, some evangelists, some pastors and teachers, for the training of the saints in the work of ministry, to build up the body of Christ, until we all reach unity in the faith and in the knowledge of God's Son, growing into a mature man with a stature measured by Christ's fullness.* (Eph 4:11-13)

To our homes He has given husbands who are to love their wives "as Christ loved the church and gave Himself for her to make her holy, cleansing her with the washing of water by the word" (Eph 5:25-26). To our homes He has also given fathers who are not to "stir up anger" in their children, "but bring them up in the training and instruction of the Lord" (Eph 6:4).

As They Hear Us and See Us, Our Families and Faith Families Should Know What Jesus Is like as a Leader

Whether we shepherd an entire faith family or just our own family, those we lead should be able to see what Jesus is like as a leader. Just as Christ shepherds, so should we. Thomas contended,

> Christian ministers are to fashion their ministry on the standards set by the Chief Shepherd. They, too, are to give their lives in service, recalling that God's flock has been purchased by Christ's blood (Acts 20:28). They, too, are to lead their flock by the example of their own godliness and devotion (1 Peter 5:2-3). They, too, as Jesus exhorted Peter, are to feed their flock with the finest of the wheat (John 21:17). They, too, are to rule over their flock; the sheep are to "submit to their authority" (Heb 13:17). They, too, are to protect their flock from danger, refuting those who oppose sound doctrine (Titus 1:9). And they, too, are to seek the lost . . . God's "under-shepherds" are to be evangelists (2 Tim 4:5). (Thomas, *God Strengthens*, 226–27)

In order to lead for the glory of God and the good of our people, every elder at our church, with the help of the Holy Spirit, commits to the following:[4]

- We commit to love God with all of our heart, soul, and mind, to love our neighbor as ourselves, and to make disciples for the glory of God (Matt 22:37-40; 28:18-20).
- We commit to lovingly care for the members of Trace Crossing and seek their growth in Christ (Heb 13:17; 1 Thess 5:12).

---

[4] This list is not unique to our congregation but is used by many elder groups.

- We commit to provide teaching, preaching, and counsel from the Scriptures that spans the whole counsel of God's Word (Acts 20:27-28; Gal 6:6; 1 Tim 5:17-18).
- We commit to helping the faith family of Trace Crossing at all times but especially in times of need (Acts 2:42-47; 4:32-35; Jas 2:14-17).
- We commit to consistently strive to meet the criteria assigned to us in the Word (1 Tim 3:1-13; Titus 1:5-9; 1 Pet 5:1-4).
- We commit to pray for the members of Trace Crossing regularly, particularly when they are sick (Jas 5:14).
- We commit to be on guard against false teachers (Acts 20:28-31; Titus 1:9).
- We commit to exercise church discipline when necessary (Matt 18:15-20; 1 Cor 5; Gal 6:1).
- We commit to help our faith family become equipped to serve Christ (Eph 4:11-13).
- We commit to seek God's will for Trace Crossing, along with our fellow elders, to the best of our ability as we study the Scriptures and follow the Spirit (Acts 20:28; 1 Pet 5:1-5).
- We commit to set an example and join our faith family in fulfilling the duties of church membership (1 Cor 11:1; Phil 3:17; 1 Tim 4:12).

As a pastor I rarely have a day where I do not consider Hebrews 13:17. In this verse the author of Hebrews exhorts his audience, "Obey your leaders and submit to them, for they keep watch over your souls as those who will give an account." As the Lord's undershepherd, I never forget I am to keep watch over those entrusted to me and I will be held accountable to the task I have been charged. I take the charge so seriously that I encouraged the church where I currently serve to clarify our membership list when I first arrived because I wanted to know for whom I would be held accountable.

Every leadership opportunity is a stewardship, particularly ministry. God entrusts His message and His means to pastors for the maturity of His people. The flock belongs to God (Acts 20:28; 1 Pet 5:2). He purchased it with the blood of His Son (Acts 20:28). So I remind myself as often as possible, it's His church, His plans, His funds, and His glory. Nothing is more dangerous than a pastor who forgets these truths. As pastors we must be careful to build His kingdom and not our own.

My initial question to you was, "Who comes to mind when you hear the phrase *godly leader*?" Now I want to ask you, "Will anyone remember us as godly leaders?" What is the legacy we will leave behind? I heard someone say recently, "My father was the same man in the pulpit as he was at home, and I was drawn into the ministry." May we leave such a legacy of influence on those we lead!

Reflect and Discuss

1. Who are some of the godly leaders God has given to you? What do you remember most about them?
2. What are some of the consequences you've seen, either in your life or the lives of others, when godly leadership is lacking?
3. Have you ever served under a leader who you believe only looked out for himself or herself? What effect did that have on you and others?
4. How can we avoid leading just for our own good and our own renown? What accountability do you have in place to help you keep leading in a godly manner?
5. What is your response to how God says He will shepherd His people?
6. What characteristics of Christ's leadership can be seen in you, and which ones are more difficult to see?
7. In what ways would you like to demonstrate greater shepherding in your home?
8. In what ways would you like to grow as a godly leader in your work?
9. What are you thankful for with regard to those who lead in your faith family? What do you wish was different about their leadership? How can you help?
10. What is your intentional plan for leaving a legacy of godly leadership?

Regeneration: How and Why God Saves His People

EZEKIEL 35:1–36:38

Main Idea: God refuses to leave His people in the condition He finds them but provides all that is necessary to conform those He loves to the image of Christ.

I. **For the Sake of His Name, God Is Going to Transform His People.**
II. **God Will Have Mercy on Whom He Will Have Mercy.**
    A. How God treats His enemies: Repayment and removal (35:1-15)
    B. How God treats His people:
       1. God restores and gathers His people (36:24).
       2. God regenerates His people (36:25-27).
       3. God reconciles His people (36:28).
       4. God commands His people to remember (36:31-32).
       5. God renews the place for His people (36:30,33-36).
       6. God wants His people to request His help (36:37-38).
III. **Why God Saves in This Way**
IV. **Don't Miss the "Alls" (36:29,33).**

The question has been asked in a folk song, "What shall we do with a drunken sailor, early in the morning?" The suggestions offered include putting him in a long boat, locking him in the guard room, tying him to the taffrail, giving him a dose of salt and water, and sticking a mustard plaster on his back. I'm not even sure what a mustard plaster is, but I'm certain I would not want it on my back. The problem with these suggestions is they deal only with the *result* of the sailor's actions and not the *cause*. The focus is on the immediate consequences of his decision rather than preventing the situation from being repeated. We have our own suggestions for helping people too: Alcoholics Anonymous, Weight Watchers, anger management courses, etc.

How often have you said, "I will never do _____ again?" When did you end up doing _____ again? Maybe even before the ink dried on your commitment card? Resolutions have no power in themselves, and worse, those who make them are encouraged to look within for the potential to keep them. Looking within is the problem. What we do is driven by who we are, and our heart determines both of these. Our decisions and choices flow from what we love and desire, which is driven by our heart (Tripp and Tripp, *Instructing*, 52). Like the drunken sailor we do not need mere behavior modification but also heart surgery.

The admonition to get our act together is a death sentence if it is not accompanied by heart transformation. The form of Christianity I was discipled in emphasized doing better and being better but without connecting me with the power of the gospel to achieve either goal. Obedience to the imperatives in the biblical text was called for, but the imperatives were never partnered with the gospel indicatives. It was like receiving Ephesians 4–6 without founding its commands on Ephesians 1–3. Or more specifically, I was called to live Ephesians 6:1-3 without understanding that the ability to obey and honor my parents could only flow from Ephesians 5:18 and being filled with the Spirit. As a result, I struggled with behavior modification because willpower alone is not sufficient. Ask most dieters.

Concerning Ezekiel 35–36 we must ask, Is God setting Israel up for failure? With the exile of His people, did He only treat the decisions of Israel rather than their desires? He's going to give them a new leader (ch. 34) and a renewed land (ch. 36), but will He send the same old Israelites back home? God can change the location of His people, but if He does not change their sin-sick situation, then He will only continue to experience frustration.

All along we have been given clues that God's aim is never just the behavior of His people but their heart. In chapter 11 we were told,

> *I will give them one heart and put a new spirit within them; I will remove their heart of stone from their bodies and give them a heart of flesh, so they may follow My statutes, keep My ordinances, and practice them. Then they will be My people, and I will be their God.* (vv. 19-20)

Do not miss the phrase *so they may*. The new heart is what will enable His people to follow His statutes and keep His ordinances.

On the refrigerator of my childhood home, a magnet had these words painted on it: "God loves you just the way you are, but too much to let you stay that way." In the depth of our depravity, God loved us

(Rom 5:6,8). But His love transforms. He does not leave us in the condition He finds us. His ultimate aim is that we will be conformed to the image of Christ (Rom 8:29). Ezekiel 35–36 contains a magnificent picture of God not leaving the people He loves in the same condition. Not only will they have the best leader (ch. 34) and a renewed land, but they themselves will also be saved **from all** their uncleanness (36:29). God is going to act for their good and His glory (36:22).

For The Sake of His Name, God Is Going to Transform His People

For many years people believed the sun revolved around the earth. They also believed you could sail to the end of the world and fall off, but that is another lesson. We know now that the earth and the other planets in our galaxy (including the rock formerly known as a planet—Pluto) revolve around the sun. At one time we lacked proper knowledge and perspective to possess a right understanding of how our galaxy worked. We do this with God as well. For some reason we are prone to view ourselves as the center of the universe and God revolves around us doing our bidding like a genie. In particular He is supposed to give us a good marriage, a fulfilling job, and an amazing house, and He is supposed to protect us from dreaded diseases. Of course, in our self-absorbed worlds, God is not the only one who is to follow our agenda but also everyone else around us.

When God acts, He always does so primarily for His glory and secondarily for our good. God wanted Israel to have a proper perspective on the actions He would take in Ezekiel 36. He was not rescuing them because they were great but because He is. He is not even delivering Judah because they have repented but so that He might lead them to repentance.

Because we tend to be dull-minded people, God clearly articulated His primary purpose. He said, **"It is not for your sake that I will act, house of Israel, but for My holy name, which you profaned among the nations where you went."** This should not have been a new thought for His people (2 Kgs 19:34; 20:6). Israel's special relationship with God was not because of anything inherent but because of what God imputed to them. He always acts for the glory of His renown.

God Will Have Mercy on Whom He Will Have Mercy

How God Treats His Enemies: Repayment and Removal (35:1-15)

Just as you might have been missing God's pronouncements of judgments, Ezekiel 35 pops onto the scene. The presence of this chapter is one more opportunity to crush any universalism that might be rolling around in our hearts with the foolish notion everything is going to turn out well for everyone, including God's enemies. Edom, or **Mount Seir**, was guilty of maintaining **an ancient hatred** and handing **over the Israelites to the power of the sword in the time of their disaster** (v. 5). The Edomites also failed to **hate bloodshed** (v. 6), they declared Israel would be their possession (vv. 10,12), and, worst of all, they **boasted against** God and **spoke many words against** Him (v. 13). Of course, God **heard** it Himself (v. 15). He did not need anyone else to let Him know what Edom was doing and saying.

Instead of extending mercy, God is going to treat Edom **according to the anger and jealousy** they showed in their **hatred** of God's people (v. 11). As a result **Mount Seir** will be made a desolate waste forever (vv. 3-4,7,9,14-15). Through His judgment the Edomites will know He is **Yahweh** (v. 15). In all these actions God will be completely fair.

One might be led to ask, Why does Edom receive judgment but Israel receive mercy? Both nations clearly deserved God's wrath. One will receive it in such a way that it ruins them, and the other will walk through the discipline and be restored. Why God extends mercy to some but not to all is determined within His own counsel. The most important question we should be asking is, How can I not be God's enemy? The answer has been provided all along the way. Turn from your sin and live. Stop walking in wickedness and walk in His righteousness. Edom is being repaid for their sin and removed from their land because they lacked repentance. If we do not want the same to happen to us, then we should heed Christ's words: "Unless you repent, you will all perish as well" (Luke 13:3,5).

How God Treats His People

Israel deserved to be treated in the same manner as Edom (36:16-21). They were just as guilty of rebellion and of lacking repentance. God's people polluted their land with bloodshed and idolatry (v. 18), and they profaned God's name everywhere they were scattered (v. 20). Their exile caused the nations to question God's goodness and sovereignty. Every other nation knew Israel was the **people of Yahweh; yet they had to leave His land in exile** (v. 20).

Yes, Israel deserved to be treated in the same manner as Edom, but they would not be. Like Edom they would be punished, but unlike Edom they would be preserved. While Edom received only judgment, Israel would receive mercy. Their discipline would not lead to ruin but restoration because God had concern for His holy name (v. 21).

In the salvation of His people, God is not passive. If He were, we would all perish. In Ezekiel 36 God's active participation in the salvation of His people is seen clearly. Yahweh will gather His people **from all the countries** and **bring** them into their own land (v. 24). He will **sprinkle clean water** on them and **cleanse** them from all their **impurities** and **idols** (v. 25). He will give them a **new heart and put a new spirit within** them; He will **remove** their **heart of stone and give** them **a heart of flesh** (v. 26). Yahweh will **place** His **Spirit within** His people and **cause** them to **follow** His **statutes and carefully observe** His **ordinances** (v. 27). He will save them from all their uncleanness and **summon the grain and make it plentiful** (v. 29). God will also **make the fruit of the trees and the produce of the field plentiful, so that** His people **will no longer experience reproach among the nations on account of famine** (v. 30). Over and over, Yahweh says, "I will," "I will," "I will." Nothing in this paragraph is what Israel will do for itself but all that He will do for them. God is not sitting back and hoping for the salvation of His people; He is accomplishing it. Let's take a closer look now at how God treats His children differently from how He treats His enemies.

God restores and gathers His people (36:24). I've heard it said what seems like a setback can be a setup for an impressive comeback. This was never truer than for the people of God. In discipline God sent His people into exile, but He would not leave them there. He was frustrated by their actions but He was not finished with them as His people. He was going to **take** them **from the nations and gather** them **from all the countries,** and **bring** His people into their own land. He can "take" them from the nations because He gave them to the nations. The other countries host Israel only as long as God wills it and not one second longer. Even if the nations or their rulers wanted to stop God from gathering His people, they could not. Just ask the pharaoh in Exodus and the one in Ezekiel.

I love that God gathers those who cannot assemble themselves. He does not tell His people, "Come to Me," but, "I will come to you. I will come and get you (which means He knows exactly where they all are), and I will lead you out of captivity." He has experience with this (see Exodus). Of course, the greatest exodus will be when He leads His people out of captivity from sin and death. What occurs in Ezekiel with God's people and the nations pales in comparison to when God will set His people free from the clutches and sting of death (1 Cor 15:55-57).

God regenerates His people (36:25-27). God does not just gather His people but also cleanses and changes them. He says, "**I will also sprinkle clean water on you, and you will be clean**" (v. 25). He is not washing away sickness they acquired while in the other nations but sins they carried there with them. He says, "**I will cleanse you from all your impurities and all your idols**." Please note: God does not say, "Clean yourself up and then come to Me." I'm afraid this is exactly what some believe they have to do to become a Christian. If that were the case, then no one would ever be clean or come to God. No, He says, "I will gather you in all of your wretchedness and I will wash you and make you new." He does the same for us (John 13:8; Eph 2:1-10).

Why the sprinkling and washing? We do not need to be just forgiven of our sin but also cleansed and healed from it (Muller, *Honor and Shame*, 56–68). There are no little sins, and no one has just a little bit of dirt on them. We are filthy, and we are sick. We need to be forgiven. We need to be healed. We need to be cleansed. Toplady said so rightly, "Wash me, Savior, or I die" (Augustus Toplady, "Rock of Ages, Cleft for Me," 1763). While our baptism is a remarkable picture of this cleansing, water can never do for us what the blood of Christ does.

The author of Hebrews contends,

> *If the blood of goats and bulls and the ashes of a young cow, sprinkling those who are defiled, sanctify for the purification of the flesh, how much more will the blood of the Messiah, who through the eternal Spirit offered Himself without blemish to God, cleanse our consciences from dead works to serve the living God? . . . Let us draw near with a true heart in full assurance of faith, our hearts sprinkled clean from an evil conscience and our bodies washed in pure water.*
> (Heb 9:13-14; 10:22)

Likewise, John says, "If we walk in the light as He Himself is in the light, we have fellowship with one another, and the blood of Jesus His Son cleanses us from all sin" (1 John 1:7). Only Christ's blood can "be of sin the double cure; save from wrath and make me pure" (Augustus Toplady, "Rock of Ages, Cleft for Me," 1763).

We do not need just to be cleansed but also changed. Salvation is not just information but also transformation. God does not leave His people in the condition that He gathers them. He gives them a new heart, and He places His Spirit within them (33:26-27; cf. Eph 1:13-14; Titus 3:4-7). The heart surgery God performs produces a change of desire in His people, which leads to a change in deeds. Having been purified and now empowered by His presence, God's people follow His statutes and observe His ordinances (36:27). What Solomon prayed for (1 Kgs 8:57-58) we know in reality (Phil 2:13; Titus 2:11-14). In bringing His people back to His land, God was not interested in business as usual but business as it had never been.

God reconciles His people (36:28). The point of the first exodus is the point of the second exodus in Ezekiel and the point of the greatest exodus through the cross of Christ: "**You will be my people, and I will be your God.**" The purpose of reconciliation is relationship. I fear many people are more excited about the secondary blessings of heaven, such as seeing loved ones, than they are about the primary blessing of dwelling with God. The point of the gospel is not that we get heaven or streets of gold but that we get God. Yahweh gathers and changes His people that He might dwell with them in a special manner.

Considering reconciliation, we often think of two parties who disagree and move in opposite directions. In God's reconciling the people of Israel, however, they walked away from Him, but He never walked away from them. In fact, He goes and gets them while they are away and brings them back into a right relationship with Himself. He will not be unfaithful though they have been repeatedly. They will be His people, and He will be their God.

How is the reconciliation of God's people achieved? There is but one means—Christ. Paul informs us, "Everything is from God, who reconciled us to Himself through Christ and gave us the ministry of reconciliation" (2 Cor 5:18). The only way for us to be His people and for Him to be our God is *through Christ.* What God declares in Ezekiel was achieved at the cross of Christ and will be ultimately experienced in the new Jerusalem (Rev 21:3).

God commands His people to remember (36:31-32). While God forgives our sins, He does not necessarily want us to forget them. Even after they are restored to their land, God commands Israel to **"remember your evil ways and your deeds that were not good, and you will loathe yourselves for your iniquities and detestable practices."** He also tells them to **"be ashamed and humiliated because of your ways, house of Israel."**

God has a twofold purpose in commanding His people not to forget their evil ways and deeds. The first purpose is that remembering will hopefully prevent repetition. He wants them to loathe the way they used to live. Only after God gives us a new heart does the possibility exist for us to hate sin. After reconciliation and regeneration, God's people should be described as running from sin and not toward it. John contends that once we have yielded our lives to Christ we cannot continue in our previous ways. He says, "If we say, 'We have fellowship with Him,' yet we walk in darkness, we are lying and are not practicing the truth" (1 John 1:6). Those who claim to have met Christ but do not forsake their evil ways and deeds have been only informed of the gospel but not transformed by it.

The second purpose God has in commanding His people not to forget their iniquities is so their only boast of rescue will be in God. They are constantly to remember that it was not their goodness that achieved their deliverance but His. Paul never forgot who he was prior to his conversion, which is why his only boast was in Christ. Duguid notes, "As we grow in the gospel we do not view ourselves in a better and better light" (*Ezekiel*, 423–24). To prevent spiritual amnesia, God wants His people to remember that He loved them in their worst state and still chose to rescue them. He alone deserves all the glory and praise.

God renews the place for His people (36:8-12, 30, 33-36). God alone brings beauty from ashes. He will see that the ruins are rebuilt (vv. 10,33) and that the land is replanted (v. 8). He will remove the curse of famine and cause the **fruit of the trees and the produce of the field** to be **plentiful** (v. 30). He will provide for His people, and the nations that remain around them will know that He alone has **replanted what was desolate** (v. 36).

God wants His people to request His help (36:37-38). Prayer is a privilege. God is not obligated to respond to every request. He is not even obligated to listen to requests (14:3). He wants His people to know, however, if they ask Him to **multiply them in number** then He **will respond to the house of Israel and do this for them** (36:37). They can know God will answer their prayer, but His answer is linked to their asking.

In His providence God has ordained our prayers to be part of the plan. If prayer is unimportant or ineffectual, then Jesus and Paul both wasted a lot of time. God wants us to ask because in prayer we admit our dependence on Him. In Ezekiel, when the **ruined cities** are **filled with a flock of people,** it will be because God has given the increase in response to His people's intercessions (v. 38).

I fear we often do not ask God too much but too little. He delights to answer prayers according to His will, and the best way to know His will is to know His Word. The prayers of His people are not a burden to Him. The God of heaven wants us to cast all of our cares on Him (1 Pet 5:7). Your congressman may not want you to do this, but your God does. He wants you to rely on Him fully. For the generation restored to Israel, they will not have a lot of children just because they are fertile but because God is faithful.

Why God Saves in This Way

The purpose of Edom's removal and Israel's restoration is the same: God's revelation. Both His people and His enemies will know He is Yahweh (35:4,9,12,15; 36:11,23,36,38). There will be no questioning who has brought about Israel's deliverance and Edom's destruction. Primarily, He does all things for the sake of His holy name (36:21-23,32). We can become egocentric and elevate God's actions as mainly being about us, but they are really about Him. His restoration of Israel is not even driven most by His love for His people but in order to demonstrate His holiness through them (36:23).

Is it wrong for God to care primarily about His glory and secondarily about our good? Nothing God ever does is wrong. His holiness means that both His attitudes and His actions are always perfect and pure. For God to seek His own glory is right because He above all others and all things is worthy of such glory. Were He to seek someone else's glory above His own, then this other would be more worthy of worship than God. So in punishing His enemies and in purifying His people, God is saying, "Look at Me." Specifically, "Look at My holiness and consider My greatness. See the folly in your idols and turn to Me. Do not set your heart in unworthy places."

Because God's greatest pursuit is the glory of His name, this should be our aim in all things as well. In our homes, jobs, schools, cities, and the world, let all we do be for the sake of His renown. May no one doubt He is Yahweh by what they see and hear in us.

Don't Miss the "Alls"

EZEKIEL 36:29,33

Before closing Ezekiel 36, I want us to consider two final verses but one major point. In verse 29 God says He is going to save His people from *all* their uncleanness. In verse 33 God says He is going to cleanse His people from *all* their iniquities. Don't miss the "alls." What God sets out to do He does completely. God does not only have the power to take away some of our sin but all of it. Through the cross of Christ, God has saved us from sin's entire penalty and has broken its power. The day is coming when the full measure of Ezekiel 36 will be experienced and God will remove sin's presence from His people forever. We will never disappoint Him again or bring reproach on His name. We will never have to seek His forgiveness but fully live in obedience to Him and delight in Him. We will know then what we sing now:

> Dear dying Lamb, Thy precious blood
> Shall never lose its pow'r
> Till all the ransomed church of God
> Be saved, to sin no more.
> (William Cowper, "There is a Fountain," 1772)

Reflect and Discuss

1. Why can true and lasting change never come from behavior modification alone?
2. Why do we so often try to deal with behavior rather than deal with the heart? How do you aim toward the heart of your children or those you are discipling and not just their actions?
3. Why is it good and right that God acts most for His name and not ours? If we considered your actions, then whose name would we think you lived for most?
4. Have you ever struggled with the truth that God is free to extend or withhold His mercy? How did the Lord bring you to peace on the issue?
5. How can we minimize causing people to doubt God's goodness and power by the way we live our lives?
6. Why is God active in the salvation of His people instead of being passive? What evidences of His actions can be seen in your salvation?

7. Why do you think some people believe they have to clean themselves up before coming to God? Why is this impossible?

8. If the point of reconciliation is relationship, then how's that going between you and God? Are you more excited about secondary blessings or the fact that God gives Himself to you?

9. Even though God forgives our sins, why does He not want us to fully forget them? How can we maintain a proper balance between remembering but also knowing they have been removed from us?

10. Is prayer a privilege to you? Are there any ways you believe you are asking for too little in prayer rather than too much? How can we pray according to His will?

Alive and United

EZEKIEL 37:1-28

Main Idea: For His glory and by His Spirit and word, God delivers His people from death and division and brings us into life and unity.

I. **Alive: God Delivers His People from Death (37:1-14).**
II. **United: God Delivers His People from Division (37:15-28).**

The angel Gabriel declared to Mary, "Nothing will be impossible with God" (Luke 1:37). Whether it is defeating a giant with a stone and slingshot, making walls fall down with horns and shouts, being in the middle of a fire and coming out of it without a hair singed or the slightest scent of smoke, or in Mary's case, being a virgin yet delivering the Son of God, nothing is impossible with God. As familiar as we are with this truth, some of us may struggle to believe it. We may believe it generally, "I know God can do great things," but doubt it specifically, "I do not believe God can do anything with some of the situations I am in." Doubt leads to despair, and despair leads to hopelessness.

Have you ever felt hopeless about something or maybe even someone? I used to feel this way about my father's salvation. I prayed and prayed and prayed, but if God was moving in his life, I struggled to see it. On December 18, 1997, however, I had the privilege of leading my father to Christ. I wept as I did, finding Luke 1:37 to be more true than ever. Some of you may feel that your current situation is not going to change, that you are never going to change, or that your spouse, children, boss, neighbor, or friend is never going to change. Gandhi encouraged us to be the change. I prefer Christ's message though: "Come to me and be changed." Whatever your "hopeless" situation is, would you give it to Him right now? Completely and fully believe He is able to do all that His holy will desires. If you have been tempted to give up and quit praying about something, do not! Keep asking. Keep knocking. Keep travailing in prayer.

Where we pick up in Ezekiel 37, Israel certainly felt hopeless. As a matter of fact, they admitted it. They said, "**Our bones are dried up, and our hope has perished; we are cut off**" (v. 11). At this point they have been in exile for at least 12 years (33:21), Jerusalem has fallen, the temple has been destroyed, many have been slaughtered, and despite all Ezekiel has preached to them, they have lost hope. I am sure somewhere deep down they knew nothing was impossible with God, but whether they believed that is up for debate. Would we? Do we?

Israel's feelings of hopelessness should not be completely foreign to us. As we encounter their struggle in Ezekiel 37, we should keep in mind we were once hopeless too. In fact, we are even commanded to remember it. In his letter to the church at Ephesus, Paul wrote 33 verses without giving a command. When he finally issues an imperative, it is for the church to "remember." What is it Paul wants them (and us) to remember? He says,

> *Remember that at one time you were Gentiles in the flesh—called "the uncircumcised" by those called "the circumcised," which is done in the flesh by human hands. At that time you were without the Messiah, excluded from the citizenship of Israel, and foreigners to the covenants of the promise, without hope and without God in the world.* (Eph 2:11-12)

Piper helps us understand more about what Paul meant by remembering our hopelessness:

> Therefore, when Paul says to us, "Remember that you were without God," he didn't just mean, "Remember that you once lacked some knowledge about God." He meant, "Remember that God was once not your God, and that he would not be yet, apart from the gospel." And if he was not our God, then he was not for us but against us; he was not our justifier but our condemner; not eternal life but eternal damnation lay before us. And it's just this that Paul wants us to remember. Remember that apart from Christ, almighty God would be against us; apart from Christ, we would be storing up wrath for ourselves on the day of the righteous judgment of God (Romans 2:4,5; Ephesians 2:3); apart from the free and unmerited mercy of Christ, we would go away into "eternal punishment" (Matthew 25:46). Or, as Paul says in a single phrase, we would be utterly "without hope." (Piper, "Remember")

We should always remember that at one time we were Christless, stateless, friendless, hopeless, and godless. We should also remember that God did not leave us this way. While we once were hopeless, we are not anymore. We can actually rejoice in hope because we know, "This hope will not disappoint us, because God's love has been poured out in our hearts through the Holy Spirit who was given to us" (Rom 5:5).

Ezekiel's generation should have been full of hope as well. They were told, "'For I know the plans I have for you'—this is the LORD's declaration—'plans for your welfare, not for disaster, to give you a future and a hope'" (Jer 29:11). They had either forgotten this word or chosen not to believe it. God, however, would not just restore their hope but resurrect His people and reestablish them in their land.

Alive: God Delivers His People from Death
EZEKIEL 37:1-14

As God's prophet, Ezekiel has been privileged to see breathtaking visions. In chapter 37 he is shown what most people probably think of when the book of Ezekiel is mentioned. It would actually be interesting to see what else our people know about the prophet besides this vision. My guess is not much.

God is going to take Ezekiel and set him down in the ultimate Death Valley. What he sees is in stark contrast to Ezekiel 36:33-36. Instead of seeing fruitful trees and vegetation bursting from the ground, he sees bones. The valley was full of them, and **they were very dry** (37:1-2). The Lord **led** Ezekiel **all around them** (v. 2). The prophet's inspection lets him know this valley is full of death and that decomposition finished its work long ago. Why does God do this? He wants Ezekiel to see that Israel is not near death but totally dead.

Both Moses and Jeremiah tried to warn God's people. Moses told them if they did not keep the covenant,

> the LORD will cause you to be defeated before your enemies. You will
> march out against them from one direction but flee from them in
> seven directions. You will be an object of horror to all the kingdoms
> of the earth. Your corpses will be food for all the birds of the sky
> and the wild animals of the land, with no one to scare them away.
> (Deut 28:25-26)

Through Jeremiah, God repeated the same message for those who refused to keep the covenant. God told them they would be handed over to their enemies and their corpses would "become food for the birds of the sky and for the wild animals of the land" (Jer 34:20). God never lies.

After God parades Ezekiel through the bones, He asks him, "**Son of man, can these bones live**" (37:3)? If Ezekiel were on a television game show, this might be the time that he wants to phone a friend. Resuscitation was not unheard of in the Old Testament. Ezekiel most certainly would have known of the experiences Elijah (1 Kgs 17) and Elisha (2 Kgs 4) had when they prayed and saw a child brought back to life. But in both of these examples, the gap between the time of death and the resuscitation was narrow. In the valley where Ezekiel is currently standing, not only had death occurred but also decomposition. All of the flesh has been disintegrated leaving just the bones, which have been exposed for so long they have been dried and bleached by the sun. An interesting question indeed, "Can *these* bones live?"

The question is never whether God has the *power* to do something but rather if He *wills* to do it. When God is referred to as omnipotent, it means He has all the power He needs to accomplish whatever He desires in accordance with His holiness. By what He has seen and heard from God over the past 12 years, Ezekiel knows God *can* raise these bones. What Ezekiel does not know is whether that is what God desires, so he responds to God's question, "**Lord GOD, only You know**" (v. 3). Great answer. Under the influence of the same Spirit as Ezekiel, Paul would write hundreds of years later that God alone "gives life to the dead and calls things into existence that do not exist" (Rom 4:17).

So, what's the plan in the valley? Is there a solution for the situation? Is God going to bring life? Yes and He's going to use Ezekiel in the process, but you probably knew that by now. The Lord told Ezekiel, "**Prophesy concerning these bones and say to them: Dry bones, hear the word of the LORD**" (v. 4). Ezekiel should not be totally caught off guard. Prior to this vision he has been asked to preach to mountains, to forests, and to people who listen like brick walls.

If Ezekiel had any questions or hesitations, they are not recorded. To my shame, I know I would have had some questions. Instead of instant obedience, I too often wrestle with the Lord's plan. Instead of saying, "Yes Sir! Right away, Sir," I tend to ask, "You want me to do what?" I'm sure I would have had a sarcastic response such as, "So, the solution for a valley full of very dry bones to live again is a sermon? Does it need three alliterated points and a poem?"

Based on what we know of Ezekiel's obedience up to this point, what do you think he is going to do? You guessed it. In verses 7 and 10 we find that Ezekiel prophesied both times as he was commanded. Because he trusted and obeyed, Ezekiel saw God do some amazing things (vv. 7-8). What about us? What are we seeing God do because we believe Him and obey Him? What are we missing out on because we do not?

Bringing the dry bones in the valley back to life will be a two-part process involving both God's word and His Spirit. Why is the word necessary? Not only because it is alive (Heb 4:12) but also because it brings life (1 Pet 1:23). Two of the greatest steps we can take to be used mightily in evangelism are praying and memorizing God's Word. If we hide the Word in our hearts, then the Spirit can bring its gospel message to our lips and use it to bring others to life. Paul says, "So faith comes from what is heard, and what is heard comes through the message about Christ" (Rom 10:17). The church at Ephesus was informed, "When you heard the message of truth, the gospel of your salvation, and when you believed in Him, you were also sealed with the promised Holy Spirit" (Eph 1:13). Without the word and someone faithful like Ezekiel to proclaim it, dry bones will never live.

The second part of the resuscitation in the valley is the work of Spirit. We are born because God forms us, but we are reborn because God fills us. Ezekiel is told, "**Prophesy to the breath, prophesy, son of man. Say to it: This is what the Lord God says: Breath, come from the four winds and breathe into these slain so that they may live**" (v. 9). Just like Adam in Genesis 2, they may look alive when they are formed, but they are made alive when His Spirit fills them. Ezekiel says, "**The breath entered them, and they came to life and stood on their feet, a vast army**" (v. 10). Ezekiel knew exactly what the Spirit's empowering felt like (2:2).

Ezekiel could preach with confidence because God promised to act as Ezekiel prophesied. God would cause breath to enter the bones and make them live (37:5). God would put tendons on the bones, make flesh grow, and cover them with skin (v. 6). Ezekiel's role was to prophesy, and God's role was to produce the results. It's the same for us. Our responsibility is proclamation, and God's work is regeneration. We may not see physically what Ezekiel was shown, but God is still bringing life from death through the preaching of His Word.

So, what was the purpose of the vision and the field trip to valley of death? Ezekiel is told, **"These bones are the whole house of Israel. Look how they say, 'Our bones are dried up, and our hope has perished; we are cut off"** (v. 11). The bones, which seem to have zero possibility of ever knowing life again, reveal how Israel feels about their discipline and exile. They believe God is finished with them. They have received the curses of the covenant and have been cut off. If God were to ask Israel instead of Ezekiel whether the bones in the vision could live again, they would answer with a resounding no! All hope was gone.

God, however, had a plan to give His people life and land. He told Ezekiel,

> *Say to them: This is what the Lord GOD says: I am going to open your graves and bring you up from them, My people, and lead you into the land of Israel. You will know that I am Yahweh, My people, when I open your graves and bring you up from them. I will put My Spirit in you, and you will live, and I will settle you in your own land. Then you will know that I am Yahweh. I have spoken, and I will do it.* (37:12-14)

Let all despair flee. God had determined to deliver His people, and nothing would stand in His way.

Even though the house of Israel felt forsaken, they were not. They were still His people, and this speaks to His faithfulness more than theirs. Despite all they had done to rebel against Him, God would still deliver His people from the nations in which they were exiled and lead them back to their land. He is not acting because they were good but because He is, which should give all of us hope.

Without Christ we are as bad and as dead as Israel ever was. Paul reminds the Colossians, "Once you were alienated and hostile in your minds because of your evil actions" (Col 1:21). To the church at Ephesus, he painted an even bleaker picture. He says,

> *You were dead in your trespasses and sins in which you previously walked according to the ways of this world, according to the ruler who exercises authority over the lower heavens, the spirit now working in the disobedient. We too all previously lived among them in our fleshly desires, carrying out the inclinations of our flesh and thoughts, and we were by nature children under wrath as the others were also.* (Eph 2:1-3)

We were no beauty queens ourselves, but like Israel God gives us life through Christ (Eph 2:4). God can bring us through the valley of death because He first brought Christ through it (1 Cor 15:20-23).

Just as the bones were resuscitated with a purpose of being an army, so we've been filled with the Spirit for a reason. We have work to do. "For we are His creation, created in Christ Jesus for good works, which God prepared ahead of time so that we should walk in them" (Eph 2:10). We are regenerated for the reason of making disciples for His renown.

United: God Delivers His People from Division
EZEKIEL 37:15-28

As further evidence that God does not want things to be as they were before the exile, He will not only bring His people from the nations but He will also bring them together. He will save them not only from death but also from division. God's people will be both alive and united. In order to convey this message, Ezekiel is given one more sign act to perform.

The prophet is told to **take a single stick and write on it: belonging to Judah and the Israelites associated with him** (v. 16). He is then told to take **another stick and write on it: Belonging to Joseph—the stick of Ephraim—and all the house of Israel associated with him** (v. 16). He is then told to join the sticks together so they become one stick in his hand (v. 17). Why is God asking Ezekiel to do this? Because He will have "one nation obedient to one king and worshipping one God" (Wiersbe, *Be Reverent*, 198). They will be united, cleansed, and walking together in God's ways and in submission to God's shepherd (vv. 20-24).

Not only will they be healed from their disobedience and their division, but also they will dwell with the Lord forever (vv. 25-28). Yahweh will make a **covenant of peace** with His people, and it will be an **everlasting covenant** (v. 26). He will never break His word. He will never forsake them. He will **establish and multiply** His people and will set His **sanctuary among them forever** (v. 26). When He dwells with His people, the aim of all the discipline will be achieved. Both Israel and the nations will know He is Yahweh who sanctifies His people (v. 28). God will do all that is necessary for His people to dwell securely in His presence forever.

Though this prophecy awaits its ultimate fulfillment (Rev 20–21), God is uniting and dwelling with His people now (1 Cor 6:19). Paul tells us:

But now in Christ Jesus, you who were far away have been brought near by the blood of the Messiah. For He is our peace, who made both groups one and tore down the dividing wall of hostility. In His flesh, He made of no effect the law consisting of commands and expressed in regulations, so that He might create in Himself one new man from the two, resulting in peace. He did this so that He might reconcile both to God in one body through the cross and put the hostility to death by it. When the Messiah came, He proclaimed the good news of peace to you who were far away and peace to those who were near. For through Him we both have access by one Spirit to the Father. So then you are no longer foreigners and strangers, but fellow citizens with the saints, and members of God's household, built on the foundation of the apostles and prophets, with Christ Jesus Himself as the cornerstone. The whole building, being put together by Him, grows into a holy sanctuary in the Lord. You also are being built together for God's dwelling in the Spirit. (Eph 2:13-22)

Through the cross of Christ, we are reconciled both to God and to fellow believers. He is working to unite His people from every nation, tribe, people, and language (Rev 7:9). Who else but God can bring together people from such diversity and see them flourish in unity as they serve one King? All of this reveals His wisdom (Eph 3:10). Piper notes,

> The point is that God aims to create one new people in Christ who are reconciled to each other across racial lines. Not strangers. Not aliens. No enmity. Not far off. Fellow citizens of one Christian "city of God." One temple for a habitation of God. And he did this at the cost of his Son's life. We love to dwell on our reconciliation with God through the death of his Son. And well we should. It is precious beyond measure—to have peace with God (Romans 5:9-10).
>
> But let us also dwell on this: that God ordained the death of his Son to reconcile alien people groups to each other in one body in Christ. This too was the design of the death of Christ. Think on this: Christ died to take enmity and anger and disgust and jealousy and self-pity and fear and envy and hatred and malice and indifference away from your heart toward all other persons who are in Christ by faith—whatever the race. (Piper, "Race and Cross")

I am so thankful all of our disagreements as a faith family are only temporary. One day God will move in our lives in such a powerful way that not only will we no longer sin against one another but we will also never sin against Him. The only way for God to set His sanctuary with His people is to sanctify His people, and this is exactly what He said He would do (37:28). While we wait for the full measure of God's deliverance from death and division let us be "diligently keeping the unity of the Spirit with the peace that binds us" (Eph 4:3).

Reflect and Discuss

1. Why do we sometimes doubt that all things are possible with God? Though we know the truth, why do we act as if some situations are impossible for God to change?
2. Have you ever felt forsaken or cut off from God? What caused this? How was it resolved?
3. What role does God's Word play in bringing spiritual life? Why should our evangelistic presentations be saturated with Scripture?
4. In what ways have you experienced the Spirit's empowering?
5. What hope can be found in Ezekiel 37 for a person who feels their sin has more power to damn than Christ's blood has to save?
6. In what ways does Ezekiel's obedience continue to challenge you? How can we move toward immediate obedience to the Lord in our lives?
7. Is your faith family united around the gospel or something else? What does it look like when a congregation strives together for the gospel?
8. In what ways are you working toward unity in your faith family, and in what ways are you causing disunity? Is there anyone you need to forgive or seek his or her forgiveness?
9. When you consider dwelling with the Lord forever, what thoughts come to your mind?
10. What do you think it will be like when sin is no longer a possibility for us? How grateful will you be?

When Bad News Is Good News

EZEKIEL 38:1–39:29

Main Idea: God always has a purpose and provision for what His people face as He works all things for His glory and their good.

I.   As Jesus Said, We Will Have Suffering in This World (38:1-16).
II. Because God Is Sovereign, Our Suffering Is Never Without Purpose (38:16,23; 39:6-7,21-22,28).
III. Because God Is Sovereign, Our Suffering Is Never Without Provision (38:17-22; 39:3-5).
IV. God's Victory in Christ Means Ultimate Defeat for His Enemies (39:6,11-20).
V.   God's Victory in Christ Means Ultimate Security for His People (39:9-10,25-29).
VI. What Ezekiel 38–39 Can Teach Us About God

How do you like to receive bad news? If you are like me, then you do not like to receive it at all. I especially dislike when someone informs me they have both good and bad news and ask which I prefer to hear first. Don't they know that as soon as they say the phrase *bad news* I cannot hear anything else? If I have to pick, then give me the bad news first. I usually cannot enjoy the good news until I know how bad the bad news really is.

When my wife was pregnant with our youngest son, Alastair, we scheduled a precautionary visit with a perinatologist. We did so because our first child, Arabella, was born with a ventricular septal defect that we did not discover until she was around four weeks old. With each additional child we have sought extra screening so that we would be as informed as possible of their medical condition when they were delivered. On this particular visit with Alastair, the technician conducting the ultrasound noticed something and for a moment forgot to hide her reaction. After a few moments the perinatologist came into our ultrasound room. He apparently noticed whatever the technician had seen because he asked, "Did you see that before?"

She responded, "Yes," and continued the screening.

When the ultrasound was finished, the doctor requested a picture be printed and then walked with us to an exam room. He placed the picture facedown and asked us what felt like a million questions. One would not need to be Sherlock Holmes to deduce that something was wrong. Because I knew bad news was looming, I prayed and asked for God to calm my anxious heart. Once the doctor got around to discussing the ultrasound picture, he revealed that our son had at least a cleft lip and most likely a cleft palate. He also shared that this "deformity" could be associated with numerous syndromes or disorders, but it was too early tell. To this day I cannot stand how that doctor drug out the process of getting to what we all knew was unpleasant news. I am happy to share, however, that Alastair was born with just a cleft lip. At three months old he underwent surgery to correct his lip. It was successful, and he is currently a precious two-year-old who exudes tenderness and joy.

To hear bad news from a doctor is one thing, but to hear it from God is another. What if God were to let you know that at some point in the distant future—when everything is going extremely well for you and your family—you would be diagnosed with cancer but everything would turn out well? Would you believe Him? Would you be mad? Would you want it another way? What if instead of cancer He said that in the distant future you would lose all your material possessions, or all of your family, but everything is going to work out? Would you believe Him? Would you be mad? Would you want it another way? The good news about God is that all of our bad news will eventually be turned to good news.

In Ezekiel 38–39 the prophet is going to temper all of the good news he has been giving the exiles with a bit of bad news from the Lord. The best part though is the bad news will ultimately be good news. Here is a summary of Yahweh's message: Many years from now, when you are living in peace, a huge army is going to rise against you. But you should know two things: I am bringing them to you, and I will completely destroy them. Why am I doing this you ask? I have two reasons. First, I will reveal my glory to the nations. Second, I will confirm my word to you that I will never turn My face from you again.

How would you like to receive this message? Would you believe Him? Would you be mad? Would you want it another way? God has a purpose and provision for everything He calls His people to experience. We will see this revealed clearly now as we examine Ezekiel 38–39.

As Jesus Said, We Will Have Suffering in This World
EZEKIEL 38:1-16

Just as God's people were basking in the promises of peace, provision, and God's presence (37:20-28), they are informed **after a long time** and **in the last years** (38:9) trouble will appear on the horizon (vv. 15-16). Specifically, their trouble will come from **Gog, of the land of Magog, the chief prince of Meshech and Tubal** (v. 2). While they are enjoying peace and living **without walls and without bars or gates** (v. 11), **Gog** will lead a **huge army** to **advance against** God's people (vv. 5-6,15-16). The army will comprise seven nations and will come from all corners of the world (vv. 2,5-6). They will be well adorned and heavily armed (v. 4). The **mighty horde** will **advance** like the **coming** of a **thunderstorm** and will be like a **cloud covering the land** (vv. 9,16).

How would you react if you received this word from God? Would panic sweep over you? Would you move into preparation mode? Would you not worry about it since it will take place many years from now? If this were all there was to the message, then this would seem like bad news indeed. Remembering God's promises, however, can often prevent panic in God's people. God had already told Israel they would dwell securely in their land (34:27). If a massive army is going to come against them, they can choose to believe somehow God will protect His people and keep His promise, or they can choose to believe God has no idea what He is saying. The fact, however, that God is the One informing them of the impending invasion means He must know something. In hearing the remainder of the message, Israel will understand the One in control is not Gog but God.

God does not just control the "who" in this invasion but also the "when." Ezekiel's audience is not given a specific date, but they do know it will occur **after a long time** and **in the last years** (38:9). So, when is this? Has this event occurred already? Was there a massive group of nations that advanced against Israel many years after their return from exile? We do know other nations like Rome ruled Israel in postexilic times, but we do not know of a situation that exactly fits what Ezekiel is describing. So, again, when will this invasion take place? Will it be within the first three years of the tribulation? Will it be at the end of Christ's thousand-year reign? Unfortunately, we cannot be more specific than the vision itself. Personally, I believe this battle is yet to occur. Because of John's employment of some of the elements of this vision (Rev 20:7-10),

I lean toward an end-time scenario of some sort, but the bottom line is, this is a prophecy that awaits its complete fulfillment.

The biggest shock in the text is not that Israel will face trouble but that God is the One who will instigate it. At some point in the recent past, I heard someone say, "God's heart is broken every time evil oversteps its boundaries." To borrow an agricultural phrase, that is hogwash. To think that evil oversteps its boundaries is simultaneously to think that God is weak and not sovereign. In essence we would be saying, "Oh, God wanted to do something, but tragedy interfered, and He was too weak to stop it," or "God was distracted counting the hairs on some guy's head, and this little evil snuck by Him." God not only sets the boundaries for evil but also enforces them. My accountability partner says, "The Bible does not reveal to us a mostly potent, mostly niscient God but an omnipotent and omniscient One." Duguid notes, "Gog has his own evil reasons for acting (38:10) but even his wickedly motivated plans can achieve nothing other than what God purposes (38:4)" (*Ezekiel*, 459).

God's reign is not limited to the regenerate. He has authority over everyone and everything everywhere. His control even extends to the enemies of His people. This truth is clearly seen in Ezekiel 38. God tells Gog, "I will turn you around" (v. 4) and "I will bring you against My land" (vv. 16-17). Honestly, I have more hope knowing evil has a controlled purpose rather than an uncontrolled one.

In all of His actions, God does not do evil. Gog is a willing participant. The Lord predicted,

> On that day, thoughts will arise in your mind, and you will devise an evil plan. You will say, "I will go up against a land of open villages; I will come against a tranquil people who are living securely, all of them living without walls and without bars or gates." (vv. 10-11)

God is not guilty of placing evil thoughts in Gog's mind. The evil desires already exist there. Gog is set on greed (v. 12) and cheered on by selfish traders (v. 13). Duguid offers a great insight on the relationship between God and Gog:

> Gog comes intent on plunder but he does so only because God's plan and purpose is to bring him. Gog's free will is the free will of a shackled lion. If you offer a lion a choice between a fresh green salad and a juicy piece of raw meat, he will choose the latter every time, without compulsion; it is his

nature to eat raw meat. But the shackled lion only gets to eat raw meat when his keeper chooses to allow him to. . . . The Bible tells us that the lions are real, but they are shackled, or rather, to change the image slightly, they are leashed. They can assault Christians only whenever and wherever God allows them to exercise their natural appetites. (Duguid, *Ezekiel*, 459)

God's punishment of Gog will be just. In reigning over Gog, He did not change Gog's heart but let his heart have its way. There is a word of warning here for us. Gog's view of Gog and God's view of Gog were not the same. Gog does not evidence any self-awareness of being on an appointed mission, but he was. This realization should move us to pray, "Father, help us see ourselves as You see us. Let our self-awareness flow from Your Word and what You declare about us." We should always want to know if God is working in us or just with us.

Nothing about the enemy ever catches God off guard, and nothing causes Him to fear. He is not surprised or fazed by Gog's profusion, power, or provisions. An enemy does not exist that God cannot crush instantly and eternally by the sheer power of His word. The psalmist asks a great question:

> *Why do the nations rebel*
> *and the peoples plot in vain?* (Ps 2:1)

He goes on to say,

> *The kings of the earth take their stand,*
> *and the rulers conspire together*
> *against the LORD and His Anointed One:*
> *"Let us tear off their chains*
> *and free ourselves from their restraints."*
> *The One enthroned in heaven laughs;*
> *the Lord ridicules them.*
> *Then He speaks to them in His anger*
> *and terrifies them in His wrath:*
> *"I have consecrated My King*
> *on Zion, My holy mountain."* (Ps 2:2-6)

Without question, "Yahweh is the unrivaled lord of human history. He raises up nations; he puts them down. Their activities are always subservient to his agenda" (Block, *Ezekiel 25–48*, 493).

For Christians this is not the world that will be trouble free. We may not face an enemy horde while we live in villages without walls and locks, but we will face enemies. One in particular seeks to devour us (1 Pet 5:8). We can walk in full obedience to the Lord and still experience struggles. Jesus told His disciples to expect suffering in our current world but also to be encouraged because He conquered the world (John 16:33). Paul told Timothy persecution is a guarantee for those who take up their cross and follow Christ (2 Tim 3:12). The good news is, no tribulation will ever separate us from Christ's love (Rom 8:35-39).

In the New Testament, suffering for Christ is the norm not the exception. We seem surprised, however, when given an opportunity to suffer as if something unusual were happening (1 Pet 4:12). As a pastor, I am constantly striving to prepare our people not to be caught off guard but to suffer well for the glory of God. If the gospel is going to advance globally, more trouble is coming for God's people (Rev 6:10-11). We know that with His grace and power we will have all we need, even if we are asked not to love our lives in the face of death (2 Cor 12:9; Rev 12:11). May we say with Paul, "I count my life of no value to myself, so that I may finish my course and the ministry I received from the Lord Jesus, to testify to the gospel of God's grace" (Acts 20:24).

Because God Is Sovereign, Our Suffering Is Never Without Purpose
EZEKIEL 38:16,23; 39:6-7,21-22,28

As we live for Christ in this world, our suffering will be real, but it will never be random. God has a "why" behind all He does. Of course, He is not obligated to reveal His purposes to us. Several years ago a pastor in my hometown lost his 18-year-old daughter in a car wreck. In a seminary class I attended, he was given the opportunity to share about his grief experience. He said, "Some people have told me that when we get to heaven then we will know why this wreck occurred. My response to them has been, 'When we get to heaven, it will no longer matter why.'" His point was that when we experience the full joy of God in heaven, we will probably not be peppering Him for explanations.

Yahweh, however, does not leave Israel in the dark about what He is doing with Gog. His first purpose in bringing Gog against them is His primary in all things—displaying His glory (39:7). He was going to display His greatness and holiness and reveal Himself in the sight of many nations so they would all know He is Yahweh (38:23). He would show Himself holy through Gog in the sight of all who were watching (38:16).

His second purpose in allowing Gog to advance on Israel was so He could demonstrate His love and commitment to His people. Despite all their rebellion God would make His name known among His people. As the nations watched how God purified Israel, they would know He is Yahweh (39:7). It will also be revealed that God's people were exiled because of their iniquity and not His ineptitude (39:23). As the nations watch God restore His people, they will know the house of Israel was not taken from Him originally but He handed them over (39:28). He was not weak; He was working. His people who profaned His name are now purified, and the nations will know He is Yahweh.

What about you? Are you struggling with something God allowed you to experience because you cannot discern an apparent reason? God's best plan for our lives may not seem best to us, but we can know it always is. He always has a why, and His why is always good.

Because God Is Sovereign, Our Suffering Is Never Without Provision
EZEKIEL 38:17-22; 39:3-5

How do you think Israel would have responded if God informed them He was bringing Gog against them and then said, "Good luck"? If we are given God's plan but not His provision, then all of our endeavors are doomed to fail. There is no way Christ's disciples would have any hope of making disciples of all nations without His promise to go with them. His presence is His greatest provision for us.

God was not going to bring Gog against His people and abandon them to their own resources. In fact, Israel would not have to do anything but trust God. He would do all the fighting necessary. God told Israel,

> Now on that day, the day when Gog comes against the land of Israel . . . My wrath will flare up. I swear in My zeal and fiery rage: On that day there will be a great earthquake in the land of Israel. . . . The mountains will be thrown down, the cliffs will collapse, and every wall will fall to the ground. (38:18-20)

And that will be just a warm up. God went on to say,

"I will call for a sword against him on all My mountains . . . and
every man's sword will be against his brother. I will execute judgment
on him with plague and bloodshed. I will pour out torrential rain,
hailstones, fire, and brimstone on him, as well as his troops and the
many peoples who are with him." (38:21-22)

While God's plan seems sufficient to protect His people, He is still not
done.

In case the outcome of the battle is still in doubt, God has a final
word for Gog. God tells him,

"I will turn you around, drive you on, and lead you up from the
remotest parts of the north. I will bring you against the mountains of
Israel. Then I will knock your bow from your left hand and make your
arrows drop from your right hand." (39:2-3)

Not a single weapon of Gog will prosper against God's people. The chief
prince of Meshech and Tubal and everyone who is with him will die
in Israel and leave their bodies to be devoured by the birds and wild
animals (39:4-5). The author of Hebrews has well said, "It is a terrifying
thing to fall into the hands of the living God" (Heb 10:31).

Fighting on behalf of His people is not a new concept to the Lord. In
2 Chronicles 20 Jehoshaphat receives word that a multitude was advancing against Judah. Though he was afraid, he called all God's people to
come together to fast and pray (2 Chr 20:3-4). In his prayer Jehoshaphat
acknowledged God's sovereignty and power and admitted, "We do not
know what to do, but we look to You" (2 Chr 20:12). God's response was,
"You do not have to fight this battle. Position yourselves, stand still, and
see the salvation of the Lord" (2 Chr 20:17; cf. Exod 14:13). While God
worked, His people were to worship. Instead of picking up swords, they
were to lift up songs. God never leaves His people to their own resources
unless they have rejected His.

The greatest battle God has ever fought for His people, of course, is
at the cross of Christ. If left to their own resources, God's people could
never win the war against sin and death. They cannot even contribute to
the battle because they are part of the enemies' cause. At the cross God's
people bring their sin, and God provides His Son. Like Jehoshaphat we
must stand and watch while God fights the battle for our eternal souls
through the death and resurrection of His Son. If God has provided a
means to overcome our greatest trouble, He will certainly help us in
everything else.

If what is described in Ezekiel 38–39 is what actually takes place in Revelation 19–20, then neither battle will be drawn out. In the first battle Jesus never even gets off His horse (Rev 19:19-21). In the second one the evil multitude will be consumed by fire from heaven (Rev 20:9). Honestly, I have no idea how an entire book in a popular contemporary series on eschatological matters was written on this battle. All who fight against God lose.

God's Victory in Christ Means Ultimate Defeat for His Enemies
EZEKIEL 39:6,11-20

Those who fight God and His people can expect not just defeat but total devastation. If one has any doubt that fighting God leads to failure, just consider Gog and his horde. Often Israel was told to raise an Ebenezer to remember something God did on their behalf. God, however, has something different He wants to use so that His people and everyone else will always remember His defeat of Gog. For Gog and his massive army, God will provide a burial place in Israel that would block anyone wanting to pass through the Valley of Travelers east of the Sea (39:11). If you are trying to use a familiar passage but find it blocked because God defeated His enemies and buried them there, then you might give consideration to the God of Israel. Likewise, it would be difficult for Israel to see the valley-turned-cemetery and forget God's protection and provision.

After the birds and beasts have had their fill of dead bodies (vv. 17-20), the burial of Gog and his army will take longer than the battle they waged. For seven months appointed men of Israel will have a full-time job burying the evil horde (v. 14). Not a bone will remain uncovered. The land will be completely cleansed. Gog's land, Magog, will be impacted as well. God will rain down fire on all the places from which Gog's army assembled (v. 6). Yahweh will not only defeat the evil horde, but He will destroy their homelands. Those who lived on the coasts and islands will find there is no security except in Yahweh (v. 6).

We cannot consider Gog's outcome and think that any contemporary enemies of God will fare any better. Jesus will ultimately put "all His enemies under His feet" (1 Cor 15:25). We long for the day when Death and Hades will be thrown into the lake of fire (Rev 20:14). But what about God's other enemies? Who exactly is considered to be His enemy? All who have yet to turn from sin and trust in Christ. This could be our coworker, our neighbor, or even the coach of our son's soccer team. Are they really enemies? Yes, according to Jesus. He declared, "Anyone who is not with Me is against Me, and anyone who does not gather with Me scatters" (Matt 12:30). James also says, "Don't you know that friendship with the world is hostility toward God? So whoever wants to be the world's friend becomes God's enemy" (Jas 4:4). Many do not consider themselves to be God's enemy, but in reality they are if they have never looked to Christ for salvation. They are still under God's wrath. The burial of Gog's body and the burning of his land should be a warning to all who think fighting God is a good idea. The psalmist has said, "Pay homage to the Son or He will be angry and you will perish in your rebellion, for His anger may ignite at any moment. All those who take refuge in Him are happy" (Ps 2:12).

God's Victory in Christ Means Ultimate Security for His People
EZEKIEL 39:9-10,25-29

Israel did none of the fighting but received all of the plunder (39:10). For seven years God's people will not have to **gather wood from the countryside or cut it down from the forests** (vv. 9-10). They will use the enemy army's **bucklers and shields, the bows and arrows,** and **the clubs and spears** to make fires (v. 9). Ironically, what Gog hoped to do was done to him (v. 12). Instead of carrying Israel's plunder away, they carried plunder to Israel. No one knows how to "flip the script" better than God.

With regard to God's provision, the best news is found in the final five verses of Ezekiel 39. After telling Ezekiel's audience about a time in the distant future (38:8), He closes this text with a more immediate message of provision. Gog will be able to come against Israel because Israel will have been restored to their land. God will not leave a single one of His people where they have been exiled (39:28). None should ever doubt God's ability to gather those who are His. Once in Israel they will receive the full benefits of covenant relationship (Block, *Ezekiel 25–48*, 493). His people will be extended the full measure of His forgiveness, mercy, and blessings. God knows no such thing as partial forgiveness. He will not do good to them while simultaneously holding a grudge. He will also not hide His face from them or send them away again in discipline. The seriousness of God's commitment will be demonstrated when He gives His people His Spirit (v. 29).

How will God cause His people to live securely in their land? Will He build a giant wall to keep all threats away? No, we already know they will live without walls, bars, and gates (38:11). Will they dwell securely because they develop a mighty arsenal of weapons? No, as we've just seen, they will burn all the weapons Gog's army leaves behind (39:9). So how will God cause His people to dwell securely? He will pour out His Spirit on them. His people will dwell securely because He will seal them with His presence. Could there be any better news for people in exile due to their rebellion? God will fully forgive them and fully bless them despite all their previous unfaithfulness.

The giving of His Spirit "serves as a sign and seal of the covenant. The poured out Spirit represents Yahweh's mark of ownership" (Block, *Ezekiel 25–48*, 488). They are His people, and they will always be His people. He knows how to both protect and provide for His children. When the nations see how God treats Gog, they will indeed know God is both with and for His people.

God's people today may dwell just as securely as the postexilic Israelites. God continues to seal His people with His Spirit. Block points out,

> It is remarkable that with every stage of the advance of the gospel, and the incorporation of new groups of people into the church, reference is made to the extraordinary manifestation of the Spirit's presence: (1) the Jews in Jerusalem (Acts 2:4,33,38); (2) the Samaritans (8:14-17); (3) Gentile proselytes of Judea (10:44-48; cf. 9:16); (4) Gentiles of Asia Minor (19:1-6). Each event signals a new phase and scope in the breadth of the embrace of the new covenant instituted in Christ. Furthermore, when Paul speaks of being sealed with the Spirit (2 Cor 1:22; Eph 1:13; 4:30), he is speaking of the possession of the Holy Spirit as the divine confirmation of the covenant. This alone is the basis of the believer's security. (*Ezekiel 25–48*, 493)

Like Israel we have done none of the fighting for our salvation but receive the full benefits of Christ's work. As we receive the blessings of Christ's substitutionary atonement and the presence and ministry of the Holy Spirit, how can we do anything but praise the Lord for these unmerited gifts? We can dwell securely knowing that He who begins a good work completes it (Phil 1:6). God never regenerates a person and then changes His mind. His Spirit guarantees He will never change His mind. We will always be His people, and He will always be our God. We can dwell securely not because we are good but because He is. Once provided His Spirit, we can join Paul in saying, "I am not ashamed, because I know the One I have believed in and am persuaded that He is able to guard what has been entrusted to me until that day" (2 Tim 1:12).

What Ezekiel 38–39 Can Teach Us About God

We can learn several lessons about God from Ezekiel 38–39. First and foremost, God reigns supreme. He has no equal in power, but He also has no equal in goodness. He is above all and threatened by none. Second, God not only knows the future but also controls it. Time is in His hands alone. He does not just ordain *what* happens but also *when* it happens. Third, whatever happens, He is actively working for His glory and our good. Even when it seems He is not in control or does not know what He is doing, He is and does. Without God the advance of an enemy army would be great cause for alarm, but with God it provides a great opportunity for trust. Fourth, He will supply all we need. God may allow us to walk through difficult circumstances, but He will also provide all that is needed. To those He disciplined He said,

> *I will be with you when you pass through the waters, and when you pass through the rivers, they will not overwhelm you. You will not be scorched when you walk through the fire, and the flame will not burn you.* (Isa 43:2)

A fifth lesson that can be learned about God is that His victory over our greatest enemies assures our victory over all lesser ones as well. In Ezekiel 38–39 God had no trouble at all demolishing Gog. It did not matter how many were with Gog or how well armed they were, God crushed them. Likewise, our greatest enemies are the world, the flesh, and the Devil, but in Christ's cross God "disarmed the rulers and authorities and disgraced them publicly; He triumphed over them by Him" (Col 2:15). God also

> *demonstrated this power in the Messiah by raising Him from the dead and seating Him at His right hand in the heavens—far above every ruler and authority, power and dominion, and every title given, not only in this age but also in the one to come. And He put everything under His feet and appointed Him as head over everything for the*

church, which is His body, the fullness of the One who fills all things in every way. (Eph 1:20-23)

If God's power has done these things, then He certainly can help us in our battles against lying, envy, lust, gossip, slothfulness, anger, and selfishness. He is able to do far more than we ask or imagine (Eph 3:20).

Lastly, Ezekiel 38–39 reminds us that God keeps His promises. He told Israel they would dwell securely. If God then brought Gog against them and let the evil ruler defeat His people, God would be a liar. God never lies. We also have the benefit of living post-Pentecost and know that God indeed poured out His Spirit on His people. He still does, which continues to be proof that He is still trustworthy. God will keep every promise He has ever made to His people. And for this He will receive our eternal praise.

Reflect and Discuss

1. As we strive to live for Christ in this world, why does suffering often surprise us? Why is it naïve to think all people will love Christians who share the gospel with them?

2. Why do we seem to forget that God knows what He is doing and is doing all things for our good?

3. How has God steered some of the troubles you've experienced for your ultimate good and His glory?

4. In what ways does knowing that our suffering has a purpose comfort you?

5. How would you encourage someone who is struggling because God's purpose in his or her experiences is not evident? Instead of finding the "why," what should they be seeking?

6. How has God shown Himself strong in provision when you've walked through a difficult season?

7. God would use the advance of an enemy army to increase Israel's trust in Him. What are ways God has increased your faith?

8. Why is receiving God's Spirit a source of security for God's people?

9. How do you express your appreciation for the provision of His presence?

10. Knowing God's enemies will be destroyed, with whom do you need to share a gospel word today? Why do we act as if those outside of Christ will not experience total loss like Gog?

The Lord Is There

EZEKIEL 40:1–48:35

Main Idea: God will purify and preserve His people so they can enjoy His presence forever.

I. **When Are We Talking About (40:1)?**
II. **Should We Start Collecting Supplies and Building a Temple in Jerusalem (40:2–42:20)?**
III. **What Was the Original Purpose for This Text (43:1-12)?**
IV. **How Will It Be Possible for God to Dwell with His People?**
    A. God's initial immanence
    B. God's incarnation
    C. God's indwelling
    D. God's infinite dwelling
V. **What Can We Learn About God in Ezekiel 40–48?**
    A. God initiates.
    B. God instructs.
    C. God is holy.
    D. God is gracious.
    E. God will be worshiped on His terms.
    F. God is sufficient.
    G. God is sovereign.
VI. **What Do We Learn About Us (44:6-31)?**
    A. Rewards
    B. Refreshing

If you have journeyed to this point in Ezekiel, let me commend you for persevering. Preaching through Ezekiel was one of the most rigorous yet rewarding experiences for me personally and pastorally. I am certain some of our people believed Christ would return before we finished our series through this book of the Bible. Of course, my prayer is that we never just "get through" Bible books but that they "get in" us. There is much to learn in Ezekiel. The true measure of our learning, however, will be evidenced in how we are living. How will a study of Ezekiel not just fill our minds but also move our hearts and hands? How can we

most profitably ponder Israel's constant disobedience and disregard for
God's Word so that we will strive not to imitate them? How can we see
a God who is really good to people who are really bad and be moved
by His mercy to us? How can we see God's desire to exalt His name and
learn not to exalt our own? How can we see God's judgment and be
motivated to share the gospel with everyone we see? How can we see
His wrath and grow in gratitude for the cross of Christ? What good will
come from this work I'm writing remains to be seen, but what good God
has wrought through His Word in my life is a value without measure.

In dealing with the final chapters of Ezekiel, I chose in my sermon
series to develop one sermon. You should feel the freedom to do what
is best for the people you shepherd or disciple. For instance, you might
choose to develop a sermon on Ezekiel 47 and connect it with Christ
(John 7:37-39). I will certainly make these connections, but I did not
develop a whole sermon just on Ezekiel 47. Also, if you have come to this
portion of the material and are hoping to have all of your eschatological questions answered, then you will be disappointed. (Actually, if you
have made it this far and this is your first disappointment, then God has
allowed you to read with eyes of grace!) My approach with passages such
as these is always the same wherever I am in God's Word: preach what is
clearest. We cannot preach what we do not know, but we should proclaim
boldly what is clear. We should also feel freedom to be honest with our
people about passages like Ezekiel 40–48 and tell them there are some
things we will not be able to figure out until God ultimately fulfills them.

As we approach Ezekiel 40–48, we acknowledge that godly scholars
and pastors claiming to be led by the Holy Spirit have not all arrived at a
point of unity in interpreting these chapters. Kaiser noted,

> Few chapters of the Bible separate interpreters into such
> strongly diverse camps of interpretation as the last nine
> chapters of Ezekiel—probably more than at any other place in
> the Scriptures. (Kaiser, *Last Things*, chap. 11)

In light of the interpretive difficulties of this portion of Ezekiel, the
words of Derek Thomas can be comforting. He contends,

> A confession of ignorance about the precise meaning of
> these passages is nothing to be ashamed of. Just because
> commentators are dogmatic about a certain interpretation is
> no guarantee that they are right. We need the illumination
> of the Holy Spirit to help us come to understand every word

of Scripture. In passages like these, meekness is the best approach. (Thomas, *God Strengthens,* 288)

Let this be our approach as we turn now to the text.

When Are We Talking About?
EZEKIEL 40:1

Twenty-five years into the exile, Ezekiel is given the vision that comprises Ezekiel 40–48 (40:1). It has been 14 years since the fall of Jerusalem. The last time reference Ezekiel noted with the visions he received was the twelfth year of the exile (33:21). If that's the case, then God has been silent for a while. Perhaps they wondered if God had forgotten them. Maybe they doubted His sincerity to rescue and restore them to Israel. What do you do when it seems God has not "spoken" to you in a while? My encouragement would be to open your Bible. He speaks through His Word every day.

For Ezekiel's audience God's silence did not mean His absence. God knows exactly when we need to hear what. How often has the Lord provided the exact word we have needed in the exact moment we needed it? When I received word that my good friend and neighbor had drowned in a canoeing accident, the Holy Spirit immediately brought 1 Thessalonians 5:16-18 to my mind. I had not even had time to ask for a word. He brought to my mind the word I needed at the moment I most needed it.

With regard to eschatological phraseology such as *latter days* or *after many years,* you will find more of this in Ezekiel 38–39 than in 40–40. If we consider these chapters literally, then obviously some of what is said is yet to occur. If we consider these chapters spiritually, then some of the promises here have already been met in Christ. I believe the complete fulfillment of Ezekiel 40–48 is still to come, which is why John uses some of the pictures found here as he writes Revelation 21–22. We are now led to another important question.

Should We Start Collecting Supplies and Building a Temple in Jerusalem?
EZEKIEL 40:2–42:20

Since my childhood, I have heard stories of materials being gathered, including a red heifer, so that all will be ready to construct a new building in the city where God set His name. What has not been certain is exactly who is gathering those materials, where they are storing them now, or why in the world they would need a red heifer. What I do know is that Ezekiel 40–48 is not intended to be a blueprint telling us how to construct God's next dwelling place. I am pretty sure He is already taking care of this, as we will see.

One reason I do not believe the intention of Ezekiel 40–42 is for us to build a Legoland like no other is because there is not a single imperative telling us to build anything. Unlike Noah, Ezekiel is not asked to construct anything. On the contrary, he is to look with his eyes, listen with his ears, pay attention to everything he is shown, and then report everything he sees to Israel (40:2-5). He was brought in a vision to see something that already exists and not something he was going to create (v. 4).

For those who remain obstinate, however, and see this as a construction plan, I just have one question: How are you going to build this if you do not know how tall it should be or what materials you need in order to construct it? Do you think God does not care about either of those details? Did He provide these for the ark? Did He provide these for the first temple? There are a lot of measurements in Ezekiel 40, but they all consist of length and width and never height. If you decide to go ahead and construct something, then you will just have to guess at how tall to make it. I am sure that will turn out well.

There are two more reasons I do not believe what is provided in Ezekiel 40–42 is meant to be a detailed construction plan. Reason number one is that when the exiles returned to Israel, these were not the plans they used. One can verify this fact simply by reading Ezra and Nehemiah. Go ahead. I'll wait here for you. The second reason is that Herod did not use these plans either. What Herod built was more for his renown than God's, but we know his temple and the one described in Ezekiel 40–42 have differences. What is most evident with both the post-exilic temple and with Herod's is that Ezekiel 43:1-9 did not take place with either. We have seen more of His glory (John 1:14) than either of those buildings ever did.

What Was the Original Purpose for This Text?
EZEKIEL 43:1-12

So, if Ezekiel 40–42 is not a construction plan for us to follow, then why was it given? One purpose revealed in 43:6-12 is the same purpose that has been emphasized throughout the book of Ezekiel: God's holiness matters. Ezekiel is told to **describe the temple to the house of Israel, so they may be ashamed of their iniquities**. He is told **the law of the temple** is that it **will be especially holy** (vv. 10-12). The vision in Ezekiel 40–42 is provided to teach God's people about His holiness and not just how to build His house.

In response to the vision of the new temple, God expected not only repentance but also other behaviors from His people:

- Because He is holy and will live among them again, God expects His people to put away anything that is unholy (vv. 7,9-10). How are we doing with this?
- Because they have seen His wrath, they should remember that closeness to God does not come without cost (v. 8). They encroached on His territory without giving it proper consideration. How grateful are we that, through Christ, we have been encouraged to boldly draw near to God (Heb 10:19-22)?
- Because they are shown the beauty of God's new temple, they should seek to diligently obey His statutes and laws (v. 11).

While challenging God's people to walk in holiness is a reason Ezekiel 40–42 is provided, I believe the main purpose is to testify of God's presence with those who are His. In Ezekiel 43:5 the prophet sees the glory of the Lord fill the temple. In 48:35 he is told the name of the new city will be "**Yahweh Is There**." When this occurs, Ezekiel 37:26-27 will be fulfilled. Thomas asserts,

> The Lord is there is the meaning of the entire vision. to point out to a despondent people in exile that God is with them. Ezekiel wants his readers to be taken up with God and His presence with His people. (Thomas, *God Strengthens*, 297)

Instead of

> the earthly temple, contaminated by the sins of the people and abandoned by the presence of God (chs. 8–11), Ezekiel has seen an undefiled temple, refilled by God's glory (chs. 40–43). (Duguid, *Ezekiel*, 547)

He does not have to dwell with us. He chooses to do so.

Have we heard Ezekiel 37:27 so often that the awesomeness of God's declaration is lost on us? Has it been a while since we just let these words wash over us: "My dwelling place will be with them; I will be their God, and they will be My people"? Do we ever pause and ask, "Why would He want to dwell with us?" Or do we have such elevated views of ourselves that we think, "Of course God wants to dwell with me. I am awesome!" An elder at my previous church used to say, "Only God is awesome."

The reason Ezekiel 40–43 is given is to provide God's people in exile with a word of hope. God will dwell with them again. His holiness will not only be important to Him but also to them. He will not move away from His people but will move in with them.

Have you ever felt like people around you could not care less whether you existed or not? Have you ever had your feelings hurt because you were not invited to do something with the "cool" crowd? If that is you, then you should know the One who matters more than anyone else has prayed to be with you. Jesus once prayed,

> *Father, I desire those You have given Me to be with Me where I am.*
> *Then they will see My glory, which You have given Me because You*
> *loved Me before the world's foundation.* (John 17:24)

Jesus desires for us to be with Him and see His glory. Has anyone ever asked the Father for anything greater on our behalf? Not even close! The vision of God's glory returning to the temple and the announcement a city would be called "Yahweh Is There" would not have been lost on Ezekiel's audience.

What about us? Can we join with Asaph in saying, "But as for me, God's presence is my good. I have made the Lord GOD my refuge, so I can tell about all You do" (Ps 73:28)? Is the Lord's presence our good? Do we take His presence for granted? Can He tell we appreciate His dwelling in us by His Spirit? How much delighting are we doing in Him? Do we wake up talking to Him? Do we talk to Him throughout the day? Do we talk to Him as we head to bed? Would we feel great devastation and utter ruin if His presence was not with us? Would we notice? How evident is His presence in our lives? Can anyone tell He dwells in us (1 Cor 6:19)?

In Ezekiel 40–48 God is saying to His people, "I will return and I will restore you. I will be with you forever." As remarkable as what He is saying is, whom He is saying these things to should capture our attention as well. He is promising to dwell with people who at one point did not appreciate His presence. How do I know? In Ezekiel 43:9 they are told to put away their prostitution. God does not mean sexually but spiritually.

God is running to people who constantly ran away from Him. The pursuit of sin always evidences disregard for God's presence. With each sin we communicate to God that we think He is not in charge, but we are; He does not know best, but we do; and He is not most precious to us, rebellion is. In spite of all Ezekiel's generation and the ones before them had done, God still desired to cleanse them and dwell with them forever. May we never cease to be humbled by this truth and to allow it to fuel our praise.

How Will It Be Possible for God to Dwell with His People?

Hearing the vision Ezekiel received in the twenty-fifth year of exile would have been encouraging to God's people, but it may have also left them with a few questions. Knowing God wanted to dwell with them and would dwell with them would have filled their hearts with hope, but their heads may have been trying to figure out exactly how this would be possible. For all their lives the temple was the only place they could meet with God, and the altar was the only means. There was only one place and one means, but it had not always been this way.

God's Initial Immanence

In the beginning there was no temple but a garden. There were no restrictions on where Adam and Eve could meet with God. Anywhere was fine because everywhere was holy. No specific meeting place had to be set because every place was appropriate for them to fellowship with God. But sin changed everything. Because of His holiness God cannot tolerate or ignore sin. As a consequence of the fall, man's relationship with God changed. Sin created a barrier that separated humans from God.

After Adam and Eve's rebellion, special locations were required in order for people to meet with God. The first location was an altar. From Adam and Eve to Moses, the Lord would meet with His people on altars they constructed for sacrifices and prayers. The second location God met with His people was the tabernacle. From the wilderness generation through David, God's people would meet with Him in this mobile tent.

The temple was the third location established for God's people to meet with Him. In Deuteronomy 12 God's people are told they will have one place for worship, one location for sacrifices, and one sacrificial altar. As we know from our journey through Ezekiel, God's people never gave up the altars on the high places. They also worshiped gods who did not exist and turned their backs on the only One who does. As we also know, God abandoned the temple (Ezek 9–11) and raised up the Babylonians (Hab 1:6) to discipline His people and destroy the temple. Now in Ezekiel 40–43, God's people are being told there will be another place in which God will meet with His people. It just may not be in the place they were thinking.

God's Incarnation

The location where God would meet with His people shifted from a place to a Person. Prior to the exile God's glory dwelled in the temple. It would not be the same postexile. God's glory instead would dwell in Christ, and He would be the perfect temple/tabernacle. John informs us that Christ tabernacled with us and God's glory was seen (John 1:14).

During His time of ministry, Jesus had a conversation about this very subject. In a discussion with a Samaritan woman, Jesus revealed that God's meeting place with His people would not be limited to a special mountain in Samaria or Jerusalem (John 4:21). He said instead, "An hour is coming, and is now here, when the true worshipers will worship the Father in spirit and truth. Yes, the Father wants such people to worship Him" (John 4:23). So, the place no longer matters? How can this be? Ezekiel's generation would have certainly struggled to grasp this.

The temple God would use to meet with His people was Christ. Jesus tried to help us understand this when He said, "Destroy this sanctuary, and I will raise it up in three days" (John 2:19). John tells us that Jesus was not talking about the building that took 46 years to build, "But He was speaking about the sanctuary of His body" (John 2:21). Jesus is the place where God meets with His people. If further evidence is needed, then just consider what happened to the curtain in the temple when Christ was crucified (Matt 27:51). In the tearing of the veil, God spoke clearly for Himself.

God's Indwelling

In promising to pour out His Spirit (Ezek 39:29), God committed to dwell not just *with* His people but also *in* them. What one person was allowed to experience in one place on one day of each year (the high priest on the day of atonement), we have the privilege of experiencing every day. Post-Pentecost, God dwells with His people in a way Ezekiel's audience could have only considered with marvel and bewilderment (Eph 2:19-22; 1 Cor 3:16-17; 6:18-20). When we think of our bodies as the temple of God, it puts sinning in a different perspective. Paul's plea in 1 Corinthians 6 was for God's people to understand that since God's Spirit resides in us, we are holy ground, and we cannot do anything we please with our bodies, especially sin.

God's Infinite Dwelling

The ultimate experience of God's dwelling with His people is what John writes about in Revelation 21–22. What was lost in the fall at Eden will be recovered in the new city. We should notice two things in relation to Ezekiel 40–48. First, John sees a city that is already built that descends from heaven (Rev 21:2). A place is prepared for God's people; they do not construct it themselves. Second, John did not see a temple or sanctuary in his vision because "the Lord God the Almighty and the Lamb are its sanctuary" (Rev 21:22). In the new creation there will be no special place where God's presence is concentrated and no holy building to go to if we want to meet with Him. There will no longer exist any distance between God and us. He will dwell with us. We will be His people, and He will be our God (Rev 21:3). We will enjoy fellowship with God, we will see Him as He is, we will worship Him, and we will serve Him (MacArthur, *Revelation 12–22*, 266–68).

Ezekiel is shown and told to declare that God's people will be in God's place under God's rule and blessing (Roberts, *God's Big Picture*, 21). God will return to His people and restore them. God will also provide whatever solution is necessary to dwell with His people forever. We have the privilege of knowing the solution is Christ.

What Can We Learn About God in Ezekiel 40–48?

We do not have to wait until heaven, however, to learn some things about God. Though we will understand all things much clearer then, we can still know some truths about God now. Ezekiel 40–48 provides multiple insights on Yahweh's character and actions.

God Initiates

Every idea presented in this vision comes from God. Finding a permanent solution to dwelling with His people eternally comes from God. Leading His people to repentance and forgiving them was God's idea and work. Even in exile God's people still did not initiate a move toward Him, but He met them where they were.

God Instructs

God gives statutes, specifications, and laws because He does not want His people to be without His will (43:11; 44–46). He wants His people taught the difference between what is holy and what is common (44:23). He gives instruction on sacrifices (46:1-15) and when to offer what. On a side note, these instructions cannot be for a millennial kingdom or heaven because what need would there be for any more sacrifices? Christ has achieved all that is necessary (Heb 10:14,18). If we do not understand all the instructions provided in Ezekiel 40–48, we cannot ignore their presence, which tells us of God's desire to inform His people.

God Is Holy

In Ezekiel 40:5–42:20 the walls that are taller and more solid, the elevated steps, the raised platform, the designation of the priests' chambers, and all of the other details point to one main emphasis: God's holiness is a big deal. In Ezekiel 44:19 the priests are informed that

> before they go out to the outer court, to the people, they must take off the clothes they have been ministering in, leave them in the holy chambers, and dress in other clothes so that they do not transmit holiness to the people through their clothes.

The priests must exercise such caution not because God's holiness is contagious but because it will obliterate you if your sins are not covered. God's presence is always dangerous for sinners left to their own righteousness.

While God desires to know His people intimately, it does not follow that their worship of Him will be informal. When considering God's holiness, just imagine drawing closer and closer to the sun. As a matter of fact, Ezekiel says, "**The earth shone with His glory**" (43:2). Ezekiel's response was to fall facedown (v. 3). We previously saw that the prophet had more interaction with God than any of his peers; yet familiarity did not breed disrespect or arrogance in Ezekiel. God's presence always comes with a price. We cannot approach Him in any way we want. He will be known and approached on His terms.

God Is Gracious

God provides a way for His people's sin to be taken care of and for them to be able to worship Him. In Ezekiel 43:13-27 instructions are given for an altar, which means God's people will have an acceptable way to offer their worship. We know the only acceptable way is through Christ (Heb 13:15). The altar is in the center of the entire compound Ezekiel is shown. As stated previously, the full purpose of this altar and the instructions for sacrifices given does not find consensus among commentators. What is clear is that in Christ, God has provided a way for His holiness not to be contaminated and for us not to be obliterated. God is gracious to reveal His holiness to us so we might see our sinfulness. In seeing our sinfulness, we then see our need for a Savior. Graciously, He has provided Him as well.

God Will Be Worshiped on His Terms

We have seen this before, but in Ezekiel 45:1–46:24 the whom, the how, and the why of worship are all important to God. In our generation I fear we have made worship too much about us. I wonder how much of what is done on Sundays is driven by preferences rather than biblical conviction. We somehow strive to make worship as convenient as possible for us. Ezekiel 45–46 provides a good reminder that worship was never intended to be offered without effort and intentionality. Our convenience is not high on the priority list when it comes to worship.

God Is Sufficient

One of the greatest verses in Ezekiel 40–48 is 47:9, which ends by declaring, "**There will be life everywhere the river goes**." In Ezekiel 47:1-12 the prophet is shown a life-giving river. It flows from the sanctuary (v. 12) and transforms everything it touches. Most notably, "**When it enters the sea, the sea of foul water, the water of the sea becomes fresh**" (v. 8). This river will transform the Dead Sea to the Alive Sea. Though it starts as a trickle (v. 2), Ezekiel sees the river become deep enough to swim in and impossible to cross on foot (v. 5). Jesus emphasized a similar point by using a mustard seed (Matt 13:31-32). Along both banks of the river in Ezekiel 47 are trees that produce fruit every month (v. 12), which is used for food. The leaves of the trees are used for medicine (v. 12). John describes something similar in Revelation 22:1-2.

So, how do we see God's sufficiency in Ezekiel 47? First, He is the source. This is not a random river but one that originates from His sanctuary. Second, He sanctifies. What was dead is made alive. Third, He sustains. The trees on the riverbanks will never fail to produce fruit.

Fourth, He cannot be stopped. No one will be able to prevent Him from giving His people life to the fullest.

God Is Sovereign

In Ezekiel 47:13–48:35 God designates which tribes will receive which portion of the land as an inheritance (47:14). God can divide the land because He owns it. It is His. God is going to provide a place He promised for His people. They will not have to fight for it, work for it, or purchase it. All that God's people will have to do is receive the land He is giving them.

What Do We Learn About Us?
EZEKIEL 44:6-31

Before concluding our study of Ezekiel 40–48, I would like us to consider God's rewards and God's refreshing.

Rewards

Nestled in the vision of a temple, a city, and a river is a tale of two priests. At some point in Israel's rebellion, they brought in foreigners who were **uncircumcised in both heart and flesh** and allowed them to occupy God's sanctuary (44:7). On top of this they failed to keep charge of God's holy things but appointed others to keep charge of His sanctuary for them (v. 8). Why did this happen? One reason is because the Levites **wandered away from** and **strayed from** God **after their idols** (v. 10). The priests who descended from **Zadok**, however, **kept charge** of God's **sanctuary when the Israelites went astray** from God (v. 15).

Both groups of priests were held accountable. The Levitical priests who chased after idols would **bear the consequences of their sin** (v. 10). Because of their disobedience they would lose the privilege to serve as priests. Instead, they would be temple guards and responsible for slaughtering the burnt offerings (v. 11). They would remain close to the temple to be reminded of what they lost. God expects fruitfulness from his servants and will hold each of us accountable for the use of resources and opportunities He entrusts to us.

The priests who descended from Zadok, however, would not be reprimanded but rewarded. They would be given the privilege of serving closest to God (v. 16). They would also be given greater responsibilities. The Zadokites would be asked to teach God's people about holiness

(v. 23) and to use God's word to settle disputes (v. 24). These privileges would also come with costs.

> For the Zadokites, access to God's presence meant heavy restrictions on their lifestyle. There were things they could not touch, places they could not go to, food they could not eat and clothes they could not wear if they were to minister in the presence of the all-holy God. So too for us, if we expect to experience the blessing of God's presence with us, then our lifestyle will be (from the world's perspective) restricted. (Duguid, *Ezekiel*, 510)

Whatever inconveniences the Zadokite priests experienced could not compare with the inheritance they received. The Lord told Ezekiel, **"This will be their inheritance: I am their inheritance. You are to give them no possession in Israel: I am their possession"** (v. 28). While the other Israelites were given land, these priests were given God. Who received the greatest gift is not difficult to see!

What about us? How often do we consider kingdom rewards? If a reward meant greater proximity to and experience of God, would you see this as the greatest inheritance? One thing is certain, we may not have all descended from Levi or Zadok, but we are all priests. Peter tells us "you yourselves, as living stones, are being built into a spiritual house for a holy priesthood to offer spiritual sacrifices acceptable to God through Jesus Christ" (1 Pet 2:5). As believers we are all ministers and are all called to a life of purity and holiness. When everyone else runs away from God, we are to run to Him. What is important to Him should remain important to us. When it comes time to give an account for our time as His servants, will ours be more of a rebuke like the idolatrous priests or a rewarding like those descended from Zadok?

Refreshing

If the life-giving river is transforming us, then others around us should be able to tell. One cannot read Ezekiel 47:1-12 without being reminded of John 7:37-39. John tells us,

> On the last and most important day of the festival, Jesus stood up and cried out, "If anyone is thirsty, he should come to Me and drink! The one who believes in Me, as the Scripture has said, will have streams of living water flow from deep within him." He said this about the Spirit. Those who believed in Jesus were going to receive the Spirit, for the

Spirit had not yet been received because Jesus had not yet been glorified. (John 7:37-39)

As the Spirit indwells us, we experience the life-giving water of Christ.

In Ezekiel 47 whatever the life-giving river touched could not remain the same. For those who are in Christ, fruitfulness is the norm and not the exception (John 15:5). If fruit is not being produced through us, it can only mean one of two things: either we truly do not know Christ, or we are not being obedient to Him. The effect of the river is not just reserved for heaven (Cooper, *Ezekiel*, 414). Even now the river grows in us and through us, and others can experience its life-giving effects as we share the gospel with them and call for repentance.

Conclusion

Ezekiel 40–48 begins and ends with a picture of a new temple and a new city. This word was meant to "encourage repentance, faithfulness, and hope: repentance over the sins of the past, faithfulness in the difficult present, and hope for a brighter future through God's grace" (Duguid, *Ezekiel*, 548). Considering our future with God should have profound impacts on our daily lives. Chester believes,

> We need to talk about our hope and inheritance when we
> are together, reminding each other of what we have to look
> forward to when we are confronted by death, hardships,
> temptation, or opposition. When we doubt or forget about
> our hope, we become focused on this world, distracted by stuff
> that seems important now, and discouraged by the difficulties
> of the Christian life. We can end up as unprofitable servants,
> wasting our time on things that won't last, while gospel
> ministry is neglected. (Chester, *God of Glory*, 62)

We should often remind ourselves that "we do not have an enduring city here; instead, we seek the one to come" (Heb 13:14). We also know "the sufferings of this present time are not worth comparing with the glory that is going to be revealed to us" (Rom 8:18).

To atone for our sin, to free us from sin permanently, and to dwell with us forever cost God the death of His Son. God was willing to pay the highest price to have a people for His namesake. This is how much He desires our fellowship and worship. God does not need us, but He knows that without Him we will all perish. If God's vision of the new temple was meant to produce encouragement and action in His people, how much more does God's revealing to us the cross of Christ move us to hope and response? We are to live life in light of the cross and the return of Christ. We have not been shown the vision in Ezekiel 40–48 or the cross of Christ just to produce feelings in us but to move us to action. He loathed the exodus group (Ps 95:10) and left the rebellious ones in Jerusalem, but I hope it will be said of our generation, "He led them."

Reflect and Discuss

1. In times when you do not think God is speaking to you, what do you do?
2. The plans for the new temple are meant to remind God's people of His holiness. What do you do to be reminded of this on a daily basis?
3. If someone were to ask you why you thought God wants to dwell with us even after all our rebellion, how would you respond?
4. Why do we fail at times to appreciate God's presence?
5. Why is Christ a far better meeting place for God and His people than the temple ever was?
6. Why do we so often make worship more about us than God? How can we avoid making this mistake?
7. In what ways are you being transformed by God's life-giving river? In what ways is your city being transformed as the river of life flows through your faith family?
8. How can we be like the priests descended from Zadok who remained faithful when all others went away from God?
9. How can we seek the city that is to come and not just settle for the cities we currently see?
10. How is what you've learned through the book of Ezekiel impacting the way you're living?

WORKS CITED

Alexander, Ralph H. *Ezekiel.* The Expositor's Bible Commentary, vol. 6. Grand Rapids: Zondervan, 1986.

Appleton, George. Originally in the *Oxford Book of Prayer.* Quoted in Kenneth Boa. *Conformed to His Image.* Grand Rapids: Zondervan, 2001.

Azurdia, Arturo G., III. *Spirit Empowered Preaching: Involving the Holy Spirit in Your Ministry.* Ross-shire, Great Britain: Mentor, 1998.

Bennett, Arthur, ed. *The Valley of Vision: A Collection of Puritan Prayers and Devotions.* Edinburgh: The Banner of Truth Trust, 2009.

Block, Daniel I. *The Book of Ezekiel: Chapters 1–24.* The New International Commentary on the Old Testament. Grand Rapids: Eerdmans, 1997.

———. *The Book of Ezekiel: Chapters 25–48.* The New International Commentary on the Old Testament. Grand Rapids: Eerdmans, 1998.

Bloom, Jon. "No More Whoring." Accessed June 11, 2015, http://www .desiringgod.org/blog/posts/no-more-whoring (written May 21, 2010).

Bridges, Jerry. *The Pursuit of Holiness.* Colorado Springs: NavPress, 2001.

Chester, Tim *The God of Glory: Ezekiel.* China: The Good Book Company, 2010.

Cooper, Lamar Eugene, Sr. *Ezekiel.* The New American Commentary, vol. 17. Nashville: B&H, 1994.

Crosby, Fanny J. "To God Be the Glory" 1875. Public domain.

Davis, Andrew M. *An Approach to Extended Memorization of Scripture.* Greenville, SC: Ambassador International, 2014.

Dever, Mark. *The Message of the Old Testament: Promises Made.* Wheaton: Crossway, 2006.

Duguid, Iain M. *Ezekiel.* The NIV Application Commentary. Grand Rapids: Zondervan, 1999.

Edwards, Jonathan. *Sinners in the Hands of an Angry God.* New Kensington, PA: Whitaker House, 1997.

Evans, Tony. *Our God Is Awesome*. Chicago: Moody, 1994.

Fee, Gordon D., and Douglas Stuart. *How to Read the Bible for All Its Worth*. Grand Rapids: Zondervan, 1993.

Goldsworthy, Graeme. *Gospel and Kingdom*. Exeter: Paternoster, 2012.

Greidanus, Sidney. *Preaching Christ from the Old Testament*. Grand Rapids: Eerdmans, 1999.

Grudem, Wayne. *Systematic Theology*. Grand Rapids: Zondervan, 2000.

Helm, David. *The Big Picture Story Bible*. Wheaton: Crossway Books, 2004.

Hoezee, Scott. "Jeremiah 8:18–9:1." Accessed June 11, 2015, http://cep .calvinseminary.edu/thisWeek/viewArticle.php?aID=890.

House, Paul R., and Eric Mitchell. *Old Testament Survey*. Nashville: B&H Academic, 2007.

Johnston, Julia H. "Grace Greater Than Our Sin." 1910. Public domain.

Judson, Adoniram. "Letter to Anne Hasseltine Before Their Marriage." Copied by Stephen Ross for WholesomeWords.org from *The Life of Adoniram Judson by His Son Edward Judson*. New York: Anson D. F. Randolph & Company, 1883. Accessed June 11, 2015, http://www .wholesomewords.org/missions/bjudson8.htm.

Kaiser, Walter C., Jr. *Preaching and Teaching the Last Things: Old Testament Eschatology for the Life of the Church*. Grand Rapids: Baker Academic, 2011. CBD Reader edition.

Keller, Tim "Talking About Idolatry in a Postmodern Age." Accessed June 11, 2015, http://old.westerfunk.net/archives/theology/Talking%20 About%20Idolatry%20in%20a%20Postmodern%20Age.

Kimbrough, Lawrence. *Words to Die For*. Nashville: B&H, 2002.

LaSor, William Sanford, David Allan Hubbard, and Frederic Wm. Bush. *Old Testament Survey*. Grand Rapids: Eerdmans, 1996.

Lewis, C. S. *The Weight of Glory*. San Francisco: Harper Collins, 2001.

Lloyd-Jones, D. Martyn. *Preaching and Preachers*. Grand Rapids: Zondervan, 1972.

Luther, Martin. "A Mighty Fortress Is Our God." 1529. Public Domain.

MacArthur, John. *Revelation 12–22*. The MacArthur New Testament Commentary. Chicago: Moody Press, 2000.

———. "The Sacrifice That Satisfied." Sermon at Grace Community Church, Sun Valley, CA, September 1, 2002. Accessed June 11, 2015, http://www.gty.org/resources/sermons/62-10/the-sacrifice -that-satisfied.

Marcel, Pierre Ch. *The Relevance of Preaching*, trans. Rob Roy McGregor. Grand Rapids: Baker, 1963.

McLaughlin, Raymond W. *Communication for the Church.* Grand Rapids: Zondervan, 1968.

Muller, Roland. *Honor and Shame.* Bloomington, IN: Xlibris, 2000.

"Newborn baby 'thrown out with the trash ALIVE after botched abortion.'" February 6, 2009. Accessed June 11, 2015, http://www.daily mail.co.uk/news/article-1137486/Newborn-baby-thrown-trash -ALIVE-botched-abortion.html.

Packer, J. I. *Knowing God.* Downers Grove: InterVarsity, 1993.

Piper, John. *Let the Nations Be Glad!* Grand Rapids: Baker Academic, 2003.

———. "Race and Cross." Sermon at Bethlehem Baptist Church, Minneapolis, MN, January 16, 2000. Accessed June 11, 2015, http://www.desiringgod.org/sermons/race-and-cross.

———. "Remember That You Were Hopeless." Sermon at Bethlehem Baptist Church, Minneapolis, MN, December 27, 1981. Accessed June 11, 2015, http://www.desiringgod.org/sermons /remember-that-you-were-hopeless.

———. *The Supremacy of God in Preaching.* Grand Rapids: Baker, 1990.

Piper, John, and Justin Taylor, eds. *Sex and the Supremacy of Christ.* Wheaton: Crossway, 2005.

"Prosecutor: NJ couple put stillborn baby in trash." May 21, 2012. Accessed June 11, 2015, http://abclocal.go.com/story?section=news /local&id=8670612.

Roberts, Vaughn. *God's Big Picture.* Downers Grove: InterVarsity, 2002.

Sibbes, Richard. *The Bruised Reed.* Electronic copy of the text obtained June 11, 2015, at http://www.monergism.com/thethreshold/sdg/ bruisedreed.html.

Smith, Gary V. *The Prophets as Preachers.* Nashville: B&H, 1994.

Spurgeon, Charles. "Now, a Sermon for Young Men and Young Women." *Spurgeon's Sermons,* vol. 20: 1874. Accessed June 11, 2015, http:// www.ccel.org/ccel/spurgeon/sermons20.xv.html.

Stocker, Abby. "'Wrath of God' Keeps Popular Worship Song Out of 10,000-Plus Churches." *Christianity Today.* Accessed June 11, 2015, http://www.christianitytoday.com/gleanings/2013/august/wrath -of-god-in-christ-alone-blocked-pcusa-hymnal.html.

Stuart, Douglas. *Ezekiel.* The Preacher's Commentary. Nashville: Thomas Nelson, 1989.

Taylor, John B. *Ezekiel: An Introduction and Commentary.* Tyndale Old Testament Commentaries, Vol. 22. Downers Grove: InterVarsity, 1969.

Thomas, Derek. *God Strengthens: Ezekiel Simply Explained.* Grange Close: Evangelical, 1993.

Thune, Robert. "How to Disciple a Transsexual." Accessed June 11, 2015, http://www.cdomaha.com/files/Transsexual.pdf.

Tripp, Tedd, and Margy Tripp. *Instructing a Child's Heart.* Wapwallopen, PA: Shepherd, 2008.

Trotman, Dawson. "Born to Reproduce," Sermon at Back to the Bible Conference, 1955. Accessed June 11, 2015, http://www.discipleshiplibrary.com/pdfs/aa094.pdf.

Vines, Jerry, and Jim Shaddix. *Power in the Pulpit.* Chicago: Moody, 1999.

Watts, Isaac. *How Sweet and Aweful Is the Place.* 1707. Public domain.

Welch, Edward T. *When People Are BIG and GOD Is Small: Overcoming Peer Pressure, Codependency, and the Fear of Man.* Greensboro: New Growth Press, 2011.

Wiersbe, Warren W. *Be Reverent: Bowing Before Our Awesome God.* Colorado Springs: David C Cook, 2000.

Wilson, Gerald. "*hîdâ.*" *New International Dictionary of Old Testament Theology and Exegesis,* vol. 2. Edited by Willem A. VanGemeren. Grand Rapids: Zondervan, 1997.

Wilson, Jared. "The Church and Idolatry." Accessed June 11, 2015, http://www.ligonier.org/learn/articles/the-church-and-idolatry.

Wragg, Jerry. *Exemplary Spiritual Leadership.* Leominster, UK: Day One, 2010.

SCRIPTURE INDEX